The Public Side
of Representation

The Public Side of Representation

A Study of Citizens' Views about Representatives and the Representative Process

Christopher J. Grill

State University of New York Press

Published by
State University of New York Press, Albany

For information, address State University of New York Press,
194 Washington Avenue, Suite 305, Albany, NY 12210-2384

Production by Kelli Williams
Marketing by Michael Campochiaro

Library of Congress Cataloging-in-Publication Data

Grill, Christopher J., 1965–
   The public side of representation : a study of citizens' views about representatives
and the representative process / Christopher J. Grill.
        p. cm.
   Includes bibliographical references and index.
   ISBN-13: 978-0-7914-7169-2 (hardcover : alk. paper)   1. Representative
government and representation—United States—Public opinion.   2. United
States. Congress—Public opinion.   3. Public opinion—United States.
4. United States—Politics and government—1989—Public opinion.   I. Title

JK1726.G75   2007
328.73'0734—dc22
2006032685

10 9 8 7 6 5 4 3 2 1

Dedicated in Memory of my Grandfathers,

Joseph Grill and John Jedrzejewski

Contents

Acknowledgments

Although a book may have only one author on its title page, it inevitably bears the imprint of many hands. I must first extend my thanks to the interview participants whose willing donation of time and energy helped make this project a reality. Their openness, honesty, interest, and perceptiveness were a constant source of inspiration to me, and helped renew my faith in the civic capacity of "ordinary" citizens.

A number of people made distinct contributions to the writing of this book. Anne Hildreth and Michael Malbin closely read the earliest versions of the manuscript and provided valuable insights and constructive criticism; the book is much better for them. Tim Gordinier's review of my work, especially the concluding chapter, resulted in numerous suggestions that greatly improved the final product. Jane Mansbridge and Paul Quirk offered instructive and encouraging reviews of the penultimate draft. A special note of thanks is extended to Sally Friedman, the earliest and most enthusiastic supporter of this study, whose knowledge of the representational literature and research methodologies helped turn a sketchy idea into a viable topic, and whose continued advice and encouragement helped bring the book to its present form. The staff at State University of New York Press, particularly Mike Rinella and Kelli Williams, deserve kudos for their skill in shepherding the manuscript from initial proposal to polished tome. Finally, I would like to express my gratitude to a select group of teachers I have known: Jack Gariepy, Dennis Shea, Paul Conway, Paul Scheele, and Bruce Miroff. Each of them deserves credit for sparking my interest in American politics, political thought, and culture, cultivating and honing my writing skills, and inculcating a belief in the importance of exploring the political beliefs of ordinary citizens. Each of them also exemplifies the enduring impact that good teaching, and teachers, can have. Of course, none of them, or the aforementioned contributors, should be held directly responsible for any of the assertions (or literary choices) that appear in the following pages!

I naturally bear a great debt to the friends and associates who helped bring this project to fruition. Among others, Karl Horstmann and especially Richard Sauerzopf were always willing to lend a sympathetic ear and boost my spirits during the long and often trying writing (and rewriting) process. Last, but certainly not least, has been the backing of my family. My mother and father have been an unwavering source of support for many years, and their continued encouragement—often framed in a gently prodding "So, how's the book coming along?"—was instrumental in keeping me going. Finally, I would like to thank my wife, Laura, and daughters, Katherine and Hannah, for all they have done to make this undertaking possible. My girls, especially the oldest, have frequently had their playtime cut short and endured many trips outside the house in order to help Daddy get his work done. Above all, this book is a testament to their sacrifices and faith in me.

Chapter One

Introduction and Overview

A Crisis of Representation?

Congress lies at the heart of both our political tradition and our political process. It also maintains a firm, if not necessarily positive, grip on the public imagination; as public opinion research consistently shows, "Congress gets more blame for the country's problems than do other institutions or the president."[1] Congress is, in a word, *important* to the American people. The institution's actions (or lack thereof) appear to have a significant impact on the public's level of satisfaction with the political process, as well as on its perceptions of the appropriate role of government in society. Greater understanding of the relationship between Congress and the public thus is of inherent value to students and practitioners of American politics.

This relationship, as the quote above hints, has been rocky for quite some time. In Robert Lane's classic study of the "common man's" political beliefs, *Political Ideology*, the section dealing with our national legislature was entitled "The Warm, Friendly Congress." How times have changed. It is only a slight exaggeration to say that public support for Congress has been in a free fall over the past forty-five years. Whether measured as confidence in the institution, satisfaction with its policy performance, overall effectiveness, or attitudes toward most of its members, positive evaluations of Congress in opinion polls have declined sharply since the late 1950s, the time of Lane's research.[2] The past two decades have been a particularly turbulent period for the institution. Early in the 1990s Congress's standing with the American people dipped to record lows, and remains near the bottom for all major public institutions.[3] The movement to limit legislative terms, driven in part by public dismay with the congressional political process, attained surprising success over the course of the decade and continues to reshape legislative politics (and careers) at both state and national levels. The 1994 elections ended the

Democrats' forty-year reign in the House of Representatives and appeared to signal a new era of Republican ascendancy in congressional politics. Yet 1998 brought both the impeachment of a Democratic president and a historically unprecedented rebound for his party in that year's mid-term elections, while the 2000 campaign resulted in an evenly divided Senate. Republicans subsequently regained control of both houses of Congress, but by 2006 disenchantment with the institution again approached record levels in the wake of high-profile corruption charges, lobbying and personal misconduct scandals, public dissatisfaction with congressional policy actions, and growing discontent with the "war on terror," resulting in a Democratic takeover of the House and Senate that year. In such a highly volatile and contentious political environment, the road ahead for Congress and its (current or future) members does not appear any smoother.

Congress's travails, however, are only one manifestation of American's general discontent with political life. Indeed, we have witnessed a long-term decline in public trust and confidence in government institutions and officials, a decline that has continued during, *and* been largely unaffected by, extended periods of peace and prosperity over the past two decades.[4] By the mid-1990s, in fact, public support of Washington reached its modern nadir, even as the country was in the midst of one of the longest stretches of economic growth in its history. Rising optimism about one's personal prospects and the state of the nation during this time also did not translate into increased support for political institutions. And while public confidence in the national government soared in the wake of 9/11, it has once again plummeted, hovering well below the levels seen in the 1960s. Books, television reports, and journalistic accounts continue to chronicle public discontent with Washington. "Why Americans hate politics" has become an all-too-familiar refrain.

It may be going too far to say that we are in the midst of a crisis of representation. A certain degree of skepticism about government, after all, is deeply ingrained in American political culture (and arguably healthy); some would even call it central to our national character. But given chronically low levels of trust in government, pervasive cynicism about elected officials and the political process, and enduring dissatisfaction with most public institutions, few would deny that the rift that emerged between citizens and government in the late 1960s and early 1970s has widened into a more substantial fissure. A fundamental disconnect appears to have developed between the American people and their governing institutions, particularly at the national level, which the highly charged impeachment process, bitterly contested 2000 presidential election, and divisive 2004 campaign only served to exacerbate. Representation provides the essential link between these institutions and the public. Investigating citizens' fundamental beliefs about representation therefore might enhance our understanding of public discontent with politics and disenchantment with representatives and representative institutions. The centrality of Congress—in our political process, in public evaluations of the national government, in many accounts of our current political malaise, and in calls for both minor and sweeping political reform—make it almost incumbent to do so.

The Missing Public

Democratic political theorists have long emphasized that effective representation is a key component in a stable and healthy political order. In the democratic ideal, government institutions (and actors) are presumed to be relatively open and accessible, responsive to public preferences, and accountable for their actions. These properties historically have been considered the special province of the legislative branch, and representation the means by which to achieve them. "Through the process of representation, presumably, legislatures are empowered to act for the body politic. . . . And because, by virtue of representation, they participate in legislation, the represented accept legislative decisions as authoritative" (Eulau 1978, p. 111). Renowned for their native distrust of politicians, Americans also consider elected representatives to be a vital, and perhaps their most essential, link to the political process. When this link is believed to be in jeopardy, public discontent with politics usually follows.[5] In this way, Congress's lifeblood as a political institution is its "representative character." At some basic level the institution has to be perceived as representative and responsive in order to be considered legitimate.

The key to understanding representation lies in defining and explaining the bond between representative(s) and represented. Over the past three decades scholars have learned a great deal about certain aspects of this relationship. We now have a much better grasp of the representative process from the legislator's point of view, for example, while theoretical perspectives on representation have become more informed and complex. Significant strides have additionally been made in explaining public evaluations of government institutions and officials, especially those regarding congressional job performance. There is also a large and increasingly sophisticated body of research on the internal processes of legislatures.

Yet significant gaps remain in our understanding of the representative process. One of the most important concerns the origin and nature of *public* conceptions of representation. Much of the research that deals with the public's view of representation has been driven by the narrow goal of explaining the "paradox of congressional support": enduring dissatisfaction with Congress coupled with generally positive appraisals of individual representatives.[6] Very little of this work touches on what citizens actually *think* about the representative process. There have also been a few, and now quite dated, forays into the representational "roles" people favor for their legislators.[7] And that is essentially it. In fact, given the plethora of academic research and political discourse devoted to the representative process, not to mention its central importance in our political system, it is remarkable how little attention has been paid to ordinary citizens' fundamental ideas and expectations about representation.

The result is that some of the most intriguing issues about the public side of representation have not been adequately addressed. At the broadest level, we have little grasp of what people believe about representation en toto: what it means to them as a political idea, how they conceive of the representative process, and whether they feel the process actually works as it should. It is certainly not clear that citizens think of representation in ways that academics have depicted it, such as in terms of policy outputs, issue congruence, or even the provision of district and constituency services. People's expectations of the representative process, including the roles that they want representatives to play, are likewise poorly understood. Finally, in part because of its particular methodological orientation, current research in the field fails to illuminate the set of beliefs that may underlie people's evaluations of their representatives and representative institutions.[8]

The implications of this are profound. This study turns on the idea that there is an integral relationship between individual political beliefs, the nature of representation, and the legitimacy of our political institutions and actors. No matter how ill-defined, citizens' basic understanding of representation—their bedrock ideas and expectations about the representative process—may condition their assessments of political actors, institutions, and events, their political attitudes, their participation in politics, and even their faith in the political process. Those who perceive a substantial gap between the way the representative process works and the way they believe it *should* work, for instance, are more likely to feel cynical and disconnected and perhaps to withdraw from political life altogether. There is, in sum, an integral link between people's political beliefs and their political attitudes and behaviors.

All of this suggests how critical people's political beliefs are to the workings of a democratic polity. *Individual-level* attitudes, which naturally are influenced by larger forces, also can have profound *systemic-level* effects. Citizens' ideas about representation in part reflect the political milieu they are in; their beliefs are shaped, and at times reshaped, by the political environment. It is equally true, however, that people's representational convictions can have real consequences for the democratic process. This interrelationship between the political world, citizens' political views, and civic attitudes and engagement underscores the importance of examining people's political beliefs. Individual political discourse is, quite simply, a major part of democratic political life. Perhaps nowhere is this more evident than in the representative process.

A Different Approach

To better understand our contemporary political process and political culture, then, it is necessary to delve into the ideas and expectations individuals have about representation—and to consider whether representatives and representative institutions are meeting them. More specifically, in order to better comprehend the public's view of Congress and its members, we need to specify the latent notions of representation that citizens use to help make sense of the political world.[9] My interest therefore lies in individuals' conceptions of representation and how these conceptions are related to the political environment. The representational issues I will address in this book fall into three overarching categories:

The Idea of Representation
The Representative Relationship
Institutional Representation

At heart, the study was designed to disclose what the concept of representation means to people. The second and third objectives were derived from this larger question; they guided my investigation of people's ideas about representation at the congressional level.

The Idea of Representation

The foremost objective of my research was to reveal people's most fundamental and global ideas about representation. There are two related aspects to this:

1. *What* people think about representation.
2. *How* people think about representation.

The underlying intent here was to uncover the actual images, ideas, and ideals citizens hold about representation and the representative process. In so doing I also wanted to find out how sensitive these beliefs are to the political universe. By listening to how people talk about representation, we may gain a better sense of the relationship between representational norms and expectations and such factors as the behavior of incumbents, institutional processes, and (changes in) the policy environment.

The Representative Relationship

The relationship between members of Congress and their constituents remains the focal point of representational research. However, the vast majority of this work has dealt only with the legislators' side of the coin. While there have been some inquiries into public evaluations of Congress and its members, as discussed above, we still know relatively little about what citizens think about and expect from the representative process. What we do know has been drawn from truncated opinion surveys rather than in-depth explorations of people's ideas about representation expressed in their own words. My project sought to address these deficiencies by examining:

1. What people look for in congressional representatives.
2. The roles members of Congress are supposed to play.
3. How people perceive the representative relationship.
4. The impact of representatives themselves on people's representational views.[10]

Institutional Representation

One of the underlying rationales for my study is that it is essential to understand what people believe about Congress as a representative body. Among its major premises are that ordinary citizens have the capacity to think about Congress as an institution and that they may also possess some enduring notions about what I call "institutional representation."[11] Therefore, I decided to investigate:

1. The expectations people have for Congress as a political institution.
2. What people think about Congress in its representative (and especially its deliberative) capacity.
3. Whether citizens appear to hold any conceptions of institutional representation.[12]

My last major concern was whether citizens feel they are being adequately represented today. It is important to tap into views on the health of contemporary representation not only because many citizens may have them, but also because they might provide a window into people's fundamental beliefs about how representation *does* and *should* work. These assessments may also have an impact on their expressed attitudes towards Congress and the political system. Accordingly, while exploring people's general ideas about representation and the congressional representative process, I tried to determine:

1. How well people feel they are being represented.
2. What people believe is good and bad with representation today.
3. How people think the representative process can be improved.

Exploring all these issues means going to the heart of representational theory to define and explain the relationship between represented and representative. There are two main elements to this. One, of course, is what Hannah F. Pitkin long ago identified as a crucial component in any representational research: pinpointing "how a representative ought to act or what he is expected to do, how to tell whether he has represented well or badly" (Pitkin 1967, p. 58). Doing so includes defining how people perceive the congressional representative relationship, such as what members of Congress should do in office, the qualities they should possess, the inherent conflicts they face, and the impediments that members and others might pose to effective representation.

The second, and equally important, side to the congressional representative equation is the link between Congress as an institution and ordinary citizens. People's conceptions of institutional representation have been largely neglected in the literature, but exploring them is essential if we are to gain a deeper understanding of the public's views about the political process. Ascertaining what citizens think about Congress as a representative body—including its primary role(s) in the political system and how well it is serving the American people—is as necessary an ingredient in this kind of representational study as any analysis of the member-constituent relationship.

Much work has been done on the "supply-side" of the representative process. We have learned a great deal about how representatives make voting decisions, the internal dynamics of legislatures, modern campaign practices, and so on. Our knowledge of how representatives serve their constituents and approach the representative relationship has also grown considerably. But the "demand-side" of the representative process remains much more of a mystery. This book is conceived as a first step toward filling this gap in the existing literature on representation. It is guided by two convictions: one, that we can greatly enrich our knowledge of contemporary political culture, the representative-constituent process, and even public attitudes toward Congress by taking stock of the ideas, assumptions, hopes, and critiques that ordinary citizens have about representation; and two, that we can best do this by engaging people to talk *directly* and *at length* about the subject in extended conversational interviews.

The work that follows is based upon twenty-eight conversations with a wide range of individuals in order to ascertain their fundamental beliefs and expectations about the representative process. Chapter two outlines the research methodology employed in this study, including the rationale for using in-depth individual interviews, the process undertaken to code and analyze the interview transcripts, and the key variables that helped guide my interpretation of the data. Chapter three presents and analyzes the central ideas—the basic "building blocks"—in the subjects' general conceptions of representation. Chapter four explores how these core beliefs are put into practice through participants' answers to a pair of hypothetical voting questions for members of Congress. By examining how these citizens expect congressional representatives to resolve classic decision-making dilemmas, we gain valuable insights into their understanding of the representative process, insights that could modify how this process is portrayed in the literature. Chapter five addresses the respondents' views about the congressional representative relationship, and offers some surprising findings that challenge the conventional wisdom of ordinary citizens as both reflexively critical and ignorant of the challenges faced by members of Congress. Chapter six looks at how these citizens perceive Congress as an institution, including their views on the state of contemporary representation and how the representative process might be improved. In the concluding chapter, we revisit the participants' fundamental ideas about representation, examine the most important and intriguing aspects of their conceptions of the representative process, and consider the larger implications of my findings for both the representational literature and the contemporary political process.

Revealing how citizens make sense of representation in a complex political world has intrinsic value for students of American politics. It can significantly enrich our understanding of the public side of the representative process, something that has generally received short shrift by scholars. It can also help provide empirical grounding for underlying assumptions about the process; theories of representation, for instance, turn on the belief that citizens' expectations of their representatives are politically significant, yet little is known about the nature of these expectations or how they matter. But considering the representative process from the vantage point of ordinary citizens takes on added importance given the long winter of our discontent with politics. Greater awareness of people's fundamental beliefs about representation might help us to get at the roots of public disenchantment with elected officials and representative institutions. It may also provide valuable insight into how, and to what extent, the contemporary political process can be revitalized.

At a time when many Americans appear to be questioning anew what they want from government and their elected representatives, it seems fitting to try to discern what representation really means to them—and to explore the implications this might have for our democratic polity.

Chapter Two

Research Methodology

Introduction

The existing representational literature, as I suggest in chapter one, has failed to adequately address the public side of the representative process. A *direct* and *systematic* exploration of people's fundamental beliefs about representation can help to rectify this shortcoming. It can, for instance, shed light on the kind of representational responsibilities citizens expect of members of Congress, and whether they see personal qualities like trust and integrity as surrogates for more direct control over their representatives. A comprehensive look at individuals' ideas about representation might also provide greater insight into their views toward Congress as an institution. Do citizens hold certain ideas about what Congress should be like and what it should do? Do they, in short, hold to some notion of institutional representation? Similarly, is responsiveness at the center of ordinary citizens' conceptions of representation, as it is in much of the literature? If so, what are its essential components in their eyes? The research conducted by Richard F. Fenno Jr., Glenn R. Parker, and others indicates that access, communication, and constituent service have become vital parts of the representative relationship. We do not know, however, if people on the receiving end of "home styles" share this perspective, let alone what they value about such processes. In sum, how does the view of representation from the top down, as portrayed by scholars, political commentators, and elected officials, compare with the view from the bottom up, from the perspective of ordinary citizens?

These are the type of basic questions about representation currently left unanswered in the literature. Fundamentally, if we are to further our understanding of the representative process, we must explore the underlying ideas, assumptions, and expectations individual citizens have about representation. These beliefs have not been, and arguably cannot

9

be, adequately addressed through prevailing research methods. Making headway on them would seem to require a different kind of approach, something akin to Fenno's work in *Home Style*. In one sense this project can be thought of as a cousin to *Home Style*—but this time exploring and explaining the representative process from the *constituents'* point of view. *How* I attempted to do so occupies the rest of this chapter.

Approaching the Subject

Some of the shortcomings of the existing literature on people's views about representation flow directly from its reliance on opinion surveys. Due to the scope of many large-scale academic surveys, inquiry into a particular subject area is often quite limited. Over time, there have been very few questions in election studies or public opinion polls that pertain to citizens' beliefs or expectations about representation. Certain approaches that are relevant to the subject have been used only once or twice, such as the representational role series in the 1978 National Election Survey (NES).[1] Existing data on public attitudes about representation thus covers only a small slice of the representational process. In fact, the bulk of the research into public expectations of Congress, including the "job performance" literature, has been based on variations of the following two queries: what people like/dislike about their own representative/ Congress, and how they rate the job _____ has been doing (and why).

These questions obviously fail to deal with the more universal aspects of representation, but they also may impose intellectual constructs on respondents. That is, they can lead people to think about the subject in highly selective and limited ways. The like/dislike query, for example, may steer subjects toward overly personalized responses about Congress and their own representatives. The way these questions are ordered may also condition how people think about the representative process.[2] Of course, these types of concerns are not unique to the survey method; they can arise in any type of research into public opinion. But the problems can be magnified when people are only asked about an issue once or twice, or in one particular way, as is the case in most surveys. Since I wished to know *how* people think about representation, I wanted participants to have the chance to express their ideas in their own way, using their own terms, concepts, and frames of reference. And because I needed to know *what* people think about representation (on a number of levels), it did not seem advisable to build this study around a few narrowly focused survey-type questions. While the survey method has proven extremely useful to political scientists, limited surveys and close-ended questions are better at producing evaluations of political figures and institutions than revealing deep-seated political values and idea(l)s. At heart, I do not believe it is possible to come by a holistic awareness of people's central political beliefs in this way, and it was essential that I grasped the respondents' fundamental views about representation.[3]

This project is therefore rooted in an alternative methodology exemplified by the work of scholars such as Robert E. Lane and William A. Gamson. Political scientists working in this tradition contend that it is virtually impossible to discern the nature of individual political beliefs through traditional survey methods. Instead, they advocate using extended conversational interviews as a way of getting at what people are thinking about politics.[4] In my view there are several advantages to the in-depth interview that make it particularly well-suited for this kind of study. These can be summarized as follows:

(a) I wanted respondents to discuss various aspects of representation *in their own terms*. People have much more freedom to do so in a conversational setting based upon a series of open-ended questions. "Open-ended questions allow respondents to establish their own frame of reference," so these queries can reveal a great deal about how people structure their political thought (Miller 1986, p. 525) and are more likely to expose people's central political beliefs and values.

(b) In-depth interviews based on open-ended questions record more fully how subjects *arrive* at their opinions—how people sample information from their memories, develop a train of thought, and justify their positions. "The way subjects ramble, hesitate, stumble, and meander as they formulate their answers tips us off to how they are thinking and reasoning through political issues" (Chong 1993, pp. 867–868).

(c) It helps guard against one of the greatest dangers in public opinion research: reifying attitudes through the interview process that may not exist outside of it. This problem can be mitigated through careful attention to question wording and design, and by approaching a subject from several different angles. The extended interview provides more opportunities to include these kind of "fail-safe" mechanisms than do limited surveys.

(d) It was commensurate with my main task: trying to uncover people's *latent* beliefs about representation. Through the interview process participants have the chance to elaborate on their answers and grapple with various aspects of an issue. In turn, the researcher has the opportunity to probe subjects' responses and cover a lot of ground. By allowing individuals to talk about an issue at length, and in their own

> words, an extended interview offers a better way to grasp
> the underlying dimensions of their political beliefs than
> by trying to divine these views from top of the head re-
> sponses to survey questions. In sum, an in-depth inter-
> view can produce a more complete picture of a person's
> political "worldview."

Since my overriding objective was to capture the various facets of,
and even contradictions in, an individual's beliefs about representation,
I needed a research technique tailored to this goal. The in-depth interview was the only suitable choice. There is no more effective means for
untangling the abstract elements and real-world dimensions of people's
political views. The opportunity for contextual analysis, combined with
the depth and breadth of information obtained, make open-ended extended interviews an invaluable tool for exploring citizens' conceptions
of the political world.[5] As Robert Lane asserted, "there is no other satis-
factory way to map [the elements of] a political ideology" (1962, p. 10).

There are, of course, certain drawbacks to using one-on-one conversations as a primary research tool. Perhaps the foremost liability is the
(often unavoidable) trade-off between quality and quantity in the interviews. The demands of conducting extended personal interviews frequently preclude researchers from canvassing a large number of people,
as was the case in this project. Most importantly, the small number of
subjects makes it virtually impossible to provide a statistically representative sample. To compensate for this problem, potential participants in
this study were screened by demographic attributes (age, ethnicity, gen-
der, educational attainment, etc.) and exposure to politics in order to
produce a sample that reflected a fairly diverse cross section of the population. By employing this kind of selected sample, I was also able to control for certain variables that strengthen our ability to generalize from it.[6]
It remains true, however, that the evidence and conclusions from this
project are based on discussions with a fairly small, and not entirely representative, group of people.

Yet this fact should not blind us to the benefits of an interview-based
research design that possess some of the crucial attributes of case studies.
Robert K. Yin (1984) notes that the case study is the preferred research
strategy when one is (*a*) asking "how," "why," and certain exploratory
"what" questions, and (*b*) investigating a contemporary phenomenon
within its real-life context. Both of these conditions certainly apply to a
study of people's fundamental ideas and expectations about representation. And unlike surveys, which provide little opportunity to examine
context, case studies are particularly useful when a researcher wants to
account for contextual factors that might be highly pertinent to the ob-
ject of study (Yin, pp. 4–13).[7] In much the same way, in-depth interviews

allow us to explore both the individual aspects and contextual dimensions of people's political beliefs. Valuable analytical generalizations can often be extracted from such evaluative "miniature case studies." In essence, individual stories, if properly contextualized, can illuminate more universal sentiments.

The inherently exploratory nature of my work further underscores the utility of this type of research strategy. In important respects I was treading into uncharted substantive and methodological waters. The study was not intended to be, nor could it be, a definitive investigation of the public's ideas about representation. What it is designed to do was furnish a much deeper understanding of what *individual citizens* think about, and expect from, the representative process. This is a crucial point to emphasize. As I suggested earlier, much of the current literature *presumes* what people think about representation. My work allows us to move beyond this to directly uncover people's fundamental beliefs about the subject. And the recurrence of certain themes about representation in these interviews, in light of what previous studies have told us, makes it possible to offer some at least tentative judgments about the public's view of representation—as well as to assess some of the prevailing ideas about representation found in the literature and the general political culture. With the appropriate caveats in mind, then, I hope to demonstrate that the data gleaned from these twenty-eight individual stories provides a much richer understanding of Americans' conceptions and assessments of the contemporary representative process.

The Research Process:
Instrument and Interviews

The research process got underway with the development of a suitable interview questionnaire. The objective here was to devise questions that (1) were both interesting and accessible to participants, and (2) were broad enough to allow them to respond in their own fashion yet focused enough to meet my needs. I wanted, in short, to create an interview context that would not unduly "lead" respondents yet would also address my fundamental research objectives.

My three major research interests defined the structure of the final instrument. After first addressing the "idea of representation" (their general or abstract conceptions of representation), respondents moved on to discuss the "representative relationship" (their expectations for members of Congress), and then their beliefs about "institutional representation" (views of Congress as a representative institution). The interviews concluded with two hypothetical questions concerning imaginary members of Congress. This analytical ordering reflected my desire not to skew how people responded to the subject. The goal was to capture respondents' most fundamental and abstract ideas first, those that transcended any particular representational context, rather than beginning with discussions of specific political figures or institutions that might influence their more general observations or judgments.

During the interview, each respondent was asked a minimum of twelve open-ended questions, several of which included designated follow-up questions (see appendix A). In most cases a large number of spontaneous probes were also asked based on subjects' answers to the initial queries. These probes were posed to let people clarify or expand upon their answers, respond to inconsistencies in their remarks, or to give me additional insight into a particular subject area. In many instances the probes proved as, if not more valuable, in eliciting useful information than the original questions.[8]

There were two overriding objectives in selecting participants for the study. The first, as mentioned above, was to obtain a reasonably diverse cross section of the population. In so doing I also wanted to control for certain contextual variables, including the congressional districts subjects resided in. Respondents were drawn from two separate House districts to help discern the effect that members of Congress have on people's beliefs about representation. Although adjoining, the districts chosen were represented by members with different party affiliations, institutional standing, political identities, and core constituencies: NY's 21st (Democrat Michael McNulty); and NY's 22nd (Republican Gerald Solomon).[9]

Participants for the study were solicited in several ways. A flyer that briefly described the project and requested volunteers was posted in various locales throughout the immediate Capital Region of New York. To obtain certain types of subjects, especially people who were actively involved in the political process and those without much education or exposure to politics, selected organizations were contacted and asked to provide the names of persons who might be willing to participate. I then called or met with these individuals, almost all of whom agreed to be interviewed. These subgroups helped to ensure that there was significant variation among respondents in terms of political interest, knowledge, and involvement. The rest of the participants were individuals who acquaintances of mine thought might be willing to take part in the project or who filled specific gaps in my sample population.

The bulk of the interviews were conducted between May 1997 and April 1998.[10] The majority of them took between 45–60 minutes to complete. All were recorded on a micro-cassette recorder. Besides ensuring that I would have a complete and precise record of the proceedings, taping allowed me to maintain constant eye contact with the respondents and to formulate appropriate follow-up questions. As mentioned earlier, a large number of probes were often asked, but in doing so great pains were taken to keep my own views from becoming part of the conversation (even when they were solicited by the subjects!).

After each interview was finished, it was completely transcribed (as soon as possible) from the cassette to my home computer. In doing the transcriptions, I was especially interested in capturing the tenor of subjects' remarks—their pauses and hesitations, points of emphasis, laughter, sarcasm, and so on. The goal was to try to bring the interviews alive on the written page, to not only render an accurate account of what was said, but also to convey *how* it was said, as well as the person's general mind-set at the time. Twenty-eight transcripts were ultimately produced, ranging from six to twenty single-spaced pages in length (with an average of approximately thirteen pages). The representational observations and assessments that begin in chapter three consequently were based on roughly three hundred fifty pages of testimony from the respondents.

The Research Process: Coding and Analysis

A number of sequential steps were taken in the crucial process of evaluating and coding these transcripts. First, the most notable or revealing passages in each interview were highlighted on the computer, to direct my attention to them during subsequent stages of coding. After a transcript was printed, it was then read through without note taking so that I could get a general feel for how the interview had played out. The third and most important step was a thorough second reading. At this stage, the transcripts were heavily marked up: key statements and ideas marked; short statements and interpretive comments inserted into the margins; and preliminary themes and ideas outlined. There were two main objectives here. From a procedural standpoint, I wanted the transcripts prepared to expedite coding and analysis. Substantively, I was trying to identify the principal ideas and expectations held by the respondents, the similarities, contrasts, and contradictions in their answers, and any recurring or widely held beliefs.

Based upon these detailed second readings, and in light of my specific research objectives, I eventually arrived at a list of approximately fifty content codes that encompassed the three major topic areas. Each of these substantive codes became the heading for one side of an index card. Ongoing review of the transcripts produced a series of subject subheadings for these code cards. Once a particular subheading was established, similar passages from succeeding transcripts were assigned to it. Lastly, notations for the most interesting or representative passages were underlined to provide me with a set of quotations for possible inclusion in the text.[11]

The final product was a comprehensive series of note cards that indexed respondents' statements by subject matter, specific emphasis, and relative merit. These code cards served as the foundation for overall chapter development, specific chapter outlines, and the organization and presentation of data in each chapter. They proved indispensable, both to my larger vision of how the book should unfold and the actual mechanics of the writing process.

Profile of Respondents

In order to get a better sense of the people behind these interviews table 2.1 on page 00 presents a basic demographic profile of the respondents. The number and percentage of subjects who fell into each category is identified (percentages may exceed 100 percent due to rounding).

Table 2.1. Demographic Profile of Respondents

Age:	18–25	26–40	41–55	over 55	
	3	13	8	4	
	(11%)	(50%)	(25%)	(14%)	
Gender:		Male	Female		
		17	11		
		(61%)	(39%)		
Ethnicity:	White	Black	Hispanic	Other	
	22	3	2	1	
	(79%)	(11%)	(7%)	(4%)	
Education Level:	Grade School	High School	Some College	College (BA/BS)	Master's/ Ph.D
	1	5	9	8	5
	(4%)	(18%)	(32%)	(29%)	(18%)
Political Affiliation:	Democrat	Republican	Independent	Other	
	11	6	10	1 (Conserv.)	
	(43%)	(18%)	(36%)	(4%)	
Congressional Representative:		Solomon	McNulty		
		11	17		
		(39%)	(61%)		

There is clearly a significant amount of variation among respondents on all these dimensions. Participants were drawn from all relevant age, ethnic, and educational categories and both genders. In addition, they held a wide range of occupations in both the public and private sectors. With the exception of ethnicity, however, it is also evident that the sample does not precisely mirror the general population. In particular, subjects were better educated and more likely to identify themselves as Democrats than would be considered average. Nevertheless, the final sample for this project was fairly, if not fully, representative of people in New York State's Capital Region. Most importantly, while controlling for certain factors that the literature suggests affect citizens' attitudes about representation, it fulfilled my primary goal of obtaining a reasonably diverse cross section of residents of the area. And this brings us to the second variable embodied in the design and execution of my project: the respondents' level of "political sophistication."

The Idea of Political Sophistication

In their study of public attitudes toward American political institutions, John R. Hibbing and Elizabeth Theiss-Morse (1995) found a clear relationship between political engagement and ideas about Congress. But they are not the only scholars to discern a link between people's personal attributes and their views about the representative process. For example, Bruce Cain, Morris P. Fiorina, and John Ferejohn (1987) observed that social class, education, and race were all significantly related to people's role preferences for representatives, with the education effect being "particularly striking." Herb Asher and Mike Barr (1994) found that politically attentive and involved citizens are more supportive of incumbents but less supportive of Congress as an institution. Samuel C. Patterson, Randall B. Ripley, and Stephen Quinlan (1992) also discovered that familiarity can breed "institutional contempt"; more knowledgeable people tend to give poorer performance evaluations of Congress.

Although these scholars were not examining the same phenomena, or would even necessarily agree on all the relevant variables, they do seem to share one assumption—that political awareness matters in people's attitudes toward Congress. An important undercurrent in this work is the idea that levels of political knowledge, interest, and involvement affect people's evaluations of political institutions and figures. This expectation naturally led me to the following question: does the same hold true regarding citizens more fundamental beliefs about representation?[12]

To address this issue, I first needed to gauge each of the subject's general penchant for politics, or their basic "politicalness," if you will. To do so I defined three analytically distinct components to political life: political knowledge; political interest/attentiveness; and political involvement. Each of these has long been of interest to scholars studying political behavior, and each arguably captures an important facet of one's political being. Each is also a matter of some dispute in the literature, but taken together these variables adequately reflect what I consider a person's political sophistication.

A respondent's level of sophistication was determined in two ways. One was through a general assessment of the interview transcript. Here I was looking for expressed interest in, and knowledge of, politics; the number of political allusions a subject made; evidence of personal involvement in the political process; and the overall tenor of the responses. These somewhat subjective appraisals were complemented by a more standardized measure of sophistication: a questionnaire administered to the participants at the end of their interviews (see appendix A). The questionnaire was designed to tap into all three aspects of sophistication. Three questions were used to divulge a subject's level of both general and current political knowledge. Three queries were also posed to probe different dimensions of political participation. Finally, participants were asked to assess their general interest in politics. Although the questions were not comprehensive or rigorous measures of the respective variables, they did provide me with a good sense of a respondent's overall political aptitude.

After reviewing the questionnaire and interview, a subject was placed into one of three categories: sophisticated, somewhat sophisticated, or unsophisticated. Assessments were based on the totality of the participants' responses to the interview and the questionnaire. Some of the assignments were clear-cut. For instance, a person who correctly identified all of the elected officials and terms in office, conveyed that he voted regularly, and was otherwise politically involved was readily labeled sophisticated.[13] Given the nature of the questionnaire, however, the assignment process often involved some discretion. Individuals who emerged as somewhat knowledgeable, neither very active nor totally inactive, and moderately interested were classified as somewhat sophisticated, yet this category ranged from subjects who were fairly unsophisticated to those who were fairly sophisticated. The point is that these were broad categorizations and rough assessments. The purpose here was not to establish fine gradations of political sophistication; it was to provide a means by which I could assess the relationship, if any, between people's ideas about representation and their political ken.

The actual breakdown of respondents was as follows:

Sophisticated: 10 (36%)
Somewhat Sophisticated: 11 (39%)
Unsophisticated: 7 (25%)

Although each category is well represented, a fairly large percentage of the respondents were sophisticated. This is not surprising when one considers that politically active and attentive people would be most likely to gravitate to a study of this kind. On the whole, subjects were probably more informed about and interested in politics than is typical. But my intent was not to produce a sample that somehow matched the distribution of political sophistication in the general population (whatever that might be). It was to obtain a mix of citizens with varying degrees of knowledge about, interest in, and involvement with politics, and to have enough unsophisticated participants to balance the "self-selection" bias toward more politically sophisticated respondents. In this I think I succeeded.

Conclusion

The methodology used in this study was a fresh application of an approach to understanding political beliefs best embodied in the work of Robert Lane. In design, execution, and spirit, this project is an heir to that tradition. Of course, a research strategy based on extended interviews does have its limitations. Foremost among them is that it often results in a relatively small and in some respects unrepresentative sample. While certainly not negating the value of this type of research, this fact does caution against making any sweeping or definitive claims on the basis of it. It would simply be untenable to assert that this study provides a full and representative account of Americans' views about the representative process. The results generated herein must continually be evaluated with this in mind.

It is also true that using in-depth interviews to probe people's political beliefs creates its own unique dynamic. The very process of thinking about a topic in a concentrated and extended fashion can alter an individual's perspective on it. In this case, respondents were compelled to think about representation more than they ordinarily would; make inferences and connections about it that they might not have otherwise; consider the implications of their initial thoughts and perhaps recast them; and apply their ideas and expectations in different, and sometimes atypical, contexts. Ultimately, in-depth interviews propel people toward a deeper appreciation of an issue—toward what they *can* think about it— rather than just revealing what is uppermost in their minds. The substance of what they arrive at might be theirs alone, but in an important sense it is a product of the interview setting.

Yet this is, paradoxically, one of the greatest strengths of the in-depth interview, for it reveals what would otherwise go unobserved and unrecorded. The research method used here gave me a unique window into people's views about representation. It enabled me to investigate facets of the representative process that have not been examined through ordinary surveys, to explore core concepts and broader ideas about representation in a way that would otherwise be impossible, and to capture nuances and complexities in people's thoughts that would ordinarily remained concealed. Tapping into people's deeply held or latent views about a subject has real value, not least because it may ultimately change our understanding of that subject. The opportunity to discover how citizens make sense of representation in a variety of contexts; the ability to penetrate beneath people's surface attitudes and document their fundamental ideas and expectations; and the richness of the material gained all accentuate the utility of extended interviews in this kind of experimental project. And the project was just that—an exploratory look at individuals' beliefs about representation, what those beliefs can tell us about the real-world relationship between representatives and represented and public views of the representative process, and the implications this may have for our political system. In-depth interviews offered the best means to address these research aims. As I hope the subsequent chapters will demonstrate, the benefits from the methodology employed here clearly outweighed the costs.

Chapter Three

The Idea of Representation

Introduction

Representation lies at the very heart of our political tradition. The republican system of government instituted by the Founders hinges on the process of representation. And students and practitioners of American politics alike pay homage to the notion that "representing the people" is a sine qua non of democratic governance. Explicitly or implicitly, the idea of representation profoundly colors their understanding and expectations of the democratic process. The same can likely be said of ordinary citizens. No matter how simple or inchoate, most people presumably carry around some kind of "picture in their heads" of what democratic politics should entail. The centrality of representation in our political process means that it is likely to be a key part of these pictures. Investigating people's basic ideas and expectations about representation is therefore essential if we are to expand our knowledge of contemporary politics and political culture.

But what does it *really mean* to people to be represented? How do citizens conceptualize representation in the abstract? What do they volunteer when asked to define the representative process? These fundamental questions about the public side of representation remain something of a riddle. The paucity of research into them also means that there are few conceptual anchors available with which to order and evaluate people's ideas about representation. As a result, I was hesitant about imposing (unsuitable) constructs on my data, especially when one of the main objectives of my study, and primary needs in the literature, is to better understand what ordinary citizens think about and expect from the representative process.[1] To more fully comprehend the nature of representation, then, we must explore the "demand side" of the representative process—and come to grips with the varied, distinct, and even contradictory dimensions of people's representational expectations and beliefs.

In this chapter, we address the first crucial piece of this puzzle: people's general conceptions of representation. Here respondents describe their essential building blocks of the representative process. Communication emerges as the single most important component in the representational perspectives of these citizens. It is both the central feature of their bedrock *ideas* about representation and the primary component in their *idealized view* of the representative process. Yet how a representative is expected to reach out to his or her constituents is problematic, exposing fundamental differences in the participants' representational beliefs and the values they assign to these core elements of representation. Ultimately, this focus on popular views of representation adds a vital dimension to the scholarly concept of representation as responsiveness. It also reveals something of the richness of the subjects' perspectives on the representative process. A cursory nod to the idea of responsiveness simply does not do justice to the depth and diversity of these citizens' views. For many of my respondents, at least, representation proved to be a tiger of many stripes.

The Nature of Responsiveness: Preface

Before examining the various dimensions of the respondents' model of representational responsiveness, it is first necessary to highlight two distinguishing characteristics of their general reflections about representation. One was the "constituency-centeredness" of their views. Somewhat less common, but no less striking, were expressions of dismay with the contemporary representative process. These threads ran through and gave shape to many of the subjects' general conceptions of representation. Their understanding and expectations of the representative process—what they believed representation both *currently is* and what it *ought* to be—often seemed to flow from these beliefs. It is to the laments about representation that we turn first.

The pervasive cynicism about politics and politicians recorded in many public opinion surveys was evident in the reactions of a significant number of respondents to the first interview question. When asked some variation of this query—"Political leaders often like to say that they are elected to represent us. What does it mean to you when you hear them say something like that?"—over 40 percent of the participants immediately expressed discontent with the representative process. The underlying assumption was that representation today clearly departs from the ideal; several people prefaced their remarks by saying something like "what it means to me and what actually happens are two different things."

For a few of these subjects, this view could be traced to their conviction that representatives really serve only certain interests in society.

More often, though, the dissatisfaction appeared to stem from a feeling that politicians basically "use" the representative process to further their own aims. Rather than fulfilling their primary representational obligations, representatives direct most of their time and energy elsewhere, particularly to staying in office: "I'd like them to be at the business of governing, I suppose . . . [but] I suspect that half the time they're not, their focus is elsewhere, most especially on elections." This overriding electoral drive turns the representative process into something of a political ploy, a device by which members secure their own interests and ambitions at the expense of the people they serve. In short, the pursuit of reelection, long considered by scholars to be one of the hallmarks of democratic politics, is essentially at odds with good representation.

The last point bears repeating: many of these citizens, as well as those who made similar comments later in their interviews, seemed to believe that the electoral imperative fundamentally compromises the representative process. As one participant responded to the first question, "usually I think it's just political jargon, I must say. Most of them seem like they are just out there to stay in business for themselves; they'll do whatever they feel will get them reelected." Others were even more caustic: "I firmly believe that politicians will tell you anything to get in office," or "I think it's just a lie to get your vote." Thus, rather than perceiving it mainly as a vital link to elected officials, these citizens' see the representative process more as an instrumental tool manipulated by politicians for their own benefit. And in this respect, the process may actually feed their dissatisfaction with political life.

Although these individuals often modified this stance, and moved on to more complicated views of the representative process,[2] their initial expressions of discontent are both revealing and disquieting. When first queried about the subject, without any (negative) references to specific institutions and individuals, a large number of respondents bemoaned the state of representation. The hollowness of the process in their eyes is perhaps best revealed in the following response: "They don't even bother to say that (I'm elected to represent you) anymore, do they? I mean, do they really even bother to say that?" Of course, this outlook might be partly attributed to Americans' natural distrust of politics and elected officials; as a national pastime, heaping scorn on politicians ranks right up there with baseball. But the reactions of these respondents suggest that for some people this native distrust has mutated into a deeper and more caustic cynicism about the representative process. As do the results of many political surveys, the pessimism about representatives and their intentions expressed here lends credence to the notion that a significant rift has developed between many citizens and their elected officials.

The Constituency

It would also be impossible to put people's conceptions of the representative process into perspective without acknowledging the importance of constituency. Those participants who offered a basic definition of representation tended to supply constituent-based versions. Even those with the most Burkean of political perspectives readily acknowledged the value of serving the people back home. For some respondents the need for a constituency focus on the part of representatives was an unspoken assumption that subtly colored their responses; for others it was the centerpiece of their answers. But no one ventured the claim that, once elected, public officials do not have a clear responsibility to the people they serve, no matter how qualified or circumscribed this obligation might (or should) be. In short, the importance of a strong constituency connection in the representative process was as close to a common denominator as emerged from these interviews.

There were three interrelated aspects to this focus on constituency.[3] The first is that elected officials should look out for, and pursue in office, the respondent's interests, those of the community, or both. Some subjects put it in precisely these terms in response to the first question:

> To me it would mean just looking out for what's good for myself, for my interests and that of my community, whether it be the state or just my local community.
>   . . . they're there to represent, um, what the people believe or identify as their interest in various legislation or administrative processes. . . . I really think it's a pretty simple equation. I mean, they're there to represent the interests of their constituents.

Or, as another respondent simply put it, "[representation] would meet some of my needs, and other people's too." In this view, representatives are essentially in office to "serve the wants and needs" of their constituents.[4]

The second facet is that properly meeting such wants and needs requires that representatives possess a familiarity with their constituents' interests, concerns, and beliefs. As will become evident, this assumption underlay most of the respondents' basic ideas about representation, especially those concerning communication and what I call "involvement." The following quote is indicative of the view of many participants when asked what would be the ideal kind of relationship between elected officials and the people they serve: "I think having a representative that's open to all the points of view within a district, who is familiar with, um, the types of people they serve, and the types of needs that are going on." In essence, representatives have to "be in contact with the people back home and know what's going on in the local situation."

The third dimension is that representatives should come to embody the values and viewpoints of those they represent. In this formulation of the representative-constituent nexus, the process works best when elected officials are (or become) *fully representative* of the people they serve. For one participant, this meant looking for a representative in his own image, someone who would "go after the things I hold dear . . . that, if he was presented with a problem he would react to that problem similarly to what I would do for the problem. You know, just act in a fashion that would represent what my thinking is." Other people contended that a close representative-constituent connection can only develop when elected officials are truly *of* the areas they serve: "When you have [officials] coming in that were brought up in the area or really have taken an interest in the districts they represent, that's when I think you can see from their background that they're . . . representing you and have your interests at stake." One respondent, the son of a longtime Westchester County executive, wistfully observed that under certain circumstances the interests of representatives and their districts can become so intertwined as to be inseparable: "I think he was unique because he really loved the town. His best interests were [tied up] with the town's." Even if so close a bond between elected officials and their constituents is atypical, most respondents would probably second the view of the math teacher who remarked that "I hope the system would work well enough that . . . the constituents and [the representatives] conscience would be more parallel than perpendicular."

Constituency unquestionably occupies a central place in the representational worldviews of most of the subjects. The belief that representatives should be closely tied to their constituents and devoted to their interests was widely held. In Heinz Eulau and John C. Wahlke's role terminology, subjects generally expected representatives to act as "tribunes" of the people. To these citizens, representation without a clear constituency focus simply would not be representation at all. Perhaps most importantly, this bedrock, almost instinctive assumption seemed to underlie the respondents' embrace of such basic representational activities as contact and communication. Ultimately, constituency matters because it frequently appeared to be the raison d'être for the various elements of responsive representation.

Yet what became equally clear over the course of these interviews is that for most of these citizens (including some of those cited above), the constituency should *not* be a representative's sole obligation or concern. While a few people did share the conviction of this individual that representatives should always "Do what the people want . . . that's what [they're] there for," a large majority of respondents highlighted other significant imperatives that elected officials must consider: their own judgment, conscience, or principles; their campaign promises; the long term impact of decisions; the "good of the country" (some view of the national interest); and even the political winds. As will become clear, subjects were often quite sensitive to the conflicting demands that inhere in the representative process, and at times struggled to reconcile their own divergent convictions. Several sought some way to combine their belief in the primacy of constituency with other key representational ideals and expectations. With these important disclaimers in mind, we can now turn to the process of untangling the diverse strands in the respondents' "model" of representational responsiveness.

Attentiveness

One of the formative elements of representation as responsiveness was attentiveness to the district. As with the focus on constituency, there were basically three aspects to representational attentiveness: being aware of constituents and their interests; listening to them; and (for certain people) fulfilling constituent demands. As one person depicted it, "I think [representation] means they are supposed to be interested in what their constituents think and that they should be listening. . . . It seems to me that they should be paying attention to what the majority of the people are saying." Over half of the respondents made similar points, emphasizing that it was important for representatives to "pay attention" to the people back home. To some of these participants, this meant *reacting* to the efforts of constituents, such as by providing prompt and thoughtful responses to mail, phone calls, and other inquiries; to a number of others, it meant actively *soliciting* constituent input on issues through things like newsletters or surveys.

Such attentiveness was seen as reflecting an underlying dedication to the needs and interests of constituents. One respondent articulated this idea in his exhortation that representatives should "[l]isten to their constituents. Don't forget who [you're] there to represent. . . . Take care of who sent you there. Congressional districts aren't that big that they should lose touch with the people." Another thought of it in terms of a "hands-on" commitment to constituent service. In this way attentiveness was taken as evidence of a true commitment to constituents. As the following subject, a recent college graduate, put it early in his interview, "I like to see that [representatives] know I'm there, that they're looking for some feedback here and there." Later on, in a reference to a specific official, he noted favorably "that we can communicate to him and expect him to actually look over whatever we happen to send to him and have us get some feedback from him. . . . If I could get that from most politicians I would be pretty happy (laughs)." Ultimately, then, attentiveness to the district was seen by a number of people, particularly the more politically attuned respondents, as one component of a vital representative process.

Openness and Accessibility

Two closely related building blocks of representation were what can be called openness and accessibility. Several respondents felt that representation would be inadequate if elected officials were not openly receptive to people's needs, ideas, or policy views. And this in turn implied that officials should be amenable to constituent influence and persuasion; that representatives' issue positions and priorities, in other words, should not be set in stone.[5] Perhaps not surprisingly, this viewpoint was espoused mainly by the "political activists." As one woman active in the NYS political process expressed it: "That if I do have a particular interest or need that I can bring it to my elected representative and that they would be willing to listen to my point of view and possibly support my position." She later hinted that because "sometimes people get down in Washington and forget who they represent," such openness can serve as a useful antidote against representatives 'going native.' A number of respondents (including the woman quoted above) used the classic image of an "open door" to signify this outlook.

Other people expressed frustration with a perceived lack of openness on the part of elected officials. One person opined that "Well, if they're supposed to represent us, I think it should be open. I don't think they should be telling us what their opinion is and then asking us to say that's really good." In a similar vein, a different respondent believed that the quality of representation was being compromised in part because of a shortage of openness: "I think they [politicians] should really be open to the people's comments and criticisms, and that's the thing. In an ideal situation they're much more open to what the people have to say, and I think that a lot of the times now . . . they vote for the larger companies rather than the people."[6]

What political scientists call access to elected officials also proved pivotal to a number of respondents. Reflecting a position held in varying degrees by others, one subject declared: "I prefer that they are reachable, you know, that you can get in contact with them and not a string of people before you actually reach them, and that they are not too far removed." Fenno observes in *Home Style* that reaching out to constituents can be facilitated by access, and that access often becomes a constitutive element of constituent trust. It may also have a kind of positive "multiplier effect" among citizens in the district: "Access to some carries the assurance of access to more; and the assurance of access carries with it the assurance of two-way communication" (p. 240).

This notion of the utility of the assurance of having access to representatives actually played out in some of the interviews. One individual even presented a remarkably Fennoesque take on the benefits of attentiveness and access: "I think it makes for a positive image for them, and for us, so that we know that they are looking out for us, if we have something that we have in mind we can go ahead and write to them [and] *that they are there for us"* (emphasis added). Considered in its broadest form, as encompassing both availability *and* certain types of attentiveness to the community, access proved to be a staple of many participants' conceptions of representation.

Involvement: Visibility and Direct Contact

Of the representational triumvirate that I call "attentiveness, open-ness/accessibility, and involvement," the last proved to be the most highly charged. Many of the participants who discussed involvement in the community by elected officials held strong feelings about it. While most extolled its virtues in the representative process, a number of them had serious reservations about it. Before turning to this, however, the components of involvement must first be detailed.

Respondents appeared to conceive of involvement with the con-stituency in essentially two ways: in a "weaker" form (as *visibility*); and in a "stronger" form (as regular and direct *contact*). Visibility includes what several participants described as having elected officials "show up" in the dis-trict, make themselves seen (or heard) by constituents, attend local functions, and so forth. In fact, a few people portrayed just being *in* the community as one of the basic responsibilities of elected officials. In this sense, visibility becomes a vital part of the representative process. As such, visibility may also help to engender constituent confidence and trust, as it apparently does for one respondent: "I think more than anything they have to make an appearance. I think more than anything they have to be seen in public. They may not get any work done whatsoever, but I think it's reassuring to the people, it would be reassuring to me, to see my represen-tative or senator at home and visible at whatever he happens to be doing."

This is an important point to emphasize. Like perhaps most other po-litical scientists, Fenno provides a different, and more critical, assessment of visibility: "Visibility requires nothing more than name recognition on the part of the constituent and, hence, requires no responsiveness on the part of the congressman. . . . He reaches them only to get their support, not to be responsive" (*Home Style,* pp. 236–237). Some of my respondents clearly shared this perspective. But others saw in visibility something more valuable. For them, visibility means more than being just a recognizable face in the crowd; it can also connote that a representative has established (or is trying to establish) a real presence—an identity—in the community. In this sense visibility, like accessibility, signals to people that the con-stituency truly matters to an elected official. Thus, it may serve as another way for citizens to gauge a representative's commitment to his district. One person expressed this view while combining elements of visibility and ac-cess in her example of a particularly good, or "answerable," representative:

In my hometown area, there's a [state] senator, Valella, he's . . . around a lot, all holidays he's around, his face is all over the place. In the Bronx News I haven't seen an issue that he's not in, and that's because he really makes a point to appear at high school graduation ceremonies and stuff like that. And he's in his office up the block, he's sitting there as much as he can, and I guess that visibility in the community and [the fact that] he is there, if you want to walk in his office and register a complaint or talk to him he is available for that.

Direct and regular contact is the second, and more frequently discussed, leg of involvement. The most commonly mentioned types of direct contact were speaking with citizens, meeting with different constituent groups, and "observing people" in the community. Involvement of this kind reflects a higher level of commitment and perhaps accountability by representatives than does simple visibility. It also implies a greater degree of intimate contact. To the subjects who discussed it, direct involvement almost always meant spending significant time with the people *at home.*

Both sides of this equation deserve attention. A few people alluded to the importance of *unmediated* contact with elected officials, of meeting them face-to-face without the filtering effect unavoidable through other forms of contact (letters, petitions, e-mail, etc.) or intermediaries like staff. These respondents felt that besides giving elected officials a better sense of people's needs or viewpoints, and allowing constituents to more clearly transmit their own preferences, one-on-one contact in the district also gives citizens a chance to see what representatives are really like, that is, a "truer" picture of who they are and what they believe. At its best, then, direct contact serves two complementary goals: helping representatives stay attuned to their constituents and letting constituents get to know their representatives. And this is more likely to occur in spontaneous situations than in more scripted settings. One respondent, a volunteer fireman, relayed a personal experience with Senator Moynihan to portray the value of representatives "seeing the people and talking to them" without any "handlers" present:

We had Daniel Patrick Moynihan swing through three years ago, and we had a community meeting, but before the meeting he was hanging out eating pizza and drinking beer with the firemen and, you know, the walls were down and we were able to talk to him about anything you wanted to talk about, he didn't have staffers at his side saying you can't talk about this or avoid this, like he did when he went out to the community meeting.

By the same token, several subjects mentioned the importance of having representatives meet and talk with constituents on the latter's own turf. These individuals insisted that elected officials must "go into the community" and observe constituents in their own environment in order to truly understand and appreciate their needs, interests, and concerns. Simple visibility is not enough; neither is contact in the "artificial" form of office hours or public speeches. What really counts is firsthand and ongoing observation of people's lives, in their everyday places of work and association. To these citizens, only this type of involvement produces real insight into the constituency and empathy for its concerns, as well as viable solutions for its problems. An *experiential* connection between representatives and represented is crucial. The following quotes from several different respondents should give some flavor of this perspective.

> Go into the community. I mean, go into different places where people are, like go to different churches and things like that to see what people think about what's happening in the community and show the people that you're really interested . . . going to the inner cities, the suburban cities, should be their job, just to see how things run.
>
> Go out into the field, and go to different places so you can see how people's living situation is and the conditions they are in, and what you can do about it, you know. You have to experience some of those things sometimes so you can actually know about it, you can't just talk about things without knowing what's going on.
>
> If they aren't already familiar with who their constituents are to seek them out and . . . find out what the people are about and what they are looking for and then proceed from there.[7]

The perceived benefits of such direct contact were manifold. As mentioned above, these respondents felt that representatives can gain much greater insight into, and therefore understanding of, their constituencies through constant contact. It enables members to stay in touch with the people they serve, to realize "that there are faces behind the constituent numbers that they need to keep in mind."[8] A number of participants noted that because "things don't stay constant in the community," regular contact helps elected officials adapt to changes in their districts. A few people felt that it would result in "more bills passed for the benefit of the public" and voting that better reflected constituent's interests (in the Miller-Stokes vernacular, more policy congruence); "if [representatives] don't spend enough time with [their] people then they're not voting correctly for their constituents as they should be."[9] A couple of subjects also suggested that ongoing contact gives people a sense of importance or empowerment in the political process. Finally, at least one individual held out the hope that greater involvement would help to restore people's faith in government: "Because if they did (go out and meet with people), then people would start believing in government more."

Interestingly, some respondents also discussed how *representatives* themselves benefit politically from regular contact. Just as with visibility, these individuals noted that contact can further the perception of good representation among constituents. And perception may be reality: "If someone sees you there (in the district) they think you're taking an interest. And I think on some level [representatives] are if they are there, so I think the more visible you are the more concerned you are about the district." Several of the more politically active subjects observed that through effective contact representatives purchase both policy freedom and political capital, which becomes especially useful in times of conflict with the district (or with district groups engaged in the political process). After recounting an experience with former Congressman Sherwood Boehlert, a lobbyist for an environmental advocacy organization revealed he had absorbed the Fennoesque political lesson that

> because of his (Boehlert's) personal attributes and the fact that he's likable, and the fact that he does spend a lot of time developing relationships with constituent groups as much as his constituents, he buys himself a lot of leeway . . . that's why if I was a legislator I would want to be directly and actively engaged with my constituents, *because it isn't just a one way kind of legislator loyalty to their constituents, but you can build loyalty the other way, and that can cut you a lot of slack when you need it.* (emphasis added)

And this brings us to two characteristics of the responses concerning representational involvement that distinguished them from those in the other categories. The first is that there was a definite relationship between the political sophistication of subjects and their views about involvement. With a few notable exceptions, the least active and knowledgeable subjects were the ones who most frequently discussed, and most strongly endorsed, regular contact with constituents *in the district*. Indeed, for some of them direct contact appeared to constitute the heart of the representative process. Several of these respondents made repeated references to this type of involvement, and in a variety of contexts. Overall, I was struck by how deeply they held to the importance of district-based contact by elected officials.

By contrast, the politically sophisticated respondents who touched on these matters were more inclined to emphasize the importance of access, especially issue access, regardless of where (or how) it takes place.[10] As discussed above, several political activists in particular mentioned the desirability of having representatives who are open to receiving information about issues and direct policy "persuasion" from constituents and advocacy groups. Several of these individuals described personal experiences with this kind of contact. For instance, a lobbyist with the NYS branch of the AFL-CIO revealed that

> Yeah, I was down for a union related conference in Washington
> . . . they asked us to lobby on something called the team act,
> which affects labor relations, and I went in and set up an appointment. Originally I was going to meet with staff, but Mike
> (Congressman McNulty) found the time to meet with me too,
> and he said he'd heard a little about the issue, and I had come
> with material. And he said, "Oh geez, I never really knew the arguments of it, thanks for taking the time." So I think probably in
> his mind he knows that issue is important to me and the organization I represent, and I think he took a closer look at it and really started reading up on it. So I think it does have an impact.

In addition, politically aware individuals were more likely to indicate that the necessity and intensity of involvement is contingent on the type of representative (local, state, or national) involved. No apolitical respondent made such distinctions (see endnote 8 for further elaboration on this distinction). Finally, politically attentive respondents seemed far more aware of the political benefits that elected officials reap through visibility and direct contact, even if these subjects did not personally endorse these behaviors. With regard to access and involvement, then, personal variables such as political awareness and participation did appear to have a discernible impact on people's fundamental beliefs about representation, as well as on their appraisal of the merits of the different dimensions of responsiveness.

The second major difference between the categories concerned the advisability or acceptability of involvement to the subjects. Unlike with attentiveness and openness/access, approximately one-third of the participants expressed some dissatisfaction or apprehension with behavior that falls under the heading of visibility or direct contact. This included three individuals who were in other respects staunch advocates of these actions. The critics tended to fall into two camps: those who considered involvement to be highly problematic or unnecessary; and those who saw it being used as a political expedient or a sham. Regarding the first group, a few people perceived a potential conflict between regular contact and the fulfillment of members other (especially legislative) obligations, either because of the unavoidable limits of time and attention ("I mean realistically I guess you can't expect somebody to be in two places at one time") or because excessive obeisance to the constituency might warp representatives judgment. One respondent felt that the benefits of direct contact, especially constituent service, could be just as easily obtained from staff or other intermediaries: "I would just basically say that the congressperson need not even come back here. I really don't care if I see you again, as long as I see somebody who represents you." Several others disparaged the representational value of direct contact, arguing that there were other means available to ensure the representative-constituent connection. Consider this example regarding members of Congress:

> I think taking care of their constituents doesn't necessarily mean being present physically, because their job is in Washington. I mean, they can find a way of [contacting] their constituents without being in that area. The work they need to do is in Washington. That's where they should be. And if they can communicate via the written word, or telephone, or computer, or staffing, I don't know that there is work they have to do in their homes (districts).

More often, however, subjects questioned the intent of direct involvement on the part of elected officials. As the respondent just quoted above skeptically remarked: "What are they going to do in Kansas, you know what I mean, except [give] free talks and get free dinners?" Some people explicitly criticized what they saw as the political artifice behind most contact: "I don't think they really need to be coming down here and shaking my hand to look good. . . . I guess they should go to see groups and meet with people and stuff like that, but I don't think they're accomplishing anything but just showing up. It's just photo-ops. I think they belong in Washington doing their jobs. . . . It's all show."

But most disturbing of all, especially for those subjects who otherwise treasured visibility and one-on-one involvement, was electorally motivated contact. As one person put it, "I think they do it up to the point when they get elected, and then it's like, 'well, I'm in there now.'" Several respondents were particularly galled by elected officials who only seem to "come out of the woodwork" during campaign seasons. Cynicism about such election-year attentiveness was unvarnished. The same man who extolled the virtues of visibility soon after sarcastically remarked ". . . during an election year, they're always around. You can't move without tripping over a politician. You go to the fair in the last weekend of August and you're tripping over Julie McCoy and, uh, they're making all the time in the world to get out and say hello, and once election year is over they disappear for three years."

To these respondents, such sporadic contact is manifestly hypocritical and actually indicative of a lack of concern for the constituency. It is, in short, a form of pseudo-responsiveness, and ultimately undermines the type of relationship that should develop between elected officials and the people they represent. The following admonition from the strongest advocate of direct contact provides a clear distinction between "legitimate" and "illegitimate" representational involvement and a fitting conclusion for this section:

> Come into the community and show people that you are really interested in the community, not being there one minute and the next minute you're not there, you know what I mean? That's how I see things. I mean you'll be there for one month and the next month you ain't going to be there. One year you'll be there putting up a façade, puttin' up something like a smoke screen. . . . I mean, people just ain't going to believe [in] you just like that. They've really got to have some faith in you to support you. . . . You've got to be there year-round. You've got to be active.

Communication:
The Heart of Representation

If I had to choose one word to describe how subjects thought about representation, it would be *communication.* As the title of this section suggests, communication with constituents was central to the representational worldviews of most of the participants. In one way or another, a large majority stressed the vital role of good communication in the representative process. Explaining the significance of communication—and proclaiming how it should take place—often took up much of their time and attention. Many of them also considered communication to be a main part of the "job description" of elected officials. Indeed, for several people it seemed to be the very essence of the representative process; as one respondent said when asked why communication was so important to her, "Well . . . that's what representation means (laughs). I don't know what else it could mean." Defining the essential features of the "model" of representational communication that emerged from these interviews is therefore one of the primary goals of this study, and the principal objective of this section.

Toward the end of *Home Style,* Richard Fenno focuses on the central role that communication plays in creating successful home styles, and therefore trust, for members of Congress.[11] Much of this communication takes the form of advertising, credit claiming, and visibility—the myriad ways that a representative presents himself to his constituents in order to induce name recognition and fashion a positive image among them. In short, *one-way* communication. Yet Fenno notes that true representation requires something more. "The idea of responsiveness assumes the existence of *two-way* communication . . . of efforts to listen to and talk to supportive constituents" (p. 238, emphasis added). As he also wrote:

> Responsiveness, and, hence, representation, require two-way communication. Although the congressman can engage in this kind of communication with only some of his supportive constituents, he can give many more the assurance that two-way communication is possible. . . . Access and the assurance of access, communication and the assurance of communication—these are the irreducible underpinnings of representation. (pp. 239–240).

Most of my respondents would surely second much of this appraisal. At heart, their understanding of the representative process generally *presumed* two-way communication—an ongoing and reciprocal flow of information, ideas, and preferences between representatives and represented. As several subjects described it, representation requires a continuous "dialogue" or "conversation" between elected officials and the people they serve. The reciprocal nature of this view of communication cannot be overemphasized. Respondents almost by definition expected that representatives would apprise constituents of their actions and decisions. But as much as they valued information about the legislative process or voting decisions, most of them also wanted to be able to provide their own input (or "feedback") to members of Congress. Actually, given the overall thrust and tenor of their responses, many of the subjects appeared more concerned about this side of the communication equation.

In fact, two-way communication appeared so important to some of them because they felt it might serve as a kind of antidote to the types of one-way communication that in their view adds little to, or even undermines, the representative relationship. It is also true that the participants might take issue with Fenno's depiction of two-way communication as the province of what he termed supportive constituents. To them, it is not enough for representatives to ensure that only certain constituents have the opportunity for real dialogue. Legitimate two-way communication should expose elected officials to the full array of groups, interests, and viewpoints in their districts. What ultimately makes this kind of communication so valuable (and necessary) is that it offers *all* citizens the chance to reach, teach, and persuade representatives about their concerns and preferences. Indeed, for some respondents' constituent to representative communication is vital precisely because it may compel members to pay attention to, and learn from, those they might not otherwise (want to) hear.

The Pillars of Communication

The first pillar of communication, and perhaps the most widely accepted by students and practitioners of representation alike, is that of *informing* constituents about the actions and decisions representatives make. Four out of every five respondents, too, highlighted the importance of having elected officials notify constituents of their activities. In different ways subjects often echoed one person's injunction that "[I]t's their responsibility to report back." For many participants, not surprisingly, reporting back proves especially important for voting decisions. Most wanted representatives to keep them abreast of legislative decision making in general and their own votes in particular. A bit more surprising was the number of subjects who explicitly or implicitly suggested that such representative to constituent communication should be constant; as one person put it, "the representative should be in contact with his people *all the time*" (emphasis added). To these citizens, an effective representative process requires not just selective and intermittent, but regular and comprehensive, communication with people back home. "Give them [constituents] more feedback with everything" was a kind of rallying cry in many of the interviews.

But as important, if not more so, for most respondents is the possibility and necessity of constituent input into the representative process. Interestingly, subjects identified two broad types of constituent input. The first encompasses things like canvassing the district, sending out constituent surveys, and taking opinion polls. In these respondents' eyes, the periodic sampling of district opinion can help members keep tabs on their constituencies, find out where various groups stand on the issues, and discover what they do or do not favor. It therefore works to ensure that the views of representatives and constituents remain in sync. "Keeping in touch" with the needs of the district in this way characterized several of the participants' views on representation, including this woman's: "I think that means they are supposed to be interested in what their constituents think and that they should be listening. If they are not getting letters from their constituents, they should be sending out surveys and things like that. It seems to me they should be paying attention to what the majority of the people are saying."

Notice, however, the passive nature of this type of input. The solicitation of constituent opinion through surveys or polls requires no interaction, no education or persuasion, no real engagement by either side. It can be a relatively static and detached affair. Many of the respondents appeared to sense this, and to think that something else was needed, for they usually moved on to discuss more involved kinds of constituent communication.

In order for members to better understand their districts, and for constituents to more effectively shape the representative process, respondents often championed interactive forms of constituent-representative communication. On one level this meant giving constituents the opportunity to transmit their views to elected officials on their own terms. This might mean having one-on-one or group meetings with representatives, or being asked to provide more individualized input to them. Concerning the latter, a number of respondents expressed the desire for more open-ended surveys from representatives that would allow constituents to frame their own responses. The subject quoted above also stated that "I do find that (surveys) don't give you much room [to respond]. They're kind of like, hey, don't you want me to believe this [laughs] . . . I think maybe if they gave you a little more space to put in your own comments instead of just check yes, no, or maybe, and here's some lines you can use for comment." A couple of people likewise wished to receive questionnaires on major issues *before* votes occur, so that constituents could be heard on the issues and perhaps influence their representatives voting positions. As one participant declared: "Very seldom am I polled up here on how I feel personally about a pressing bill or a major issue. I mean, they should if it's a major . . . let's say like the minimum wage issue that's coming up for a vote in Congress. They should [say] on a questionnaire, "do you agree that the minimum wage should be raised or stay the same?" Most of all, subjects were looking for the opportunity to engage in true "conversations" with elected officials. They wanted to be able to *directly* educate and be educated by, to persuade and be persuaded by, their representatives. And the most oft-mentioned vehicle for such representative-constituent interaction was some variant of the town meeting.

Town Meetings: Realizing Two-Way Communication

More than anything else, open public meetings between representatives and their constituents embodied the respondents' ideal of two-way communication. Nearly 60 percent of the subjects spontaneously mentioned or endorsed town meetings at some point during their interviews, and a large percentage of this group dwelt on them at some length. The depictions of town meetings made by certain individuals were almost romantic musings on the nature of the good representational process. And what is it about such public gatherings that so fired the participants' political imaginations?

In part it may be their link to one of the most powerful and enduring images in American political life—grassroots local democracy. The New England town meeting is perhaps the foremost symbol of this participatory impulse; two respondents specifically mentioned it in reference to their ideal political process. But in the contemporary political context, constituent-representative meetings seem to be valued mainly because they are seen as the embodiment of both one-way and two-way communication. That is, subjects at all levels of political sophistication considered town meetings not only to be one of the best ways for representatives to inform and enlighten their constituents, but also for citizens to make themselves heard and understood by those in positions of power. They allow constituents to both receive and give the most essential kinds of political "feedback." In this sense, then, town meetings embody all the facets of true representational communication.

First of all, community meetings were considered one of the best platforms from which representatives can inform their constituents about legislative developments, major political events, and issues or decisions of local import. Respondents believed that by having representatives come home to directly face citizens and be questioned about their issue positions and political actions, people can gain a firsthand, unmediated, and richer understanding of the political process, as well as of the character and convictions of the representatives themselves. Town meetings were similarly viewed as an excellent arena for members of Congress to explain, and perhaps justify, their voting records. The gatherings therefore serve as a way for voters to hold elected officials accountable. When asked if she would trust representatives more if they held more town meetings, one subject replied, "Oh, absolutely. Because then they could see us. . . . They could see us, and they'd be held accountable. Because they would have to come back to the meeting next month. You know what I'm saying?"[12]

At the same time, town meetings were thought to give representatives a better grasp of their constituents problems, preferences, and interests, and thus to help members set their own legislative priorities. When questioned how legislators can accommodate local political pressures and still keep the "big picture" in mind, one participant stated that it "probably boils down to open communication. You know, perhaps going out and having town meetings here and there, and you still get the local point of view from each spot but you can get a better picture of the whole through several town meetings, you know, [and] keeping an open door to phone calls and to visits."

An underlying thread in many of the discussions about town meetings was the idea that they are truly public and reciprocal: both the representative and the constituents have the opportunity to speak, react, and present their cases.[13] The subjects' faith in the inherently interactive nature and potential benefits of this "great medium" was perhaps best disclosed in this answer to a hypothetical question about a representative's vote choice:

I think there should be open debate in her district in terms of a town hall meeting. Let her come home before the people and let them know how she feels, and why she feels this vote will neg-atively impact that district. Then let the constituents speak. Let each constituent have, say, five minutes at the microphone. En-courage her constituents to come forward with letters that her staff can review. But the constituents also, a lot of them are very intelligent people who can shed light on a situation. That's how I think it should be done, through a town hall meeting style.

In sum, town meetings supply citizens with a widely accepted mode of engaging, and perhaps directly influencing, their elected officials. Sev-eral subjects approvingly noted that town meetings can help get ordinary citizens involved in the political process and even empower them. To these individuals, a main selling point of such gatherings (what one de-scribed as "open-mike meetings") is that they give constituents the chance to speak openly and directly to representatives about their views, priorities, and concerns without the limitations inherent in some other forms of communication, or when information is filtered through inter-mediaries like staff or party officials.

A few participants, in fact, contended that town meetings (like cer-tain other types of involvement) might be the only time that represen-tatives would have contact with "real people" or marginalized groups in their districts. As one of these respondents opined, "You know, a lot of these guys, the only time they are going to hear anything from some-body who is down and out or poor is in a situation like that. You know, to come into contact with real people who are having a tough time." Town meetings may therefore serve as a useful corrective to the other sources of information and advice that representatives rely upon. And such gatherings might also compel officials to deal with issues of real concern to ordinary people. The intrinsically positive relationship be-tween two-way communication, town meetings, and the representative process to these citizens is best crystallized in the following quote from one subject:

Well, I think the ideal relationship would be one where there is a lot of contact, where the legislator is kind of actively engaged in bringing his or her constituents into the legislative process, so that her constituents are well-versed in what's going on in terms of what's at stake for them, so they can better understand what their interests are [and] so they can have ample opportunity to provide input. . . . I think one of the ways that legislators educate their constituents or attempt to get feedback from them are through public meetings.

The Benefits of Communication

This brings us back full circle to the perceived benefits of representative-constituent communication. On the whole, subjects believed that citizens profit in three major ways from good communication. First, of course, is that constituents who are regularly well-informed by members gain better and more extensive knowledge of government, especially of individual and institutional decision making. Many of the respondents' answers implied that effective citizen understanding of the political process could be foreclosed without the information and insight gleaned from ongoing communication with their representatives. Having elected officials "report back" thus appears to be an essential component, and perhaps even a precondition, of effective representation in their eyes.

When combined with two-way forms of communication, such contact was also thought to enhance responsiveness to district needs and concerns. Interestingly, a number of the more sophisticated respondents observed that elected officials generally *will* try to respond to constituents' entreaties, so citizens who engage their representatives and provide input are more likely to get results. When people make their views known, in short, attentiveness follows. As one individual stated: "I think people can make an impact when they follow an issue by talking to their congressman directly. Most congressmen do listen to you when they get phone calls and things; it has an influence on them." A few subjects intimated that regular constituent input might also reduce the number of election-year converts to district attentiveness. Soon after tartly issuing the injunction that "I think they should be paying attention," a respondent often critical of members of Congress asserted that

> RES: Well, I think people—citizens—should be a little more outspoken as well. I think they should be good listeners, and they should be speaking their opinions, and I think that people should have opinions and contact their officials . . .
>
> INT: How would that change the way representatives act?
>
> RES: Maybe they would pay more attention, not just to think election time means come out of the woodwork to put their pictures everywhere and litter on my front lawn, *they would pay attention the whole time they are in position.* (emphasis added)

Greater sensitivity to constituents' political and issue preferences was a third and related benefit of good communication noted by several respondents. One participant even contended that communication would increase representatives' legislative effectiveness: "A congressman that communicates with his people on a personal and political basis could get more done." A few people put this idea in broader institutional terms. For instance, one subject asserted that openness to constituent input—"to what the people have to say"—would result in "more laws that would better serve the people instead of the bigger interests." Or, as another individual expressed it: "I think if representatives did ("ask and listen"), Congress or whatever's voting record would reflect more reality in what's happening with people."

Finally, as with direct contact, many of these citizens also surmised that representatives themselves could gain from regular communication. From a representational standpoint, it was thought that such communication invariably expands elected officials understanding of their districts, as touched on earlier. But some participants recognized the potential political benefits as well. Representatives who "pay attention" to their districts through frequent communication are more likely to be viewed as truly concerned about their constituents, which in turn may inspire greater confidence in them. Along with this possible increase in public support, several people mentioned that regular contact with the district can reduce constituent misunderstanding of a member's positions or behavior and the political fallout from controversial decisions. In the words of one respondent who conveyed this idea,

> I think there always has to be a good flow of communications between a congressman and his district, because you can fight so hard for it and people will be like, "well, why did you do it?" The general public, they don't know what's going on, so I think the benefits are that, you know, you don't have any lag, you don't have any [misunderstanding].

And another:

> RES: Even if a lot of people may not agree with him, they should be able to understand him and respect that and know the reason why he's going against them, or why he's going for something that's not so popular. . . . Being very informative helps all the time, communication must be positive and constant.
>
> INT: Do you think that would help him in this situation?
>
> RES: Definitely it will help, even though the certain decision is not really favorable.

Thus, rather than spelling certain political disaster, honest, open, and continuous communication about one's actions and voting decisions could nurture constituent understanding and respect—trust.

Concluding Remarks

This chapter has presented a comprehensive portrait of the subjects' abstract ideas and expectations about representation. It has defined and explored the respondents' basic building blocks of the representative process—attentiveness to the constituency, openness and accessibility, involvement in the district, and (especially) communication. It has delineated the representational *and* political blessings that they believe can accrue from the proper operation of these processes. And it has outlined how these views do and do not match up with the portrait of the representation found in the literature. But understanding what citizens think about representation in general, while essential, is just one part of the story. To more fully grasp the public's view of representation, we must also recognize how such general beliefs inform people's convictions about the actual representative process and their priorities for the representative relationship. What, for instance, do ordinary citizens want representatives to do in office, and how do they expect members of Congress to make decisions? How do people perceive the contemporary representative relationship? And how are these viewpoints and expectations conditioned by their global beliefs about representation? These are some of the fundamental questions that animate the following two chapters.

Chapter Four

Representation in Practice

Introduction

Explication of people's overarching representational ideals and expectations can significantly increase our understanding of the public side of representation, as the preceding chapter demonstrates. But it is equally important to know how such abstract beliefs inform citizens' views of the *actual* representative process. How well, for example, do people think representative-constituent communication really works? How do they think members of Congress should come to make voting decisions? And what do they expect congressional representatives to do when faced with some classic decision-making dilemmas? These bedrock concerns may lie at the heart of the representative relationship, but they have received scant attention in the literature. Addressing them could greatly enhance our knowledge of the dynamics of the representative process.

In this chapter, we investigate some of the practical implications of people's primary representational beliefs. We first examine the respondents' views about the state of representative-constituent communication. We then inquire how their core convictions about representation—the constitutive elements of responsiveness—are "put into practice" in responses to two hypothetical voting scenarios for members of Congress. By exploring how subjects expect members to resolve these voting quandaries, or how they view the representative process when placed in a member's shoes, we get a glimpse of how ordinary citizens conceive of one of the most important aspects of the representative relationship, as well as a better understanding of their foremost representational ideals. Through all this we will also chronicle the vital importance of two other representational functions: *explanation* and *education/persuasion*. The evidence presented here offers the first inkling that ordinary citizens can appreciate the underlying complexity, practical political difficulties, and conflicting

imperatives members of Congress confront in the representative process—
and that these realities may be integrally related to people's diverse and divergent expectations for the process. It also indicates that people believe
such representational processes as communication, explanation, and education can serve both narrow political aims and larger democratic ends—
but that significant obstacles stand in the way of this realization.

Communication: Opportunities and Pitfalls

The critical importance of communication in the subjects' representational perspectives prompts consideration of their views about the state
of contemporary representative-constituent communication. To begin
with, a number of respondents appeared quite sanguine about the impact of modern technology on this relationship. The telephone, e-mail,
internet, and television were all portrayed as instruments that could improve both the informative and interactive sides of communication. To
give just one example, the following subject suggested that representative-to-constituent contact could be simultaneously institutionalized and
energized, and the audience for such contact significantly broadened, by
linking town meetings to that most pervasive of modern communication
mediums—television. In her words,

> I think town meetings should be televised on cable. Not every-
> one can make a town meeting. I would like to know what's going
> on, so I think a way it could be helped would be for us to know
> what's happening. The meetings should be televised so we could
> tape it . . . communication is the key. How they can make that
> work would be four times a year representatives would have to
> have a televised program. Four times a year, every spring/sum-
> mer/fall/winter on a certain date, it would be on TV. Everything
> that happened during the last three months, what we'll be work-
> ing on the next three months.

Notwithstanding the apparent promise of technology, however,
a sizeable percentage of subjects were cognizant of the many obstacles
to effective communication. Although some people (especially the
most politically active subjects) felt that representatives generally do
a good job of corresponding with their constituents, a larger number bemoaned both the quantity and quality of representational
communication today.

Some of the impediments to communication are endemic to the
modern representational process, as a surprising number of respondents
seemed to realize.[1] They are not, in this sense, anyone's fault, nor are
they easily remediable. The problem most commonly recognized by sub-

jects in this vein was the geographic size and number of constituents in legislative districts. How can today's representatives possibly contact and communicate with, and therefore be responsive to, all or even a majority of the people they represent when their constituencies are so large? A third of the somewhat sophisticated and sophisticated subjects wrestled with this representational dilemma directly, while several others touched on it in more indirect ways. As the following individual put it, in fairly typical fashion: "It's tough with the system we have, with populations as they are, I don't think they can get around as much as they would like or would be optimal to get to people and make sure that each small group of people feels that they're represented."

Many of these respondents appeared to conclude that there is an inverse relationship between the size and complexity of the constituency and the quantity (and/or quality) of communication and contact. The following response from one participant to a question about the ideal kind of representative relationship illustrates this view: "Obviously there should be an awful lot of communication somehow. That's hard to accomplish. Keeping up with the people is a more attainable goal, you know, in a very small constituency like my alderman. I know my alderman and I think I should. . . . But a congressman personally can't know everything like that." And respondents were often concerned that the kind of communication most likely to suffer today was the kind they valued most—the interactive variety. A few even pointed out the effect of constituency size on that bastion of two-way communication, the town meeting. As one subject who described town meetings as "wonderful" later agonized, "Yeah, I think they're great. But we're so big now. We're so big. I don't know, how do you do that? Something like that can only work in a small . . ." and then her voice trailed off.

Yet many of the problems with representative-constituent communication identified by respondents are not so rooted in the basic structure of the political system. Rather, they can be traced, in a manner of speaking, to someone's negligence. For instance, some participants believed that effective communication was being undermined by representatives' aversion to informing constituents about their actions and their unwillingness to engage in sustained, worthwhile contact. Several opined that elected officials try to shroud at least some of their voting record and political actions from the public: "So often these guys vote and you don't even know when they're voting or what they're voting on." Apathetic, uninvolved citizens only compound the problem of noncommunication. One occasionally politically active respondent pointedly observed that

> they're (representatives) all fairly responsive. I think the thing is, you hear people piss and moan about government without being willing to take an active role, without being willing to accept the

responsibilities of citizenship. And if you make the effort—if you write the letters and round up your friends who are like-minded and you go have the meetings—then I think, you know, you can see some effect. . . . So I believe that for the people who are willing to put in the effort it works. It's just that it takes more effort than some people like to expend.

Respondents' grievances, however, usually centered upon a perceived dearth of legitimate communication from their elected officials. There were several parts to the critique here. One concerned an overall lack of communication from representatives. A number of people remarked that they rarely receive contact or information from their representatives, even in the form of tax-subsidized newsletters or surveys. Some respondents also thought that two-way communication was hampered because members simply aren't "out there" enough in their constituencies.[2]

But most prevalent were often biting remarks about what people regarded as phony, banal, or entirely self-serving communication. The subjects' animus was usually directed at what they perceived to be the electoral motivation behind communication in the form of surveys or newsletters. For example, the participant quoted below charged that

I don't fill [surveys] out anymore because they're *so slanted.* . . . I think all of their newsletters are for self-aggrandizement. I don't think they're really asking us so much as telling how wonderful they are. So it's certainly slanted only on reelection and image. I don't see them truly asking (pause) I mean, they'll ask you this and that, but I think they've almost already decided what they want to hear back. (emphasis in original)

In fact, more than one respondent simultaneously extolled the educational or interactive potential of surveys/newsletters and derided those they do receive as being transparently dedicated to what David R. Mayhew called advertising and credit-claiming. A couple of these subjects were particularly interested in learning more about the underlying dynamics, the "ins and outs," of the legislative process. The following quote from one such individual illustrates this point nicely:

I would like more (newsletters). . . . I'd like to know more in-depth about what is really going on. Instead of just the frothy, "oh, we're great, we just did this, this and this." How about, "you know, what's going on in Washington is we're fighting for this or we're having trouble because this PAC is against it. The person over here is causing us to have to give a little over here." I want to know about that kind of stuff.

In the view of these citizens, most representative-to-constituent communication is simply not geared toward raising the level of political awareness among constituents or soliciting their (informed) opinions—which they believe should be its ultimate purpose. As another individual put it: "I don't want a cheap survey. I want a comments section. It's like they're trying to pigeonhole you. . . . 'I'm going to vote this way, can I talk you into it with these questions?!'" It is not so much the form itself that is fatally flawed; it is the current substance. If used "properly," that is to educate and engage citizens, then it might become a valuable link in an interactive communication chain, as this concluding passage from the same individual who called newsletters "so slanted" suggests:

> RES: I think those newsletters could be used well in their own districts. . . . I'd like to see more questions or presentations of, "this is the way it is, here's the problem and here's the bill, and these are the possibilities, and let me know what you think about it," rather than I've been such a good guy or girl and I got you all of these things, and don't forget that on election day.
>
> INT: What kind of improvements would that kind of communication bring?
>
> RES: I think they would get many more responses, they might get people to think about it more. And it would probably be more cumbersome to collate and analyze, but it might be worth it. It certainly would make their constituents feel better [*laughs*].

Making Voting Decisions:
The Hypotheticals

To conclude the interviews, respondents were presented with realistic voting scenarios for two imaginary members of Congress.

1. Suppose a bill to increase environmental regulations was being considered by Congress. Congresswoman Y thinks the bill will hurt the economy, but the people she represents support such environmental regulation and are in favor of the bill. What do you think she should do in this situation?
2. Now let's say Congressman Z believes it is important for the country to reduce government spending to balance the budget. A bill to do this has come up for a final vote in Congress. However, some government programs will have to be cut under the bill, including programs that benefit the congressman's home district. What do you think he should do when faced with that kind of choice?[3]

In most cases, a series of follow-up questions was asked to give participants the opportunity to clarify or expand on their answers, react to inconsistencies or contradictions in their previous remarks, and/or address other representational dilemmas that surfaced in the course of their replies.

There were essentially three objectives behind the hypothetical queries. First, I wanted to know how (and whether) previously expressed ideas or assumptions about representation reappeared in true-to-life voting contexts. Second, I was trying to gain a clear sense of how respondents expected the decision-making process to unfold, what they expected members to do in these situations, and what they considered to be most important in the overall process.[4] Third, I wanted subjects to ponder the real-world implications of their stated beliefs about representation. The questions were therefore designed to let them face some of the inherent decision-making conflicts in the representative process from the vantage point of *both* ordinary citizens and representatives—and to try and resolve them.

Exploring how people apply their abstract beliefs to the reality of being a representative can help us to distill their basic expectations for the representative relationship. In this way the hypothetical questions helped supply the raw materials to construct a model of what many subjects might consider an "ideal" representative process. They also provided an opportunity to examine something oft-scrutinized by political scientists—how members of Congress make voting decisions—but this time from the standpoint of ordinary citizens. Ultimately, these queries gave me another window into the respondents' representational belief systems, as well as valuable insight into the public's view of one of the most crucial aspects of the representational process.

Resolving Decision-Making Dilemmas

The first hypothetical question essentially presented subjects with a version of the classic trustee-delegate dilemma: in times of conflict between them, should a member of Congress defer to the wishes of her constituents or follow her own judgment? A slight majority of respondents (approximately 60 percent) expressed the view that the representative should vote according to her constituents' preference. Yet few of the participants offered the kind of unequivocal delegate position offered by this individual: "I think congresspeople should be voting the way that their constituents want them to vote." Most were much more hesitant and studied in working out what they believed would be a viable position, one that finally conformed to their basic assumptions about representation.

In this vein, over 40 percent of the respondents presented some kind of stipulation(s) that qualified their original stance. For example, one person argued that while the representative should consider both sides of the issue, she should give greater weight to the short-term impact of the bill even if this ran against the grain of constituent opinion. Someone else proposed that she should "argue like hell with as many people in [the] constituency her views, listen, and come up with a consensus of what the people want and vote that way." A few subjects submitted what might be called a "contingent delegate" position. One of these individuals argued that as long as constituents were sufficiently "educated" on the issue, the representative should accept their informed judgment; outside that, however, she needs to vote for "what is right." Another suggested that the representative should vote the constituency unless there is "a real overriding issue like morality." A third indicated that the crucial variable in the representative's decision should be the amount and strength of opposition in her district.

Those respondents with a more Burkean perspective offered similar types of decision-making provisos that affected whether, and under what circumstances, the representative should act as a trustee. These voting contingencies ranged from the nature of the issue involved and the depth of the representative's personal conviction to what she had promised her district as a candidate and whether constituents could persuade her to change her position during the two-way communication process. One individual enumerated a whole series of steps that the representative should take before voting her judgment. The overall effect, as was true with the subjects who favored a delegate position, was to restrict the member's voting freedom. And all of the proposed contingencies could be taken as evidence that the respondents were searching for some way to reconcile a commitment to the constituency (or the member's own judgment) with other vital representational responsibilities.

Another common reaction, regardless of the subject's role orientation, was to try to circumvent the dilemma through some kind of compromise solution. For instance, two respondents—one sophisticated and the other relatively unsophisticated—intriguingly contended that the representative could utilize the political process to turn this problem into, as they both termed it, a "win-win situation."[5] A number of others similarly proposed that the member should try to modify the bill so that it would satisfy both environmental and economic interests, or produce a companion piece of legislation that would mitigate what she believed would be the negative economic impact of the measure. For these subjects, such behavior is a standard, and acceptable, part of the legislative process, especially since politics usually "plays in gray areas." It may also be, as one respondent suggested, the only politic thing for a representative to do: "I think what they normally do is what she should do. They water it down so it's acceptable as a compromise, and it goes both ways.

That's what they usually do, and I think that's what she should do as a politician." Thus, rather than being characterized as a deplorable part of the political process, political maneuvering and policy compromise were portrayed by these subjects as necessary (and even beneficial) ways for members to meet their conflicting representational obligations.

The second hypothetical question placed another imaginary representative in an all-too-real predicament: voting in a way that reflects his political platform/principles, or abandoning them in order to protect programs that benefit his district. Interestingly, but perhaps not surprisingly, approximately two-thirds of the subjects in this case concluded that the representative should adhere to his personal beliefs even at the expense of the constituency.[6] But a sizable portion of this group (nearly half) also emphasized that he should take steps to blunt the impact of the decision on his district. And once again, participants often seemed torn about the proper decision to make, and ended up advancing rather complicated or provisional positions. Through all this many of them displayed a good feel for the underlying representational dilemma in the situation, the conflicts it could create for their ideals, and the member's own trying political circumstances.

The first inclination of a number of subjects was to try to find a way out of the quandary. Almost one-third of them, in fact, argued that the representative should initially take steps to soften the blow of a balanced budget on his district or possibly even eliminate the cuts. One person advanced the old standby of first reducing wasteful government spending, preferably in "someone else's district." More typical were calls for the member to negotiate, or "wheel and deal," in order to reduce the severity of the spending cuts, introduce alternatives that wouldn't hurt the district as much (or at all), or at the very least ensure that all districts made equitable sacrifices. Although few people discussed how successful they thought the representative might be in doing this, it was clear that they considered the effort to be an essential demonstration of his commitment to the district.[7]

However, most of these subjects eventually concluded, after some agonizing, that the member should make the decision he believes is in the national interest. Yet they (like several others who did not discuss such compromises) also emphasized that it would be both just and politically imperative for him to help the constituents directly affected by the bill rebound from their losses. One of the least sophisticated participants concisely expressed this perspective:

RES: . . . because it's probably going to affect them big, a lot of people out there need some of them things to get by, and he probably won't get elected again, you know. So try to work around it, try to make sure they don't cut the things that are going to affect his people.

INT: Now what happens if he does all he can to try to work around it, but there's still going to be some programs that are going to be cut?

RES: It isn't the end of the world. People can try to get around it, the same way he tried to get around it. The people have to try and support him. He did all he can. It's not in his hands no more.

In making this case respondents sometimes touched on the fundamental representational dilemma confronting the member. As another individual explained,

> If he is making votes that hurt the livelihood of his constituents . . . it is ultimately politically wise and part of his responsibility to support his constituents. That's a thorny and difficult problem. On the other hand, he should make decisions and let the chips fall where they may. It ultimately boils down to where Congress is supposed to help the general welfare, but needs to provide fallback and mitigate the impact of those decisions.

A different subject spoke of the political importance of

> trying to justify to the people that it would be better for everyone, and perhaps looking for work in other areas for the people that would be affected . . . because I think, you know, local constituents here in Albany would say, "geez, we elected you and here you go voting for a bill that put us out of work," so I think there would be some necessity in going back to the people and pointing out the positive aspects of it, like saving money for the government or being able to allocate money elsewhere . . .

As an unsophisticated participant distilled the member's obligation, "I think he should keep his promise—balance the budget—and still try to come up with something to help the people back home. So it's like nobody is left hanging, you know?" For these citizens, being able to "feel that [he] was representing the district" and to contain the attendant political damage requires that a representative take some steps to assist his constituents, regardless of his vote preference in this kind of situation.

Finally, as was true of the first hypothetical, respondents often added a disclaimer to their voting recommendations. Thus, one subject thought that the representative should vote his principles unless an "overwhelming majority" of his constituents disagreed. Another person advised the member to "stick to his beliefs," unless he concluded that the budget deal would unfairly hurt his district; in that case "he has an obligation to defend his people." And a third resolved that "[l]eadership is one of the most important jobs of the representative. He has a responsibility to get out in front of the people and say we can do something better with our money . . . *But it really depends on the basis of the issue*" (emphasis added). The same general rule applied to those people who expected the representative to vote his constituency over his platform. Although two of these subjects took unequivocal stands in favor of protecting the district, several others introduced extenuating circumstances, such as the importance of the issue to the member or how badly the district would be affected, into their opinions.

Ultimately, what both of these hypothetical questions revealed about the respondents were their varied, and often conflicting, convictions about the representative process. A few people, it must be said, seemed blissfully unaware that they had embraced potentially contradictory positions. One participant who repeatedly emphasized that "I believe they're supposed to make the right decision on an issue" later concluded in the first hypothetical that "I think she should always do what her constituents say." And another individual who repeatedly stressed the need for representatives to fulfill their campaign promises decided that hypothetical member number two should forego his commitment to reaching a balanced budget if enough of his constituency objected: "If that's what his constituents want, he's got to vote the majority."

More often, however, respondents sensed the potential dissonance in their answers and attempted to reconcile their divergent beliefs. The dilemma of how to fuse responsiveness to the district with other deepseated representational expectations became particularly evident and acute during the hypothetical voting questions. Many subjects seemed torn over how to combine responsiveness with imperatives like a member's own judgment or campaign promises, a "long-term" orientation, or a commitment to the national welfare. Besides the conditional answers cited above, the attempt to do so led certain people to backtrack from their initial response, veer abruptly from one position to another as they realized the implications of their assertions, and then move toward what they hoped would be an acceptable resolution.[8] The following exchange with one of the participants during the first hypothetical question should give some flavor of this:

> RES: I think she should look to the people in her district. That doesn't mean she shouldn't try to balance it, but if this is an overwhelming concern of the people. . . . I think she should listen to the people in the district.

> INT: I know that you mentioned earlier that you valued someone who was independent and—

RES: I do, and maybe there's a contradiction there. [*Pause*] I mean, they are certainly entitled to their opinions and they have to have a different perspective, they can't help it.

INT: But on the other hand you think they have an obligation to follow the people in their district?

RES: Well, I think they ought to give heavy weight to it, how's that. They ought to really, really think about it if it's something the people in the district favor. I don't know why she can't say, "I think this is going to be the effect of this," but if they say "yes, but we still feel this is right," then I think she should listen to them. I'm not sure you ever get anything as clear-cut as that, do you?

In grappling with these issues, some respondents exhibited another telling reaction—that of sympathy for the representatives' problems. A number of people seemed quite sensitive to the members' representational dilemmas and political predicaments. Consider, for example, the following halting response from one participant to the second hypothetical question:

That's tough. But it's his job. Do what's right, if you're in the national level then I think you better [*pause*] tough job. I wouldn't want that job [*laughs*]. There's no way he's going to persuade the people they should lose their jobs. Maybe it means, um, maybe that's why they start sticking in all those strange amendments, so then they can get new jobs, different jobs, the world changes . . . I think that he—that's tough. I guess if he was personally, truly convinced that some places needed to be closed, then he votes against keeping the arsenal open and his constituents would be upset, but hopefully then he would also negotiate within that bill what you do for the people. You don't just close the plant and leave them. So then he could say, "listen, it had to be done, but at least I've gotten this accomplished." That's ideal. . . . It's kind of like looking at the big picture. No easy task.

In essence, many of these citizens appeared to grasp the underlying complexity and potentially conflicting imperatives of the representational voting process. As one person said about such decision making, in words that would apply to many others: "I think a lot of it, well some of it anyway, is situational."[9] Several respondents also displayed a keen appreciation for the difficult personal and political choices that representatives face in these circumstances. As one of these individuals concluded, in a pithy phrase that captures the human crux of the problem: "What's this poor joker to do?"

Once again, such evidence illustrates how in-depth study of people's representational beliefs may alter our view of the public's understanding of the political process. When given the opportunity to fully and carefully consider the topic, as they were here, citizens may exhibit fairly thoughtful and realistic views of representational decision making. In a variety of different ways, a majority of the respondents demonstrated that they were cognizant of at least some of the representational conflicts and political perils that members must negotiate in making voting decisions. And the frequently thoughtful "solutions" people offered for these voting dilemmas reveal an awareness of the complexities of the representative process that is certainly not disclosed in public opinion surveys or existing studies of public attitudes toward Congress.

Vital Representational Functions: Explanation and Education

In the course of answering the hypothetical questions, most of the subjects provided further insight into their view of the essential qualities of the representative process. The most significant idea to emerge here was the vital importance of explanation and education-persuasion. Both of these concepts, of course, are intimately related to the praxis of communication. A number of participants, in fact, introduced them at earlier points in their interviews, typically in their general discussions of communication. Put another way, explanation and education reflect the extension of communication into the sphere of representational voting and decision making. There is another quality about these processes worth noting: they had almost universal appeal. We turn now to these crucial representational functions.

Essential Function I: Explanation

In both hypothetical questions a majority of respondents, regardless of their role orientation or sophistication level, emphasized that representatives should communicate and explain these types of important decisions to their constituents.[10] And the way such explanation was usually depicted indicates that these citizens consider it to be an integral part of the representative process. The following quotes from a pair of subjects readily convey this attitude about explanation:

> . . . the member I would say should tell the people, "I believe this is a good bill, this bill is going to do this, this, and this," but don't lie about it. That's the main thing. Say it's going to do this, this, and this, and I believe this is good, and I am supporting it

because I believe in it. I think she should explain until she turns blue and then make the decision on what the people feel.

I think she should go back to the people and explain to them why she [voted] no . . . because I think that people would respect her more if she came back, you know, to put some kind of closure on it than just leaving it. Because then they're going to be like, "Pfff, who are you?" [L]et the people in the district know about the effects, don't pull punches. Be honest, come right out . . . just tell the people, let them know what's going down. And if they agree with it, fine.

What these excerpts also suggest is that explanation goes beyond merely transmitting issue positions or voting decisions to the people back home to include *justifying* them as well. In a manner of speaking, participants often believed that elected officials have the obligation to fully defend their decisions in the "court" of public opinion in order to convince citizens of the propriety of their actions. This is a key point. These citizens were effectively embracing a deeper form of representational accountability that goes beyond the basic "monitoring and sanctioning" of members posited in most contemporary models of representation to include a more interactive process of explaining and justifying one's actions. And respondents most often emphasized the need for this kind of explanation (*a*) when a representative votes against what the respondent and/or a majority of constituents favor; and (*b*) when a decision will somehow hurt the district (as in the balanced budget hypothetical question).

These are, of course, the kind of political circumstances where one might expect representatives to be the *least* forthcoming about their actions or least willing to actively engage their constituents. Yet for many participants this is precisely when such in-depth communication is most critical. As one person noted, "I'd like a little more explanation as to why they do it when they go against something I think they should have voted for." Another individual even hoped that such explanation would be provided prior to the voting process: "He should first of all before he does vote bring his opinion [before the people] and his reason why it's important for him to go against his district's choice. He should be able to explain that fully."

To these respondents, the value of explanation seemed to rise in direct proportion to the political magnitude of a decision and its potential impact on the district. The underlying presumption was that constituents are particularly entitled to understand the rationale for representatives' behavior when an issue really hits home in the district or when members are not immediately deferring to constituent opinion. The following strong admonition from one subject provides a good glimpse of this view: "When he's going to do this [vote to balance the budget], he better be informing his constituents what's happening, man, because you don't just cut things without . . . even if he gets flack he's got to do this." Or as two other individuals responded to the balanced budget hypothetical,

> I can deal with that. *He's got to explain to us, though, exactly why he's doing it.* "I want this bill to go through, we're taking a cut in this, this, and this, and we're taking a cut in road building, which means we've got to take better care of our roads for the next four years." I could buy that. (emphasis in the original)
>
> He favors cutting spending. Well, you can't say that everyone else is going to cut but I'm not in my district, so he's certainly going to have to communicate that in some way if he feels that's a fair thing. If he feels that's fair, and this is not the only area of the country that's being hit, and you're not closing all kinds of things in this one area and ignoring another, I would think he would have to lay that out for his constituents.

In effect, representational explanation is most important to citizens in those contexts where it is most likely to be seen by representatives as political dynamite.

Nevertheless, about half of the participants believed that candid and thorough explanation would actually help *minimize* the political damage wrought by controversial decisions and/or boost a member's standing in his district. For instance, several people noted that such explanation would allow a representative to highlight the positive aspects of his decision. In the words of one individual, "even if it hurts his district, he can always rally back by saying, 'look at what we're getting in the long run, the benefits for the country.'" Another respondent folded this long-term emphasis into her discussion of the political benefit of being "up front" with constituents:

> I think the best policy is to be honest with people, because then they can't say, "well, you didn't tell us and you hid this from us, and why didn't you tell us?" It's better to be up front and say, "this is the way it is, we had to do this because . . . , I realize you may be disappointed right now, but if you look down the road to this, this, and that, I think in the long-run you will agree with me."[11]

Still another subject advised members to "Go back and say, 'look, this had to be done, this and this and this, but I'm working on this and this and this.'" To do otherwise would be at their peril: "I think it would hurt her more if she didn't. . . . They (constituents) are really going to be [left] hanging."

Respondents were quick to point out related benefits of explanation for members. Several people suggested that this type of open communication might increase public understanding of and support for a legislator. As one subject declared: "At least you know that they're able to tell me they've thought about it a lot, that their experience has been this, and they've finally come to this conclusion . . . that person is more valuable to me." Consistent explanation might also result in more favorable perceptions of representatives among constituents. Respondents tended to frame this in terms of gaining citizens' trust or respect. For example, one person claimed "if they explained it to me, no, I wouldn't lose trust. If they explained it and I understood why they had to do it . . . and you're like [you] did your best. That I can live with." Or, as another participant concluded, "[i]f it's from her heart, then that's the way I expect her to vote, and I've got to respect her for that. *I may not like it, but I'll respect her for that. If she explains it*" (emphasis added). Given this clear advocacy of explanation, some subjects, especially the more politically attuned, lashed out at what they perceived to be the failure of *real* representatives to adequately report and justify their positions, particularly while important legislation is being considered or key decisions are being made. The following individual pointedly remarked that

> It bothers me that you don't see . . . what the hell these guys are doing the whole time they're in session. You know, maybe after the session you might get a mailing that these are the laws that are passed this session, but you don't see, you know, here's a letter to you constituents saying, "here's what's going on and this is a concern to you and to this region, and here's the way I'm going to vote on it, here's my position." You don't see that.

Another participant similarly commented that "what's missing is it's hard to know where they stand on anything. Like I'd appreciate it if they would say 'well, thank you for telling me that's how you view this; however, the reason I voted against this is this.' And I'm not unreasonable. If they have a good reason I'll go, 'oh, I never thought of that before,' and I'd appreciate that."

The perceived scarcity of this kind of up-front and detailed explanation, the "pervasive evasiveness" of elected officials and their reliance on what one person called "catchwords . . . these little sound bites," was all the more disturbing given the positive impact that subjects believed regular explanation would have on the representative-constituent relationship. Several of them emphasized that representatives' explanation would demonstrate to constituents that their opinion mattered and that they had a meaningful role to play in the representative process. While responding to a question about how continual explanation would improve the representative process and reduce public cynicism, one respondent even proposed that it might eventually engender greater public participation in politics. In explaining this, he also inadvertently touched on some of the daunting obstacles to really putting this kind of explanation into practice.

> Yeah, without asking me how it would happen, if you could set up some ideal situation in which it wasn't burdensome and was presented in things other than in sound-bite format, if there was a way that congresspeople could be required to explain their position to their constituents, to explain their votes, I think they should do it all the time. It would get people eventually, probably over generations, out of their seat in front of the TV and get them more [active].

Explanation of representational decision making clearly occupied an important niche in most of these citizens' conceptions of the representative process. As respondents described the purposes of explanation, it sometimes seemed as if they were taking a page from Hanna Pitkin's guidebook of "acting for" citizens: when constituents' interests and desires do not appear to coincide, representatives have the responsibility to look after the interests of their constituencies and *publicly justify* why they have violated district wishes. From my observation one would add that they should also do this when a decision harms the immediate well-being of their districts. And in ways that Fenno would appreciate, a number of participants highlighted the political benefits of explanation and explicitly drew a connection between it and constituent trust; for other subjects these remained unexpressed, but no less real, assumptions. On the other hand, what actually passes for "explanation of Washington activity" by members did not seem to sit well with respondents. Their fundamental view of explanation—as a regular, candid, and thorough explication of representational position taking and decision making—(perhaps unrealistically) requires something more from representatives.

Essential Function II: Education-Persuasion

The education and/or persuasion of constituents by their representatives seemed equally, if not more, valuable to many respondents. As was the case with explanation, a clear majority of subjects, including almost all of the sophisticated respondents, touched on some aspect of representational education and persuasion in their replies to the hypothetical questions. What quickly became evident upon reviewing the discussions was the critical role that these functions played in their images of a sound representative process. "Good" representation often appeared to hinge on whether elected officials are willing and able to engage constituents during and after the decision-making process. For many of the subjects, there were clear benefits to thoughtful and continual education-persuasion for representatives and citizens alike. In a very real sense, the representative process would be woefully inadequate without them.

In *Home Style*, Fenno defines representational education "as an effort to persuade people to change their attitudes when the effort itself cannot be seen, in the short run anyway, as electorally beneficial" (p. 162). This definition is too narrow and election-driven to describe the subjects' view of education. Instead, education would more broadly encompass all efforts made by representatives to apprise constituents of their issue and policy positions, present all relevant sides of current policy debates, and let citizens in on important legislative and political decisions. The defining point here is not a bid by members to sway constituents to their side or alter their long-term beliefs, but rather the attempt to *fully inform* citizens about pertinent facets of current policy issues and the members' policy stands. From this perspective, education becomes less politically charged but necessarily more routine; the way education was often portrayed by subjects suggested that they envisioned it as a familiar part of the representational process. And, as we will see, to fully inform is emphasized for a reason, for it captures the essence of how people conceived of representational education.

Although respondents thought of education both in proactive terms (provided during important policy debates or before major decisions are made) and reactive terms (to give constituents a better understanding of why the legislator/legislature acted as they did), the proactive side generally received more attention. The most recurring theme in this vein was that education is necessary to give constituents the "big picture" about an issue, to let them understand the key dimensions of a policy dispute, and even to impart new ways of thinking about a problem.

To some participants this implied that representatives should furnish balanced and inclusive coverage of important political matters. For example, several respondents emphasized that members of Congress should present information about all sides of an issue or have "open discussions with both sides" in a policy debate. As one person put it, "I guess I'd like them to indicate that they do understand there's another position and then state their own. It's like debate. They ought to be able to present that in some fashion so the rest of us could come to our own conclusions and let them know." A few subjects also highlighted the importance of a candid appraisal of a bill's impact on the constituency. The first reaction of one of these individuals to the balanced budget hypothetical was "let the people in the district know about the effects, what the effects are going to bring, don't pull punches. Be honest, and come right out."

Many of the subjects suggested that this kind of comprehensive education ultimately serves larger (and related) representational ends. In the first place, education was thought to enhance constituent understanding of the policy and political implications of legislation and to help citizens make more informed judgments about policy issues, that is, to arrive at thoughtful "public opinions."[12] This in turn promotes the second major purpose of education: gaining informed constituent feedback on important issues or major pieces of legislation. Numerous respondents alluded to the importance of having representatives actively seek out constituent opinion and guidance in these situations. What emerged was advocacy of what might be called "two-way education," essentially the decision-making corollary of interactive communication. The following quotes from a wide range of subjects illustrate their view of the integral relationship between education, informed public opinion, and constituent influence in the decision-making process. They also exemplify what people meant by truly educating, and then listening to, constituents.

> Talk to the people somehow, have a public forum and ask the people if they've considered the economic effects, which they probably have, and then I think she needs to listen to why they think the environment would be more important than the economics to them on that particular bill.
>
> Well, I think she should be . . . presenting both sides but highlighting her point and then seeing how her constituents felt. And then asking them, "are you willing to feel it in your pocket, are you willing to take a pay cut for that bill or have more taxes taken from your paycheck?" That kind of thing, letting them know full out how she feels, saying "I know you feel this way, I feel this way, this is why." And then seeing their response after hearing that.
>
> I think she should say until she can't stand it anymore, "this is the situation; it's going to affect our economy because of this," and just tell people "I believe in this wholeheartedly," honestly telling people, and then if they say, no, we still want this, we are willing to take the losses economically, then she has to go with that.

As was often the case with interactive communication, several participants submitted that such two-way education could be advanced through town meetings. This view was perhaps best expressed by the following respondent: "Well, I know this would never happen, but she has the responsibility to go back and explain to people why she has that position, and I think the perfect medium for doing that is having a town meeting. That's saying like I want to hear what you people think, and she can say, "well, I've heard what you think, and I'll consider your opinion, but have you considered these, these, and these alternatives, and here's why I still hold this position."[13] A few people similarly alighted on the (largely untapped) educational potential of constituent newsletters and surveys. As one subject wryly remarked, "I'd like to see more presentations of, 'this is the way it is, and here's the problem and here's the bill, and these are the possibilities, and let me know what you think about it,' rather than 'I've been such a good guy or girl and I've got all these things, and don't forget that when voting on election day.'"

For many of these citizens, support for representational education was linked to a concern with political persuasion. As one participant quickly responded to the first hypothetical, "Has she approached her constituency to try to persuade them to see it her way? I don't know if that's a given or not . . . her first job is to persuade her people to see it her way, and the people have to finally decide what they want done." These respondents noted that besides allowing representatives to clearly communicate their views to their districts, and thus minimize constituent misunderstanding of their stances, the educational process can help members build public support for their positions and perhaps even convince people to change their perspectives.[14] It is the latter idea that most closely resembles Fenno's conception of representational education and leadership.

Interestingly, people who tended to favor deference to constituent opinion most often made this linkage between education and persuasion. Several of these respondents basically contended that persuasion of the constituency is a prerequisite if representatives are to act as trustees. In her discussion during the first hypothetical, for instance, one individual asserted that

> I think she should educate her constituents as to why she opposes it, let them know why it's going to hurt the economy and why she's opposed to it. She should let them know, and then she should find out, after she's educated them, how they still feel about the issue. If they aren't convinced by her concerns about the economy and they still want it, then she should vote for it. If she gets to the point where they are like, "oh yeah, you're right, we've changed our minds," then she should vote the way she feels about it.

In this view, issue congruence on representatives' terms should not simply be predicated on their superior judgment, experience, and access to information, let alone the cultivation of "policy freedom;" rather, it should occur only if members can successfully induce constituents to alter their short- or long-term viewpoints.[15] Another participant took this argument to the national level. When asked if representatives should not abide by their constituents' preferences if they believe those wishes might be harmful in the long-run, she replied that "No, I think they need to follow their constituents, and if that means the whole country has not been persuaded yet then they need to, if it's really important to them, get out there and start being persuasive, instead of when election time comes they can bring up that issue, "I voted for this because you people wanted it. I don't think you were right because blah, blah, blah.""

One of the most politically uninformed subjects even made a case for "deliberative persuasion" on the part of members: "Um, she should try speaking to her people to try and change their minds. If not, she has no choice but to go with them . . . try to reason with them. Show a reason why it's no good, and then show a reason *why* it's good, you know. Not just say it's no good and not show a reason *why* it's no good" (emphasis in original). These delegate-oriented respondents valued persuasion as much as those who condoned trusteeship; the major difference was that the former stressed that attempts at persuasion should occur *before* important legislative decisions are made. The shared assumption was that the value of education-persuasion rises in situations where members of Congress are not immediately responsive to their constituents.

Respondents identified several blessings of representational education-persuasion for citizens. As alluded to earlier, they frequently mentioned that education and persuasion would increase constituents' knowledge and understanding of important policy issues, political debates, and members' positions on such questions. A few subjects also thought that it would engage people in the representative process and give them a greater sense of political influence. As one participant optimistically intoned, "at the most generic level, maybe we would have a different kind of politics than we have right now, where we have a lot of cynicism. . . . I think you would have real politics where people were actively engaged as opposed to the media campaign politics which is how I would characterize what we have now." In the view of another, explanation and education might let constituents know that "they have a little more power than just watching things go by." The end result would be better informed, less cynical, and more politically active citizens.[16]

Once again, some of the respondents also noted that constituents would not be the only ones to benefit from this kind of responsiveness. Just as with explanation (and direct contact and communication, for that matter), a number of subjects felt that honest education-persuasion could reduce the political fallout that representatives face from difficult or unpopular decisions. The underlying premise here was that an informed constituency will be more forgiving, less likely to exact electoral revenge, than an uninformed one. As one of the unsophisticated participants concluded during the second hypothetical, "Don't just cut it and leave it there, because then people are going to get angry because they don't know. You can deal with a situation better if you know the whole thing." In much the same way, education-persuasion could reduce public anxiety about representatives' intentions or actions and therefore preserve constituent trust. In the following observation of one subject,

> I think persuasion [*pause*] seems to be really important to me. Because I don't think people are unreasonable in general, and if they (legislators) take the time to think it through and they came back and said, "no we can't do it that way *because* . . . ," I think we would figure it out. And it just seems like if they can't state their opinions that makes me suspicious. It makes me suspicious, you know, why can't you persuade me? *Were you bought by somebody?* (emphasis in original)

Finally, a handful of participants intriguingly hinted at the idea that education and persuasion can help reconcile divergent representative-constituent viewpoints, priorities, and interests. As one of these respondents put it, "it's better [for members] to be up front and say, "this is the way it is, we had to do this because, I realize you may be disappointed right now, but if you look down the road to this, this, and this, I think in the long-run you'll agree with me." Better issue and policy congruence, and hence representation, thus could issue from members' efforts to enlighten and win over their constituents.

And what did these respondents think was the likelihood of such education and persuasion from *actual* representatives? Placing herself in the shoes of the representative from the first hypothetical, one of the political activists argued that members can and often do pursue an interlocking strategy of advertising, education, and persuasion: "What I would do if I were her with every decision I made I'd make sure I had a lot of stuff to back up my decision, to try to persuade the other side that this is the best thing, and I would do some kind of PR thing to make sure everyone knew that. *A lot of them do that*" (emphasis added).

More often, however, participants remarked about the paucity of educational efforts from their representatives. In fact, many of the same people who touted the virtues of education-persuasion also criticized its absence or superficiality in the contemporary representative process. These citizens basically echoed Fenno's judgment about representational education in *Home Style*: "I [do] not see a great deal of it." Their attitude was perhaps best summarized in this tart assessment from one subject: "I think [representatives] would rather be evasive than persuasive."

Assessment: Fenno, With Some Twists

What conclusions can we draw about the subjects' view of representative-constituent communication, its decision-making corollaries explanation and education-persuasion, and the representative process writ large? Above all, and worth restating, is the central role these processes played in their basic view of representation. The way communication was portrayed, for instance, suggests that respondents consider it to be one of the most important aspects of the representative process, arguably *the* most important one. Not only did many of these citizens appear to equate good representation with effective communication; they tended to have high hopes about its ability to elevate the representative process. In their eyes, real responsiveness simply cannot be sustained without effective communication. A number of them thus seemed genuinely distressed when they talked about how representational communication was falling short of their expectations.

In important respects these conclusions also apply to the subjects' global conceptions of representation. The elements of "responsive representation" delineated by Fenno and others do appear to be vital components of people's views of the representative process. When asked to define and describe what representation meant to them, participants touted the importance of such elements as accessibility, attentiveness, contact, and (especially) communication. On the whole, then, this study bolsters the idea that responsiveness has become an essential part of the representative process.[17] With the notable exception of district and constituency service, which relatively few people emphasized, respondents seem to value many of the things that the literature indicates representatives try to shower on their constituents. This suggests, of course, that citizens' fundamental ideas and expectations about representation are integrally related to the "representational universe"—to the totality of what elected officials say, do, project, and make available to them. Both directly and indirectly, people are continually exposed to political cues that may reinforce, conflict with, and even alter their basic representational inclinations and preferences. Immersed in a political environment that in many different ways accentuates the importance of being responsive to constituents, citizens understandably may have come to make this a centerpiece of their beliefs about representation.[18]

But acknowledging the importance of responsiveness does not get us to the heart of respondents' understanding of the representative process. To do that, one must also appreciate that responsiveness was seen not so much as an end in itself but as a *means* to achieving other worthwhile goals: greater insight into constituents needs and concerns; legislative priorities and outcomes that more closely reflect people's views and interests; citizens with an increased capacity to understand government and arrive at informed public opinions; enhanced public confidence and trust in government; and, yes, better issue and policy congruence between constituents and their representatives. From the subjects' perspective, responsiveness should ultimately be in the service of larger representational ends, including promoting greater accountability on the part of representatives.

None of these ends seemed more important than promoting citizen influence in the political process. In their discussions of the ideal type of relationship between representatives and the people they serve, participants tended to place the most emphasis on having legislators interact with, listen to, and absorb from their constituents—on true constituent to representative contact. The subjects' overriding concern with two-way communication and contact was driven in large part by the desire for citizens to play a meaningful role in the representative process and the opportunity to educate and influence their representatives. At its best, then, responsive representation ensures that the arrow runs both ways; that *citizens* too have sufficient and continual opportunities to engage members on their own terms.[19] In this sense, Fenno's concluding remarks about communication, though given from the point of view of the representative, also fit my respondents perfectly: "Members of Congress believe that whatever they do to enhance two-way communication . . . they also enhance the representative relationship" (*Home Style*, p. 241).[20] Or, as one of the more unsophisticated participants summarized his understanding of the ideal representative process:

> Besides more communication, and, you know, direct meetings, I would say probably more, uh, contact, representatives sending more letters and keeping in touch with the public of what they're doing before they do it. Okay. So people would have a say before big bills are passed, you know, on certain issues. I would have a say-so as a citizen, that would be appreciated, because it makes you feel that you are a part of the decisions that are being decided. That's what democracy is supposed to be, for the people, I guess.

Yet, to judge from the replies of many of the subjects, the apparent symmetry between the abstract representational views of citizens and members does not hold up in reality. In *Home Style* Fenno spends much time detailing the instrumental and sometimes brazenly self-serving uses of communication and contact by House members: how it helps to underwrite advertising, ensure name recognition, bolster home styles, and garner trust. Respondents often seemed quite aware of, and disturbed by, the instrumental political motives behind responsiveness. Indeed, an underlying theme in many of the interviews was that members of Congress use the tools of responsiveness solely for their own electoral benefit, rather than to discern constituents' true needs and interests or to encourage public involvement in the representative process. A number of participants took pains to emphasize that (at times) the forms and (at times) the substance of "legitimate" contact, communication, and explanation/education are missing.[21] In effect, these citizens believe that they lack the kind of two-way contact and communication the literature suggests representatives go out of their way to provide. The *assurance* of this kind of responsiveness does not seem to be enough, as Fenno infers; and even if it was, the subjects' responses indicate that, for whatever reason, they do not believe they have received it.

Thus, while the idea of responsiveness broadly captures what these citizens think about representation, their conceptions of the representative process are richer, more varied, and more complicated than the literature would lead one to expect. And when it comes to their assessments of the *actual* representation they receive, the process appears a bit more hollow than as portrayed by scholars like Fenno. The notion of a disconnect between representatives and the people they serve takes on new meaning given the respondents' beliefs about the lack or distortion of constituent to representative input. In fact, to the extent it was made manifest, subjects' dissatisfaction and disillusionment with contemporary representation often seemed to stem from their sense of the absence and/or superficiality of constituent-representative communication and participation.

The irony of this outcome is unmistakable. While congressional representatives have helped to sow a political culture in which citizens esteem responsiveness, they may also be reaping the negative rewards of failing to meet the public expectations such a culture generates. Along with the respondents' abiding faith that access, involvement, two-way communication, and explanation/education might help recast the representative process came the disheartening conviction that numerous obstacles stand in the way of that vision. In terms of ideational impediments, perhaps none is more intractable than their belief that the essential building blocks of responsiveness are often compromised by electoral and political considerations—put another way, that at some level politics and representation are incompatible.[22]

Chapter Five

The Representative Relationship

Introduction

Scholars have approached the congressional "representative relationship" from a variety of theoretical and empirical fronts. But there is one common denominator in almost all of their work: the centrality of the behavior and beliefs of members of Congress themselves. As is true of the representative process writ large, the public side of the representative relationship has generally received scant attention in the literature. Much of the research that does touch on people's views of this relationship has been driven by one goal—explaining the paradox of congressional support. This job performance literature, like most of the other inquiries into ordinary citizen's beliefs about representation, has rested on a handful of national survey questions. As a result, important questions remain about how ordinary citizens conceive of the representative relationship. What, for instance, do people really expect from members of Congress in terms of job responsibilities, personal attributes, and political characteristics? What impact, if any, do members themselves have on people's views about this relationship? And how do citizens perceive the job of the contemporary representative?

This chapter addresses these issues through an expository look at the participants' own reflections on the representative relationship. There are a number of benefits in doing so. Exploring these citizens' underlying ideas and expectations reveals a surprisingly sophisticated and sympathetic understanding of the dynamics of this relationship, as well as of the daunting array of expectations and obligations contemporary members of Congress face. The effort also exposes the disparate and sometimes conflicting views about this crucial dimension of the representative process that may be held by different portions of the citizenry. And all this can help us to better comprehend why ordinary citizens feel the way they do about the contemporary political process—as well as the larger political implications of their beliefs.

In order to get at their underlying convictions about the relationship between congressional representatives and constituents, all of the respondents were asked the following set of questions:

- What is your definition of a good congressperson?
  Probes: What would you say you value the most in a congressperson? What do you look for in a member of Congress?
- When you vote for a candidate to Congress, what do you expect that person to do in office?
  Follow-ups: Anything else? How do you think members of Congress should balance between their work in Washington and spending time at home with their constituents? (This question was often expressed in percentage terms).

Once again, most participants were asked a number of additional probes inspired by responses to these questions. Relevant answers from other parts of the interviews were also incorporated into the analysis here, as were any spontaneous comments made about congressional representatives. All of this material was designed to pinpoint the respondents' primary ideas and expectations about the representative relationship. The operative assumption was that by letting people talk at length, and in their own way, about members of Congress, we might illuminate the set of beliefs that underlie citizens' attitudes toward (and evaluations of) their representatives—and thereby enhance the portrait of the representative process currently painted in the literature.

Representatives Defined

My first and most fundamental objective was to document participants' general images and expectations of congressional representatives. I defined two main dimensions to this: one, the essential qualities that members of Congress should possess; and two, their most important responsibilities on the job. In other words, I was interested in knowing what respondents believed representatives should be like *and* what they should be doing. This evidence in turn was used to delineate the roles that members are expected to play, as well as the similarities and differences in people's expectations. Of course, all of these concerns have been dealt with to some degree in the literature on representation. The crucial differences in this study are the depth of the analysis, the idea that participants were able to address the subject in detail (and in their own words), and the fact that this process occurred as part of a larger examination of their representational worldviews. The subjects' views about the congressional representative relationship thus could be readily aligned, and placed into context, with their more global beliefs about representation.

One of the most basic questions about people's views of the representative relationship is this: What do citizens "look for" in a member of Congress? What do they consider to be crucial characteristics in a congressional representative? The qualities mentioned most often by participants in this study fell into two broad categories: the *personal* and the *political*. In a nutshell, most subjects want representatives who combine essential personal qualities with vital political attributes, whose individual traits are complemented by certain political strengths. Participants generally appeared to think that these two dimensions are related; for example, that someone with desirable personal characteristics would likely be politically appealing and effective. The underlying assumption was that members' personal qualities have a direct impact on their conduct in office and their political efficacy. It is to these personal attributes that we turn first.

Personal Qualities

The most frequently mentioned, and for many seemingly the most important, personal qualities fall under the heading of *personal integrity*. Nearly three-quarters of the respondents emphasized the importance of this attribute in representatives; terms like "honesty," "honor," and "personal integrity" arose repeatedly in the interviews. Related references included being a "straight-up person," "someone who is straightforward," or someone who is "straight with himself."

There were several aspects to this focus on integrity. A few subjects highlighted the need for probity in representatives' dealings with other politicians. More often respondents hoped that members "would be truthful with their constituents," whether about issue positions, relationships to interest groups, the impact of legislation on their districts, or their voting records. As one individual replied when asked to define integrity, "Honesty. Honesty with his constituents on how he feels about voting on certain issues. Don't say one thing and then vote the other way." Another touched on the importance of living up to one's political principles: "Honesty means that a person would say things and go by what he says, you know, not a person that waffles back and forth on how the public is in the mood." A few participants even touted the importance of having representatives who can serve as models of personal virtue. For example, one subject opined that "it would be nice to have people representing us that stand on a more moral path. . . . I think it's important for us to be able to look up to the congressmen." And a handful of people connected the rise in public cynicism with politics to the increased evidence (or at least exposure) of politicians' moral and ethical failings. To these respondents, political leadership depends on moral standing, and personal character therefore is relevant when deciding if members are really going "to look out for our interests." Personal integrity, in short, promotes public credibility.[1] Thus, one subject emphasized that it is imperative for members of Congress to "be of the moral best. Because they're our leaders, and nobody trusts them [now], nobody buys it."[2]

This was not the only evidence of respondents broaching the political impact of personal integrity. For example, one person felt that honesty among representatives would improve legislative outcomes; his view was that voters should elect candidates based "on their honesty and things like that, because overall if you get a group of honest people together even if they have different opinions, which they would, hopefully they will come up with a good solid answer that represents all of us out here."

But the political manifestation of personal integrity was most evident in the yearning for representatives who cannot easily "be bought." For most of these citizens not being bought had the obvious monetary connotations; it meant having members who are resistant to the blandishments of campaign contributors ("I like a man who isn't selling himself to . . . the interests that gave him money for his campaign"), or the temptation to use the office to feather their own nests.[3] Others, however, conceived of it in broader political terms, as referring to someone who is politically independent, often votes according to principle or judgment, and is not unduly susceptible to public or special interest pressure. When asked what she valued most in a congressperson, the following respondent replied that "If they're not easily bought by corporate lobbying, that they are more willing to look at the repercussions of their behavior and what [will happen] in the long run. If they vote for something, it's because they really think it will benefit people for a long time and not just for an election year."

A second oft-mentioned personal trait was intelligence. For those participants who discussed it, the emphasis was less on pure intellect than on what might be called "political intelligence," the capacity to grasp the policy and political dimensions of a wide range of issues and then to convert that understanding into effective legislative action. In this sense, intelligence is clearly associated with political creativity and leadership ability. This perspective was perhaps best expressed by one of the sophisticated subjects:

> You need to have a rep. who is, you know, a strong intellectual, not intellectual in the sense of being a professor but a guy who is capable of understanding a lot of different facets of a thing and being able to translate that into a leadership role and being able to work with other people in government bodies to develop a policy more. . . . It's a complicated world out there, and he

has to be able to understand a lot of different issues that are unrelated. And so you need someone who is intellectually capable with leadership qualities who can go in and translate that understanding into policy . . .

A closely related quality was thoughtfulness, the ability and proclivity to reflect on issues and arrive at informed judgments rather than adhere to knee-jerk positions or the dictates of interest groups. As the following individual put it, "You don't have to agree with me, but I like to know that they're really thinking about (an issue) and that the opinion isn't something of a pressure group but more likely the congressman's own." A number of respondents likewise alluded to the importance of an open mind or flexibility in a representative. For one person this meant the willingness "to weigh all sides of an issue"; for another to "get out of the rut and try new things." To a third, openness to different perspectives seemed to be one of the defining characteristics of a good representative. When asked what a responsive congressman is, she replied: "I guess I'd like him not to have a certain set 'this is what I believe.' I'd like to see a little flexibility . . . [being] able to rethink a question or look at it from two sides, or three." A few of these subjects additionally noted that such receptivity to new ideas can help a representative adapt to constantly changing policy and political tides, and thus be a better (and more viable) agent for his constituency.[4]

The final characteristic embraced by several participants was a sense of personal commitment: to the constituency, people's interests, one's own political beliefs, and so on. These citizens preferred members with demonstrable passion for their job and dedication to the people they serve, or what one person described as "heart and soul." To some of them, this elusive quality of having one's heart in public service is revealed in a member's political assertiveness, the willingness to speak out (and act) on what he believes in. It also may help him prosper in the rough and tumble world of legislative politics. In the words of one subject: "I think it helps to be a little bit aggressive. You're not going to get a lot done if you just sit there and keep your mouth shut." The combination of openness to information and the willingness to act on it was particularly attractive. As another individual described one of her favorite representatives, "Well, he's a good listener, and he will also take action. And we need that kind of person."

Respondents clearly valued these personal qualities in their representatives, and many of them explicitly or implicitly underscored the political relevance of certain personal qualities. In this way the evidence here, and particularly the accent placed upon honesty and integrity, bolsters the literature that finds personal attributes are key criteria in people's evaluations of their representatives, and that citizens often look to such qualities as markers of good representation. Yet given the subjects' global conceptions of the representative process, it appears that these qualities are viewed as a *supplement to*, rather than a *surrogate for*, more direct forms of involvement with (or control over) their members. Still, it was clear from their responses that a perceived lack of integrity and commitment works to jeopardize that vital element of trust underpinning the political relationship between citizens and members of Congress, or any representative body.

Political Qualities

The relationship between the personal and political was equally evident in the political qualities respondents tended to emphasize. Somewhat surprisingly, only five participants mentioned the importance of prior political experience or "a good background in government." More common were references to the need for political courage and independence among members of Congress. A politically courageous representative was depicted as someone willing to "take a stand," whether on behalf of his own platform, conscience, view of the national welfare, or district's interests. Although few of the respondents made a direct connection between personal integrity and political courage, one can reasonably infer from their remarks that many of them consider the former to be a necessary precursor of the latter.

In much the same way, political independence was usually described as the willingness of representatives to buck party control or to separate themselves from what several people dubbed the "party line," especially when the interests of their districts are at stake.[5] For example, one person stated that she valued "someone who is not swayed by party leadership, party direction, someone who will take a stand that just because Dick Gephardt says we've got to vote this way, you know, he will take his district in mind and vote that way."[6] Another subject intriguingly defined independence as the ability to stand apart from, yet still work to define, the "party line" in his response to what members should do in office: "The other thing that is important is that even though they represent a party, they can't just vote the party line all the time. They really have to be conscious of representing their districts on issues where their own districts would be adversely affected by the party line, and they also have to be very adept at working within the framework of the party to influence what the party line will be."

Members' Job Obligations

The second dimension of people's representational expectations concerns what members should do in office. Subjects offered a wide variety of responses when it came to depicting the most important job responsibilities for members of Congress. Nevertheless, virtually all their answers fit into one of three categories—the individual, the constituency or district-based, and the institutional. Each of these will be taken up in turn.

The most frequently mentioned individual job expectation was for members to adhere to their issue/policy positions or political agenda. About 60 percent of the respondents touched on this concern, and many were quite adamant about the need for representatives to fulfill their public commitments. A sampling of responses from subjects at different sophistication levels should give some idea of the importance they attached to this trait:

> The reason is, he's already run on that platform and said this is what I believe in. So when you elect him and send him out there you should know what he's going to do. . . . As soon as he goes back against his word, he has to get [another] job.
>
> I'd expect them to stick to what their campaign promises were, if they say they are for a particular issue that is reflected in their voting patterns. If I vote for someone on the platform that . . . they believe in making sure all children are vaccinated, I expect them to act on that. If they don't, if their voting record shows six years later that they've not done the things then I'm less likely to vote for them.
>
> Well, I think they should . . . like you know, they give you this big whoop-dee-do speech before they get in and get elected, they make all these promises, you know. I think they should be of their word, you know what I mean?

These respondents were not necessarily looking for elected officials to promise them the world. In fact, several wished that members of Congress would stop making grandiose pledges or campaigning on overly expansive platforms.[7] But they did make it clear that they expect representatives to live up to their word and produce tangible proof of attempts to fulfill the promises they do make. What these citizens evidently cannot brook are transparently political bids to change positions, clearly unattainable promises, and/or an apparent lack of effort in fulfilling one's agenda. From this perspective, living up to campaign pledges becomes the embodiment of political integrity.[8] Secondly, half of the (mainly sophisticated and somewhat sophisticated) participants reported that they expect members of Congress to use their own judgment or make what they believe to be the "right" decision, notwithstanding the potential political consequences or cost to the district. One subject asserted that "I've always felt bad about grass roots or pork barrel stuff, even when it affected us, [because] I'm the type of person who wants to do what's right or just in a given situation, even if it hurts me. So I expect my representative to look at an issue, and base it on what he thinks is right." Some of these individuals presented the willingness to do this as one of the calling cards of a good representative.

In certain cases, respondents noted, making the right decision means saying no to people, making "tough choices that isn't for the majority," or telling constituents "I know you may not like this, but I'm doing this because I believe that it's good for you."[9] One person offered a little vignette to illustrate his admiration for the representative who is willing to challenge, and not simply curry favor with, the voters:

> Let's say they're giving a speech in a certain low income area of the city, and there's three candidates up there. And somebody asks: "What're you going to do to keep our kids in school?" And the first guy says, "when elected I'll appoint a blue-ribbon committee." And the other guy says something similar. And the third guy says, "It's not my job to keep your kids in school. It's not the government's job; it's your job." Now, he's not going to get elected for saying that, but it's the absolute truth. That's who I'd vote for. But I also want to vote for somebody who's going to get elected. But that's who I hope the people would listen to.

Once again, in a variety of ways, respondents expressed a desire for more political courage from representatives. In the concluding assessment of another subject, "I would rather have a representative that did not sugarcoat things. I'd rather know up front this is where we are, this is where we are going, and this is how we are going to get there."[10]

The third major personal job expectation was that members should possess (and be influenced by) a long-term vision for the country, should consider the future implications of their decisions, and/or should pursue the national interest while in office. In the words of one participant: "I'd like them to be taking the long view of things, not the quick fix . . . to try to take that tack at the same time that they're trying to address everyday problems." As another person understood it, "If they vote for something, it's because they really think it will benefit people for a long time and not just for an election year. . . . If they actually think about it—will it help the entire country?" The following subject expressed this idea in a kind of Federalist-style injunction to New York's congressional delegation: ". . . I expect our congressmen to take issues and ideas from our state and take them to the federal level and try to get things passed for the betterment not only of our state but our country in general. . . . I expect them to act responsibly, for the welfare and benefit of our country and the good of all people."

A few people similarly condoned the classical ideal of public-spirited representatives driven to serve by a sense of civic duty. The underlying presumption in all these cases was that members of Congress have a responsibility to more than their own or their constituents' short-term (and narrow) interests, that they need to be aware "of the situation that's going on not only in the district, but also for the people as a whole. Not just being selfish and just representing one district, but the people in general." And this implies that representatives must continually find ways to balance the pursuit of parochial aims with the larger public good. As one respondent articulated this challenge, members must "maintain that juggling act of stepping back and looking at the whole versus looking at the parts." The prevalence of such expectations in these interviews suggests that the "trustee" vision of representation continues to resonate among citizens, even in the face of what scholars have characterized as a home style, constituency-centered, "Washington Establishment" congressional political universe. No matter how much they may be conditioned to think otherwise in the contemporary representative relationship, many of the people I interviewed hold onto the idea that members of Congress have important representational responsibilities beyond that of merely serving their constituencies.[11]

At the same time, however, constituent-centered job expectations were also prominently featured in participants' answers to this section. Responsiveness to the constituency was alluded to fairly often, as were accessibility to or familiarity with the district. The avowed desire for representative-constituent communication was also underscored here. This preference was expressed in various ways: as keeping constituents well informed; as opening and maintaining a "dialogue" with people; as looking "for feedback from constituents on certain issues"; or as generally staying attuned to the district. The following individual summarized this set of constituent-centered expectations when asked what a representative should do while in office:

RES: First, if they aren't already familiar with who their constituents are to seek them out and go into the community and to find out what the people are about and what they are looking for and then to proceed from there.

INT: Anything else?

RES: Um, I think they should initiate the dialogue . . . and that would be by going into the community.[12]

These preferences, of course, conform closely to the subjects' general conceptions of representation. One exception to this correspondence between abstract beliefs and specific expectations was the greater number of references made to some form of constituent service in this section than in the general discussions of the representative process. As one of the respondents, a self-proclaimed "radical socialist," enumerated the job obligations of a member of Congress, "Um, to propose legislation that is in the interests of the working class. . . . And as well, to provide constituent service. If there's one thing Al Damato has been good at, it's constituent service" [*laughs*]. A second expressed his support for the "Washington Establishment" in terms that would have made Fiorina proud: "I shouldn't say manipulating, but influencing government bureaucracies to act in favor of his constituents. . . . Knowing where the federal money is, how much money is available to help his local community, seeing that his community gets its fair share of that money."

A few participants similarly described the representative as a kind of ombudsman; as one of these individuals put it, "typically representatives also serve as troubleshooters for their constituents, which is another role they can play, to kind of light a fire under bureaucrats and agencies." In all of these cases, district service and/or constituent problem solving were considered to be prime components in, if not necessarily the foremost part of, a member's representational obligations. This stands in stark contrast to those subjects who failed to mention constituent service at all in this regard, or criticized it as embodying the worst aspects of the political process.

Many of the respondents also outlined institutional obligations that representatives should meet. The most prominent among these was to attend to their legislative duties. For some people this meant having members take an active part in the legislative process: studying issues in depth, being heard as bills are written and considered, and making informed voting decisions. In the words of one of these respondents: "I expect him to give his full time to legislation. That he attends to the sessions of the legislature and votes regularly."[13]

For others, however, being real legislative players meant that representatives have to craft and shepherd their *own* legislation. As the following subject insisted: ". . . I expect them to be sponsoring legislation. You know, not just signing on to a whole bunch of bills made by someone else, but creating and trying to get approved their own stuff." Another person held that "we want someone who is also astute enough to create or spearhead legislation and take the lead." The mark of a good member, then, is proactive policymaking enterprise, the capability to identify important needs and interests and then translate them into legislative action, as opposed to just reacting to the initiatives of others. In either case, though, the ultimate objective was the same: to "make sure the law represents the broad interests of constituents" and/or the nation. A few participants also emphasized the institutional corollary (or prerequisite) to such legislative success—the capacity to build and sustain support for one's bills. These citizens regarded the ability to develop effective coalitions as an important quality in a member of Congress. In the most succinct depiction of the representative as legislative advocate, one individual stated: "What I would look for in a representative to Congress is . . . [s]omebody who is going to be really for the things that I am for, and agree with them, and fight for them and lobby for it and try to get it done, try to get as many people behind it as possible, you know, and take the heart to things."

Finally, when it came to balancing between institutional and district responsibilities, respondents tended to believe that representatives should devote more attention to their work in Washington. Ten of the seventeen participants who expressed this in percentage terms felt that members should spend somewhere between 25–50 percent of their time in the district and 50–75 percent in Washington. Four believed that members should be in the Capitol at least 75 percent of the time; no one made the same claim about the district. A handful of people, mainly those with some familiarity with the congressional calendar, felt that a schedule of weekdays in Washington, and some/most weekends and vacations in the district, was reasonable or "about right."

Role Expectations: The Rank Scales

The qualitative evidence I gathered of people's expectations for their representatives was supplemented by a more quantitative measure: a job responsibility ranking scale administered to respondents at the end of their interviews. Subjects were asked to rank in order of importance six distinct job obligations for members of Congress. The list provided a fairly comprehensive set of representational duties for participants to evaluate.

There were a variety of reasons for asking them to do so. Having all of the participants' rank the same set of obligations permitted standardized comparisons within the sample, while simultaneously giving subjects the opportunity to consider responsibilities that they failed to mention during their interviews. I also wanted to see how the rankings compared with the interview narratives, both individually and as a group, as well as to the representational role series from the 1978 NES. At the same time, I hoped to discern any relationships between levels of sophistication and job expectations, as well as to see how my results compared with previous studies of people's representational role expectations. Most of all, I wished to gain a better picture of what the respondents valued most and least from their congressional representatives, not least because these expectations may shape citizens' actual evaluations of members of Congress.[14]

The six responsibilities and their corresponding role designation (in parentheses) were as follows:

- Helping people back home when they have problems with the government (constituency casework);
- Discussing and debating important and controversial issues (deliberation);
- Bringing federal money and projects back to the district (district service);
- Spending time in the district meeting with constituents (direct contact);
- Keeping people informed about what's going on in Washington (communication);
- Passing bills that deal with important national problems (lawmaking).

Respondents were also given space to describe any other important responsibility not included in the scale (see appendix A for the complete ranking scale).

Table 5.1 below presents the overall results of the congressional rank scales. The ratings were combined into three categories to facilitate comparison. A ranking of 1 or 2 for each option was deemed "very important"; 3 or 4 "somewhat important"; and 5 or 6 "least important." Both the total number and percentage of rankings for each category are listed (percentages may not equal 100 percent due to rounding).

Table 5.1. Job Responsibility Rankings for Members of Congress

	Very Important	Somewhat Important	Least Important
Keeping people informed . . . (communication)	12 (44%)	10 (37%)	5 (19%)
Discussing and debating . . . (deliberation)	11 (41%)	13 (48%)	3 (11%)
Passing bills that deal . . . (lawmaking)	10 (37%)	5 (19%)	12 (44%)
Helping people back home . . . (constituent service)	9 (33%)	8 (30%)	10 (37%)
Spending time in the district . . . (involvement)	7 (26%)	11 (41%)	9 (33%)
Bringing federal money . . . (district service)	5 (19%)	7 (26%)	15 (56%)

What is perhaps most striking here is the lack of consensus about representatives' job responsibilities. No role(s) emerged as the overriding favorite or majority choice. The participants in this study clearly hold divergent expectations for members of Congress, a result consistent with the range of viewpoints about representatives and the representative process expressed during the interviews. The diversity of opinion in even this small sample points to the pitfalls in trying to speak about what the "public" expects from members of Congress. These citizens were far from one mind when it came to what they most want congressional representatives to do.

This conclusion is bolstered by the polarization in the job rankings. Some subjects gave the lowest rating to the same role that others bestowed the highest. This was particularly true for certain roles. Opinion was strongly split, for example, over constituency service, while the conflicting attitudes about direct contact that surfaced in the interviews were essentially replicated in the rank scales.[15] Respondents were even more sharply divided over the lawmaking function. No other category received more "1" ratings, yet nearly half of the subjects deemed this role relatively insignificant.[16] By comparison, the district service, or "pork barrel," function fared consistently worse. Ten participants rated this as the least important job obligation; over 70 percent ranked it from 4–6. Of course, this result contrasts sharply with the conventional wisdom about the public's craving for representatives who "bring home the bacon." At least on a conceptual level, many of these citizens do not appear to regard district service as a key part of the representative process or members' duties.[17]

There is another distinctive pattern in the rank scales: the value that subjects attached to the communicative and deliberative functions of members of Congress. Only a handful thought that either role was unimportant. The desire to have members keep their constituents informed is quite consistent with the emphasis placed on representative-constituent communication in the interviews. The weight attached to the deliberative function is a bit more surprising, but may reflect our general perception of representatives' primary institutional roles, a deeply ingrained collective vision of what being a legislator means. Consider, too, the informative and expressive overtones to this function; one envisions members conveying their (and their constituents) views on the issues of the day, and in turn possibly persuading others.[18] Thus, members of Congress may be valued as the public "voice" of their districts, the political spokespersons and advocates who ensure that their constituents' perspectives and preferences are heard on the national stage. Representatives give the people they serve a say, however limited and indirect, in the councils of government, and in this sense may confer a measure of public legitimacy on its actions. In any event, this role clearly remains an essential part of these citizens' conceptions of representatives' duties.

Additional insight into the participants' expectations for members of Congress can be gained by examining which representational roles they deemed to be the most important. Table 5.2 below portrays the number and percentage of respondents who gave a 1 or a 6 ranking to each function. The table thus sheds greater light on the representational responsibilities that are most (and least) critical to people—those that are regarded, in essence, as defining obligations of congressional representatives.

On the whole, this table mirrors the results from the overall rankings. No one or even two roles stand out as overriding preferences. Each category, *including* district service, received support as the most important obligation, and no function was chosen in this regard by more than a quarter of the participants. The polarization in beliefs is equally apparent. While nearly 25 percent of the respondents basically dismissed constituent service, for example, four ranked it as a member's foremost obligation. Deliberation and communication again emerged as favored roles, although lawmaking received more top rankings than either of these categories. The upshot of all this? The citizens interviewed for this study do not concur on a representative's most important jobs. The rank scales, like the interviews, hint at substantial variance in people's expectations for members of Congress.

They also bolster some of the previous research conducted in this area. In particular, my rankings are quite similar to the results from the representational role series in the 1978 NES. In that survey, as men-

Table 5.2. Supplemental Rankings for Members of Congress

	Ranked 1	Ranked 6
Passing bills that deal . . . (lawmaking)	7 (26%)	4 (15%)
Discussing and debating . . . (deliberation)	5 (19%)	1 (04%)
Keeping people informed . . . (communication)	4 (15%)	3 (11%)
Spending time in the district . . . (involvement)	3 (11%)	3 (11%)
Helping people back home . . . (constituent service)	4 (15%)	6 (22%)
Bringing federal money . . . (district service)	4 (15%)	10 (37%)

tioned earlier, communication was ranked as the most important activity for members of the House, followed by policy making.[19] District and constituency service were also deemed comparatively unimportant in the 1978 NES.

Equally important, these findings are somewhat at odds with members' actions and the documented growth in constituent service over the past few decades. There appears to be a disjunction between members' behavior and the representational expectations of the participants in this study. More generally, citizens assert that district service and (to a lesser extent) constituent service are of secondary importance to them, yet members of Congress regularly engage in, and appear to benefit politically by, the provision of these services.[20] One is tempted to conclude, then, that many people find the idea of trafficking in these services contrary to their basic representational beliefs, but still want such assistance available if they need it (and come away with a better evaluation of their representatives if they, someone they know, or their communities get it). In this respect, as in several others, citizens' representational ideals and the actual representative process appear to diverge.

Finally, the results suggest some systematic differences in people's representational beliefs that may be linked to political sophistication. The lawmaking function provides the strongest evidence for a "sophistication effect"; sophisticated subjects were most likely to consider this a primary role, whereas all but one of the unsophisticated respondents gave it a 5 or 6 ranking (somewhat sophisticated people were evenly split). Somewhat and sophisticated individuals also had a more favorable view of the deliberative function. By contrast, politically involved participants typically gave constituency service a low ranking, while those deemed somewhat sophisticated were overwhelmingly skeptical of district service. Unsophisticated subjects, on the other hand, were likely to rate communication highly and were most favorably disposed toward involvement in the district.

The more unsophisticated the respondent, therefore, the more important that contact, communication, and district services seem to be in the representative relationship. Put another way, politically unattuned citizens are more likely to feel a sense of connection and responsiveness when representatives surface on their "radar screens" or provide assistance to their districts. For them representation is best defined by the direct bond that members of Congress establish and must continually renew with their constituents. As one moves up the sophistication scale— to people with greater resources and inclination to follow or participate in the political process—the less vital (one-way) communication, visibility, and constituent services appear to be. For politically active citizens, representation may be embodied more by what members do *in* the institution than what they (directly) do *for* their constituents.

What else might account for these divergent preferences? One factor may be people's underlying representational convictions. The ranking results tended to parallel and underscore the general views about representation articulated during the interviews. Involvement in the district, for example, was a centerpiece of the representational outlook of several of the unsophisticated respondents, a predilection reflected in the rank scales. The biting comments about direct contact made by several of the somewhat sophisticated respondents were also echoed in the rankings; these subjects rated involvement as the least important job responsibility. Similarly, those individuals who emphasized the significance of issue accessibility, fulfilling policy commitments, and legislative activism usually awarded high marks to deliberation and lawmaking. People's role expectations appear, in sum, to be related to their underlying beliefs about representation and their political attributes. In this case, what someone expects from a member of Congress is at least partially conditioned by his or her knowledge and interest in politics.

Assessment

The composite picture of congressional representatives and their job obligations outlined above contains some striking ambiguities. One, of course, is that it embodies starkly divergent ideals. Some of the respondents, for instance, want a representative who will always reflect the constituency's views, strive to secure projects for the district, and/or provide constituent service. Others are strongly opposed to some (or all) of these actions, preferring representatives who in some respect act like political trustees. Certain subjects appear to care deeply that members be role models in their personal conduct, while others could care less. And what it means to make the "right" decision was defined in markedly different ways.

Beyond this, it is also evident that we have a portrait of congressional representatives who must meld disparate, uneasily coexisting, and even conflicting actions and expectations. These citizens want members to exhibit responsiveness and fidelity to district interests plus use their own judgment, show political courage and independence, and doggedly pursue the public good. Representatives are expected to maintain a strong constituency connection and concentrate on their work in Washington; to stay closely attuned to their districts, but not at the expense of their institutional obligations. Similarly, members are supposed to "stick to their guns" and meet their public commitments, yet also be receptive to new ideas, willing to compromise to get things done, and constantly open to constituency input and influence. Finally, as the job rankings best demonstrate, there is considerable variation in the roles people expect members to fulfill.

In short, respondents have expansive expectations of their congressional representatives; put less charitably, they want to have it both (or all) ways. This is perhaps most true when one considers their views as a group, but it also characterizes a significant number of them as individuals. Members of Congress are supposed to fulfill numerous, challenging, and sometimes crosscutting roles and obligations. It certainly seems plausible that their ability, or inability, to meet such a diverse set of expectations in today's highly charged political environment in no small measure affects citizens' level of satisfaction—or rather dissatisfaction—with government.

Representatives as Political Models?

In *Home Style*, Richard Fenno posits that members of Congress can have a significant impact on their constituents' attitudes toward the representative process. On an even deeper level, he suggests that the way people *think* about representation may be conditioned by their representative's behavior. Although Fenno was primarily talking about members' influence over people's views of Congress as an institution, his portrayal of the home style connection implies that they are also in the business of trying to shape citizens' conceptions of what I call the "representative relationship." The fact that representatives encourage people to "think only about their relationship with their member" (p. 257) suggests that they strive to do so.

Taken to its logical conclusion, Fenno's analysis raises some intriguing questions. To what extent do members of Congress serve as political "models" for citizens? Do they really function as a kind of benchmark against which citizens gauge what politicians should or should not be like and should or should not do? More broadly, do people derive their notions of the ideal representative and/or representative process from the characteristics and behavior of elected officials, especially their current representatives? If so, *which* representatives? And what types of people are more likely to be so influenced? My study allows us to gain important insight into these issues.

First, my research suggests that Fenno overstates the impact that House members have on people's views of the representative process. Their own congressman appeared to have little hold over the subjects, including those who were otherwise politically knowledgeable. Even with Representative Solomon's prominent position in the House leadership, and both representatives multiple terms in office, few people (with the notable exception of the activists) made spontaneous or cued references to either member. More tellingly, when asked "who would you say best represents you today," only one respondent mentioned either Solomon or McNulty, and then in a decidedly half-hearted fashion. Indeed,

Solomon seemed to serve as a kind of "anti-model" of the ideal representative for some of the more sophisticated respondents. Consider the following subject's response to a probe about why he disliked Solomon:

> Well, he's very parochial, he's unthoughtful, he has knee-jerk positions that he always falls back on without making any decision. [*Pause*] I think he is, what is that word . . . self-aggrandizing. He likes to stand up and pompously say how he's for the little guy and he's down to earth. He grandstands more than he takes thoughtful positions on things.

Another respondent, a self-described "very conservative" Republican, was equally critical:

> . . . I have a lot of problems with Solomon. He supports lots of causes which are strictly political, he's doing a favor for somebody out in California or Texas, and we have to pay for these things. He's playing the game. I don't consider that the conservative way to do things. . . . And he makes statements that I think just are not really too educated, and I have problems with people like that on either side of the fence.[21]

Despite these exceptions, my work reinforces the voluminous literature that accentuates the relative invisibility of rank and file House members to the public. Fenno's representative-centered perspective exaggerates the degree to which citizens are affected by, or even aware of, their own members' home styles, as chronically low levels of name recognition for House incumbents also indicate. Most importantly, my research indicates that representatives have little direct impact on their constituents' images of the ideal representative relationship or the ideal representative.

The interesting deviation from the rule here was the political activists. Regular involvement in politics gives activists a vantage point on the representative process that is unavailable to other citizens, including those who are otherwise politically knowledgeable. It may also shape their conceptions of that process. Most of the activists relayed anecdotes about personal experiences with House members (not necessarily their own representative) that seemed to influence their view of the representative relationship. In this case, House members did appear to serve as models of representational behavior. To give just one example, the following subject, a lobbyist for an environmental advocacy group, relayed the impact of his experience with Representative Sherwood Boehlert, another member of New York's congressional delegation:

I had some direct experience with Boehlert organizing around NAFTA back in '92. The thing that was interesting about Boehlert was in that case he did vote the wrong way on the environment, from our perspective. We had a coalition that included labor groups, environmental groups, human rights groups, a wide variety of interests, but when it comes down to the day of the vote we got the call from Washington that said Boehlert was going to vote the wrong way and pull out the stops to try to see what we could do to turn him. And as I started calling, particularly the labor leaders, [they] were saying things on that day like, "Sherry"—they all call him Sherry—"called me up last night and explained what he's going to do, vote his conscience." So in essence he's created this personal relationship with these folks that in many respects he's not held as accountable as some other schmo who might not have created the personal relationship . . . because of his personal attributes and the fact that he's likable, and the fact he spends a lot of time developing relationships with constituency groups, he buys himself a lot of leeway . . . that's why if I was a legislator I would want to be directly and actively engaged with my constituents, because it isn't just a one-way kind of legislator loyalty to their constituents, but you can build loyalty the other way, and that can cut you a lot of slack when you need it.

While not conclusive, such evidence implies that House members are much more likely to make an imprint on the consciousness of politically active and sophisticated citizens. Intentionally or not, members may serve as representational touchstones primarily for the politically involved.[22]

If Representatives Solomon and McNulty were not portrayed as political exemplars, were any members of Congress? The person most often alluded to in this way was the late New York Senator Daniel Patrick Moynihan. To those respondents who mentioned him, Moynihan appeared to possess many of the personal and political qualities most desired in a representative. The descriptions provided of him were remarkably similar: of someone who combined fierce intelligence and understanding of the issues with an uncommon degree of political courage and independence. As one person put it: "I love Pat Moynihan . . . I think he's real, and I think he is terribly, terribly smart. I think he is a true liberal who cares about the people, and he makes sense. I don't think anyone's going to mess around with what he says because they know he's right." Such attitudes were not limited to liberal Democrats. Several of the Republican subjects also expressed admiration for Moynihan, none more so than the following individual:

If you look at Patrick Moynihan, here's a guy who has more than your average intellectual capacity, who is a guy who has synthesized new ideas that certainly are not mainstream political thinking, who shows a lot of leadership, he's one of the few guys in the Democratic Party who stands up to the president and says, "I'm sorry, Mr. President, but you're wrong on this issue." There are very few people who have the kind of stature and authority who will do that, who have the personal integrity to stand up and be counted. I have a lot of admiration for him. I don't agree with his policies, but I have a lot of admiration for him.[23]

In this sense, Moynihan was the closest to being an ideal type, a kind of trans-party paradigm of the good representative. Several participants also mentioned former Senator Al Damato, but usually in a less flattering light. In any case, the relative prominence of these two men suggests that there is something of a "senatorial effect" at work regarding people's representational models. That is, respondents' tended to make references to more prominent and/or highly visible officials in their discussions. Next to the president, of course, senators are typically some of the most recognizable national political figures. At whatever political level, though, high profile elected officials were more likely to occupy people's political imaginations, and therefore to potentially influence the latter's representational ideals and expectations.

A host of other individuals or groups were chosen as best representative. They ranged from the president and other members of Congress to governors and the city of Albany's mayor.[24] One person picked the Sierra Club. Two women mentioned former Secretary of State Madeleine Albright; one even selected Oprah Winfrey. The allusions to unelected public figures, and to elected officials subjects were not directly represented by, are particularly instructive, indicative of the range of people's conceptions about being represented (or who qualifies as a representative), as well as the perceived absence of good representation from their own elected officials. The handful of people who were unable, or unwilling, to choose a best representative also speaks to this. As the most sophisticated of these respondents said, "That's kind of hard to say. [*Pause*] I mean [*pause*] I wouldn't say that anyone sticks out."[25]

"A Tough Job": Being a Representative

As the previous paragraph hints, many of the participants were not terribly sanguine about the state of congressional representation. Once again, however, we encounter an intriguing paradox in their representational views. While often critical of today's members and the contemporary representative relationship, the respondents also expressed a surprising sympathy toward the job of being a representative. In fact, approximately 60 percent of them conveyed some appreciation of the personal or representational dilemmas faced by the modern congressperson, and some of the harshest critics of the representative process were especially quick to point out that "I wouldn't want that job." In essence, many of these citizens combined criticism of the "failures" of contemporary members with an awareness of the real-life occupational challenge of being a representative.

Taken together, subjects tapped into three major dimensions of this challenge. Some highlighted the personal trade-offs and sacrifices representatives make during their tenures. For instance, several people noted that the job and its many demands, including those that come from maintaining a close attachment to the district, can consume a member and take a huge toll on his family life. One of these respondents commented: "I don't think that being a politician is a great life. It takes you away from your family. I was just reading about all the organizations Manning (his state senator) belongs to. No way would I do that." A related drawback is a lack of down time. As another person observed: "It's a terror job being a representative, because you don't really have free time for yourself because you're either in Washington or your district, and you have to be out and be visible. So it's a tough balance." A few subjects also mused on the strain of having to endure myriad kinds of personal assaults while gaining little in the way of public esteem. Being a career politician may be unappealing to more than just the public today, as this respondent sensed: ". . . it's such a hard thing now, I don't think they can do it anymore, the game's too rough now, and people don't want to have politicians for life, it's not all that well respected. So I think you see people who go in it are in for eight years and getting out. I don't know if that's good or bad." The same individual later concluded that the personal toll on members has become so high that the kind of "people needed to fill these positions" are turning away from politics, to the detriment of the representative process itself:

> And that's why it is so discouraging the way that campaign laws are set up, and, you know, media attention on personal things, that the most capable people are not being elected now, sometimes they are scared off, and can't put up with the campaigning that's required, and the personal sacrifices, and the loss of privacy. Now that's another reason why I think you should pay politicians well. People are like, "why is this guy getting paid so much?", but you're expecting a lot of them, and if you want the most capable people you should be willing to pay them well.

The second major difficulty mentioned by respondents is the institutional demands of the job, including the number and complexity of issues. "It's a lot of work, a lot of issues," said one. "A lot of issues. And how do you get the big picture?—I don't know." Information overload, both within Congress and from the constituency, was similarly cited by a few people, including the following participant:

> The staff is here, the staff is in Washington, the communications that come through must be enormous. I can't even imagine what it would be. Someone else has to distill that for them, I suppose, because they can't possibly deal with it all. Just trying to get through even that must be a problem because of the committee meetings and the attendance in Congress and whatever else they're expected to do.

This individual also speculated that members of Congress may become so immersed in everyday legislative responsibilities that they lose sight of the "big picture": "Maybe they are so caught with the day-to-day things, they forget all about whatever they had intended [to do] when they began. . . . I would imagine their time is taken up with minutiae sometimes, and there's not a real good way around that." A few other respondents broached the issue of trying to make informed judgments in a legislative environment awash in different issues and bills. In an otherwise critical account of representatives' unwillingness to educate constituents, one subject also acknowledged the difficulty in fulfilling the role of deliberative legislator:

> They use these catchwords, they use these little sound-bites, because most of them don't know what's going on in the bill to begin with [*laughs*]. They really can't, in a way. If you take a look, there's fifteen thousand bills introduced just in the [New York] state legislature every year. Now many of them are duplicates, so maybe you end up with five or six thousand that are new. But you can't read all these and research them. You've got to rely on what somebody tells you.

The third major facet of members' "hard job" concerns the fundamental conflicts that inhere in the representative process, such as choosing between one's own beliefs or judgment and the interests/preferences of the constituency. These kinds of stark realities led some subjects to question their representational ideals. For example, the following person submitted that his "classic representative image" of the citizen legislator "climbing on his horse and riding off to Washington and making decisions to make us a great country and then coming home" runs headlong into the reality of modern politics, "because how can you do this highly complex job and still come home and plow your fields? You really have to be a full-time congressman to really know the ropes and do it the right way, so what I like about it (serving in Congress) is an ideal that doesn't exist."

This is not to say that all participants were sympathetic about members' occupational hazards and personal travails. When asked to give Congress some advice on how to do its job, one subject replied bluntly, "First of all work some more. I don't think the actual representatives work as hard as they should. They're busy courting their beneficiaries, for one thing." As you will see in the next chapter, respondents often believed that members of Congress, especially long-term incumbents, become increasingly complacent and unresponsive in their jobs. And a few people lampooned the attitudes and worries of what the Anti-Federalist's dubbed the "first class." Consider the following broadside launched against contemporary representatives by one such individual:

I know people that work for $5.00 an hour, two or three jobs, just to make ends meet. Just to have a roof over your head. These guys (representatives) have no idea. They think middle-class America is [pause] do they know anyone making less than $100,000 a year? They think $50,000 a year you're poor? . . . work for $5.00 an hour. You know, oh, they need raises because they have to have a home in Albany or Washington and then they have to have their home down in the state or town they come from, and they have all these expenses, oh me, oh my. Jeez, doesn't your heart just bleed. It's a joke. It's heartbreaking; it really is.

On balance, however, the evidence from this study challenges prevailing assumptions about ordinary citizens' attitudes toward and understanding of a representative's job. Reflexive hostility toward the personal concerns and job obligations of members of Congress was surprisingly rare in these interviews. Indeed, most of the participants who touched on these matters displayed a fairly keen sensitivity to the personal and professional burdens that members may face, even as they were often critical about various aspects of today's representative relationship.[26] In essence, these citizens seemed able to distinguish between the nature of the job (inherently demanding and problematic) and representatives' ability/willingness to discharge their responsibilities (in some respects inadequate). Perhaps nowhere was the respondents' awareness of the underlying complexity of the representative relationship more evident than in their elucidation of the intrinsic dilemmas of representation.

Members' Burdens:
The Inherent Conflicts of Representation

Participants addressed many of the "classic" dilemmas of representation over the course of their interviews, suggesting that the more complex facets of the representative relationship may not be a complete mystery to ordinary citizens. A large number of subjects discussed either of two of the most significant conflicts faced by members of Congress: promoting the good of the whole versus its parts (i.e., advancing the nation's interests or those of one's district/main constituencies); and pursuing a long-term agenda versus satisfying short-term demands or interests. The following individual provided one of the best accounts of the first predicament while mulling over the most important obligations of elected officials:

> I think their overall responsibility would be to look out for the welfare of their territory, not necessarily what their constituents want but generally what would be best, which is a difficult line to walk, I think, because people and interest groups want certain things, not necessarily what's good for the whole but . . . what each group wants. So it's difficult to try to decipher what's good for the whole versus what's good for some parts, but I think [they have to consider] that and what's good to keep them elected, you know, fudging along with partisan politics.

Befitting the importance they attached to having members possess a commitment to the long-term public good, several people wrestled with the challenge of squaring this imperative with constituents needs and desires in the here and now. As one somewhat sophisticated respondent tried to navigate the issue,

> I guess sometimes you have to go with your heart, and sometimes you have to go with your people, and sometimes if you go with your heart you have to be thinking what is the best for my constituents, because the way it should be is like the Indians, think of the seventh generation. What is not good for you, what is good for the children of the children of my children. That's what it comes down to. That's the way it really should be.

For many respondents this quandary emerged most clearly during the second hypothetical question, which heightened the constituent-centered political imperative that members face yet provided circumstances in which they might feel obliged to resist it. These subjects often emphasized the inherent difficulty of the situation. To illustrate, one person stated:

You see, this is hard, because politicians sometimes want to satisfy everybody, so it's a difficult position to be in. . . . This is a real difficult question, because you are kind of in between, you know, how to benefit the people and how to cut the budget at the same time. So in order, we might have to do things that aren't very popular in order to achieve something that will be beneficial in the long run. So he may have to face difficult decisions, but he will have to make those difficult decisions because in the long run, you have to look at the outcome in general for the future, not just temporary.

The problem became particularly acute for those respondents who were compelled to reconcile their *own* conflicting ideals. Take this exchange with one of the staunchest advocates of a long-term national focus on the part of members of Congress.

RES: You need a representative who can deal with people saying, "oh, but we want it now, who's going to give money to our town." People who are elected really need to have, I even think there should be a law that would force whoever ends up making a decision to have to come up with a plan for the long-term. And I think most people want that.

INT: Now what happens, though, if what you mentioned is important to you is that we're signing their paychecks, and their job is to represent what the people want, or what their interests are . . . ?

RES: I know I said before that they should represent the people, but I also think common-sense has to come into play. And to vote for something that you know is going to be harmful, you're not being honest with people. There are fine lines in everything . . .

Arrestingly, a handful of participants also latched onto one or more of the quandaries that can flow from members' attempts to stay closely attuned to their districts, reflect constituents' needs and viewpoints, or even heed their own judgment—exactly the kind of diverse representational ends championed by most of the respondents. One of the district-driven dilemmas that has already been examined arises from the clash between constituent preferences and a member's own beliefs or judgment. Several people, including the subjects cited below, additionally emphasized the political price representatives may pay at home for taking unpopular stands or resisting district opinion:

> If you get a decent guy, and he dares to speak out in the short run, the majority of people that are his constituents are, you know, going to vote him out. They might get really ticked off. So it's a hell of a job for, well, this hypothetical person who I think would be ideal. It'd be a hell of a job. It would be really easy if you're in there for your own self-bettering, self-serving.
>
> I think they definitely should; it's not always that it's politically possible. I mean, there was a case of a congressman who voted against something that would have benefited [his] home district and he was out the next time. He thought he would gain nationwide fame by doing that but he was voted right out. . . . I know I would tend to vote for a guy like that, but I know if I lost my job I'd probably vote against a guy who did that. So you have to count on losing those votes, and you have to be pretty secure in your position to do that.

These citizens recognized that the (actual or anticipated) wrath of constituents can dissuade even the most independent and seemingly secure representatives from following their own judgment. As another individual pointedly observed, "It's pretty tough to tell a man or woman to commit [political] suicide, huh?" Therefore, even as they castigated members for being unwilling to make tough decisions or show political courage, some respondents also acknowledged the potential political cost of failing to reflect the "will of the people".

But perhaps the most surprising argument made about public opinion was that there is simply too much of it. A few respondents seemed to think that inordinate public and interest group pressure is distorting the representative process and members' decision making. For instance, in her discussion of the ideal kind of representative relationship, this participant remarked that

> Ideally we wouldn't have too many little gripes, and they would listen. So I think if I were a politician I would be overwhelmed with people saying this, this and this. You know, they have to deal with it because they're supposed to be caring. . . . I think as a whole country we just gripe about the littlest things, and our politicians have to sit there and listen. I think it's crazy. I guess it does affect their job, because they have to listen, they have to deal with this crap, and I think it's a waste of time.

Thus, burdened by "trivial and excessive" public demands, caught up in an endless spiral of constituent service and rising expectations, contemporary members of Congress are no longer really free to attend to their primary responsibilities. One of the foremost critics of today's politics also touched on this issue, although he pointedly suggested that members had brought much of it down on themselves:

> . . . an awful lot of problems that people bring should not come to a congressman to begin with. You can't spend your time dealing with hundreds of thousands of people now in your district, and they come to you with every little problem they can think of. But they are afraid to tell the people this, "don't call me, call your city councilman," because this person won't vote for them. And I think it's a trap. I don't know how you get out of it, because people will get very angry, and they don't know the difference.

One of the more unsophisticated respondents nicely captured the ultimate paradox of members trying to fulfill their obligations in an age of heightened public expectations: "I think it would [be] kind of hard just to please everybody across the board, to meet each and every person's needs, you know what I'm saying? You'd be doing that for the rest of your life, you know. And even still, people are not gonna be satisfied."

Nevertheless, it must be emphasized that relatively few of the participants pondered the impact on the representative process when, as one person put it, "everyone is clamoring for what they want." Most importantly, they generally failed to consider the larger representational implications of the kind of continual contact/communication and responsiveness to the district that they favored. Ironically, the potential dilemmas posed by a strong constituent connection were the ones most likely to slip beneath subjects' radar screens.

The Balancing Act of Representation

Perhaps the best way to finally depict how many of these citizens perceived the representative process is as a "balancing act." Reflections of this sort occurred most often during responses to the hypothetical questions, but they surfaced at all points in the interviews, including the section dealing specifically with the representative relationship. The obligations or interests that participants thought members need reconcile were diverse, and often reflected the respondents' primary representational concerns: the short and the long term; personal judgment and constituency preferences; district and national interests; and so on. As one individual articulated the fundamental challenge (and opportunity) for representatives early in his interview,

> . . . you have to when you are representing a district represent that district's interest, and even though that may not be to everyone's interest, you know that is what you'll have

to do. But I think you can temper, there's so much gray area in being a politician and passing laws and I think you can play the game so that you seem to be representing your own special interests, yet not in such a way that the best interest of the public is endangered.

Most often, however, respondents alighted on the need for members to balance their political aims with constituents interests, to calibrate political imperatives and their own beliefs, to juggle the drives to "get reelected *and* to do good."[27] As the following subject observed: "Personally I would like to see them doing what's better for the whole, but for them being in office, they do have to look at what will keep them in office." In one way or another, all of these citizens would concur with the succinct appraisal of the representative relationship offered by this person: "It's a balancing act, you know." The kind of assessment that might very well be offered, and in all likelihood endorsed, by members of Congress themselves.

Concluding Remarks

The portrait of the representative relationship that emerges from these interviews is rich, varied, and complicated, composed of both thoughtful perspectives and troubling incongruities. Taken together these citizens conveyed a surprising sensitivity toward the complexity and manifold demands in the relationship between constituents and members of Congress. This was particularly evident in references to the intrinsic dilemmas of representation and the difficult job of today's member. Such an outlook, however, did not preclude frequent and often sharp critiques of contemporary representatives and the current representative process. The representative relationship may be inherently difficult, participants seemed to be saying, but that does not mean there isn't substantial room for improvement in it.

This complex perspective was mirrored in subjects' hopes for their representatives. Respondents harbored an abundance of personal and job-related expectations for members of Congress. At best these convictions, like the view of the representative relationship described above, might be taken as evidence of a "realistic idealism" among citizens—of a reasoned and reasonable wish for members to balance disparate and sometimes competing representational ends as best they can. At worst, their views lend credence to the argument that representatives are expected to be all things to all people today, a certain recipe for political cynicism and disillusionment. The expansive and crosscutting beliefs held by the small group of citizens studied here hint at the myriad of competing representational expectations that likely swirl in the public at large. Like officials in other public institutions, members of Congress—indeed, all representatives—may now be subject to heightened (and contradictory) public demands, even as trust in government institutions and official has waned. In other words, people's expectations for the representative process probably have grown, in part because of the behavior of members themselves, over the same period that their faith in representatives and the political process has sharply declined. The ultimate irony is that members' inability to fulfill these divergent expectations in all likelihood reinforces citizens' disdain with politics.

Chapter Six

Institutional Representation

Introduction

Over the past three decades, increasing scholarly attention has been paid to the political relationship between Congress and the American public. Much of this research springs from the recognition that it is essential to examine the institutional dimensions of the representative process. For the most part, however, this focus has not extended to people's conceptions of what I call "institutional representation." As is true of representation in general or the congressional representative relationship, ordinary citizens' beliefs about Congress have been largely neglected in the literature. Yet the connection between our national legislature and the American public is an integral part of the representative equation. This study turns on the idea that it is vital for us to know what ordinary citizens think about Congress as an *institution.* Investigating people's views about institutional representation can give us a better grasp of public attitudes toward, and evaluations of, legislative actors and institutions. Most importantly, it could significantly enhance our understanding of the representative process and our political culture.

In this chapter, we address this third important dimension of people's representational views. A number of fundamental, yet mostly unanswered, questions drove this enterprise. How do ordinary citizens perceive Congress? What basic images and expectations do they have of the institution? What do they consider to be Congress's most important roles, obligations, and contributions in the political system? And what do they think about the state of the contemporary representative process? Here we will see that, to many of the citizens I interviewed, Congress is both a great abstraction and an indispensable actor in our political process. We will find that political sophistication matters in how, and how well, people conceptualize Congress as an institution. And we will discover that while the respondents are often critical of representation today, their attitudes toward the congressional legislative process are far from, as some research would suggest is typical, summarily undemocratic.

By delving into what these citizens consider to be the most important functions of Congress and the major impediments to effective representation, the suggestions they offered to improve the representative process, and their perspectives on term limits and incumbency, we cast valuable light on their beliefs about contemporary representation and their deepest representational ideals. We also glimpse some of the implications that the participants' views about institutional representation may pose for the actual political process. Ultimately, this chapter demonstrates that exploring citizens' ideational beliefs about Congress is as essential for understanding the public side of representation as examination of the representative-constituent relationship.

Conceptions of Congress

The institutional segment of the interviews began with two questions designed to tap into respondents' overarching view of Congress. Rather than opening with queries about specific facets of the institution, or asking subjects to comment on the current Congress, I first wanted to record their fundamental images and expectations, or "sense," of the institution, unaffected by any current contextual referents. The intent was to get at people's basic beliefs about institutional representation, including the essential functions of our national legislature, which may shape their attitudes toward today's Congress.

To do so, each respondent was asked the following questions:

- In general, what do you like about Congress? In general, what do you dislike about it?
- Congress does many things in our political system. What do you think are the most important things that Congress does?

The subjects' first impressions of Congress were defined by abstract appreciation of the institution combined with more specific qualms about the way it currently operates. Regarding the former, several participants voiced support for Congress's place within our constitutional system. For example, a few expressed admiration for the historic continuity of the institution, the fact that it has endured and still "works" after more than two centuries. In this vein Congress serves as perhaps the foremost symbol of the success of our brand of constitutional government. As one of these respondents said, "what I like best is you know it's what we're all about, it's got hundreds of years as a system, and I think that they haven't changed much of that, so I think it's historic."

More common were general references to the blessings of our political system. Some participants expressed this in the most generic terms: "I like the set up. It's a good set up, they did a good job, our founding fathers. The structure of it." A few respondents extolled the advantages of a Madisonian system of checks and balances: how it helps to protect minorities, prevent policy/political "radicalism" or extremism, and so forth. Others touched on the benefits flowing from the basic structure of Congress. Several people, for instance, touted the virtues of having a federal legislature. To them, representation by both population and state/region helps to provide a proper "balance" of interests in Congress and ensures that a wealth of differing views and groups will be reflected in the political arena.

This last point proved to be a recurring theme. In fact, the expressive/representative capacity of Congress seemed to evoke the most positive associations among respondents. The open airing of ideas and viewpoints was cited by a number of subjects, as was a decision-making process that people can see and try to affect; in the words of one of these individuals, "I guess that's what I really like about it . . . [y]ou, uh, have the ability to influence, the public really has the ability to have some input." Perhaps most of all, Congress was perceived as the political institution that best embodies the country's great social and political diversity. As the following subject described it, "the positive of Congress is that it's America, you know. . . . It's the country fit into a little building. So to that extent that shows a lot, that shows a lot." Or, in the succinct assessment of another, "What I like about it? That [it is] representative of the entire nation." From this perspective, Congress's greatest strength and appeal lies in the fact that it, however imperfectly, "mirrors" American society and serves as the people's political forum.[1]

Most Important Responsibilities

As part of the effort to identify their beliefs about institutional representation, subjects were canvassed about the essential roles of Congress. The lawmaking function, not surprisingly, was mentioned most often. When asked about the most important things that Congress does, about half of the respondents alluded to making laws or passing legislation. Determining the federal budget was another oft-cited obligation. Congress's crucial role in setting tax and spending priorities, the power of the purse, figured in the responses of about a third of the subjects, including the following individual: "In terms of the budget, then clearly that's absolutely crucial, it's the most important thing that Congress does."[2]

Interestingly, some of the participants outlined broader visions of the institution. Several emphasized the importance of attending to national issues and needs—of promoting the general welfare. A number of others went even further, charging Congress with the obligation of setting national priorities and providing national leadership. As one of these respondents put it, Congress should "decide what issues the country is going to be moving on." Or, in the words of another subject, "I think they're supposed to be setting the course of the country, in whatever way, whether it's financially or socially in some cases, and they certainly ought to be giving us national direction as well." One individual even opined that by its actions and decisions (or lack thereof), the institution helps to set a particular tone or "atmosphere" in the country that can have important social repercussions. There is little doubt that to all of these citizens, Congress is a—and possibly *the*—driving force in our national political process.

Institutional Roles: The Rank Scales

As was the case with the representative relationship, the narrative evidence I gathered was complemented by a job responsibility ranking scale administered at the end of the interviews (see appendix A). Subjects were asked to rank in order of importance six discrete roles for Congress as an institution. The list offered a fairly comprehensive set of institutional duties for people to evaluate. The overall intent was to gauge the relative importance of major institutional roles to the respondents, pinpoint any relationships between sophistication levels and job expectations, and see whether the rankings were consistent with the interview narratives. Above all, I hoped to gain an inkling of what ordinary citizens prize most in legislative institutions. The six responsibilities and their corresponding role designation (in parentheses) were as follows:

- Representing the different groups and interests in America (expressive);
- Discussing and debating important or controversial issues (deliberation);
- Keeping people informed about what's going on in Washington (communication);
- Preventing the president from becoming too powerful (constitutional—checks and balances);
- Providing federal money and projects to local districts (district service);
- Passing bills that deal with important national problems (lawmaking).

Respondents were also given the opportunity to describe any other important responsibility not included in the scale.

Table 6.1. Job Responsibility Rankings for Congress

	Very Important	Somewhat Important	Least Important
Discussing and debating . . . (deliberation)	13 (48%)	11 (41%)	3 (11%)
Representing the different . . . (expressive)	12 (44%)	8 (30%)	7 (26%)
Passing bills that deal . . . (lawmaking)	11 (41%)	12 (44%)	4 (15%)
Keeping people informed . . . (communication)	11 (41%)	9 (33%)	7 (26%)
Providing federal money . . . (district service)	6 (22%)	9 (33%)	12 (44%)
Preventing the president . . . (constitutional)	1 (04%)	5 (19%)	21 (78%)

Table 6.1 presents the overall results of the institutional rank scales. Once again, the ratings were combined into three categories to facilitate comparison. A ranking of 1 or 2 for each option was considered "very important"; 3 or 4 "somewhat important"; and 5 or 6 "least important." Both the total number and percentage of rankings for each category are listed (percentages may not equal 100 percent due to rounding).

These results bolster my initial appraisal of the importance of the expressive and deliberative roles of Congress. Almost half of the participants considered representing the nation's different groups and interests to be a primary mission of the institution (and another quarter gave it a ranking of three). The deliberative function, which has some expressive overtones, was rated even more highly, with only three subjects deeming this role relatively insignificant. Thus, respondents appear to value Congress as a center for national political discourse and debate. In their eyes one of its main "reasons for being" is to provide a forum for the articulation and sifting of vital public needs, interests, ideas, and concerns.

The importance of the legislative function was also underscored in the rankings. As was true of the results for individual members, no other category received more "1" ratings; this time, however, only a handful of subjects deemed this role to be relatively unimportant. Keeping people informed also garnered its share of support, befitting the weight that respondents attached to representational communication.[3] But while each of these roles gained significant backing, it is important to note that not one emerged as a clear choice as the most important function. Finally, although not quite as evident as in the rank scale for individual members,

there is still some polarization in the institutional rankings. Over a quarter of the subjects, for example, deemed the communication and expressive roles to be relatively unimportant activities.

Additional perspective on these matters can be gained by examining
which institutional obligations respondents considered to be the most
and least significant. Table 6.2 presents the number and percentage of
subjects who ranked each function 1 and 6. This table therefore provides
further insight into what these citizens do (and do not) regard as the
quintessential responsibilities of our national legislature.

Three functions emerge as favorites here: communication, lawmaking, and expressive. Unlike lawmaking and communication, however, almost as many people ranked the expressive role as least important as
ranked it the most important congressional activity. "Representing the
people" therefore stands as the most contentious, as well as one of the
most critical, institutional functions. While only three participants chose
discussing and debating issues as Congress's most important obligation,
this was also the sole category not to receive the lowest ranking of six.
And a few respondents did hold district service in high regard.

Again, what both of these tables indicate is the great diversity in people's representational role expectations. Further illustrating this point is
the fact that four of the six functions overall were considered very important by at least 40 percent of the subjects. And while the most respondents chose lawmaking as the key institutional role, eleven people
(or 41 percent) rated it from 4–6. On the whole, then, participants

Table 6.2. Supplemental Rankings for Congress

	Ranked 1	Ranked 6
Passing bills that deal . . . (lawmaking)	9 (33%)	2 (07%)
Keeping people informed . . . (communication)	6 (22%)	3 (11%)
Representing the different . . . (expressive)	6 (22%)	5 (19%)
Discussing and debating . . . (deliberation)	3 (11%)	0 (00%)
Providing federal money . . . (district service)	3 (11%)	7 (26%)
Preventing the president . . . (constitutional)	0 (00%)	10 (37%)

evinced little agreement about Congress's major responsibilities. The one exception to this is the "checks and balances" function; all but three ranked it from 4–6. To the citizens in this study, regardless of their level of political sophistication, Congress's obligation to ensure a constitutional balance of power is clearly superseded by other duties, at least under normal political circumstances.[4]

Overall, however, political sophistication played an even greater role in the institutional rankings than in those for individual members, albeit much to the same effect. Somewhat sophisticated and sophisticated respondents typically awarded high marks for the lawmaking and deliberative functions (for example, all but two of these individuals ranked the latter from 1–3), but were quite skeptical of district service. Those considered sophisticated were also most likely to give communication a low ranking. By contrast, unsophisticated subjects were highly supportive of providing federal money and projects to the district and keeping people informed.[5] Lawmaking and deliberation were less important to them, usually receiving rankings from 3–5.

These findings bolster the thesis that representational expectations vary according to people's personal attributes, including what one could call their "aptitude for politics." The politically active and informed participants in this study tended to value the classic "civics book" functions of Congress, its legislative and deliberative roles, whereas the more apolitical citizens seemed to prize the representational communication and district services provided by the institution. In other words, more politically sophisticated people generally expect Congress to engage in discussion, debate, and lawmaking, while less sophisticated individuals look to the institution to dispense both information and benefits to the American people. What Congress is expected to do (or not to do) therefore hinges to some degree on the audience involved. One important systemic implication is that the institutional actions and processes that are vital to some people or groups may be insignificant, or even a source of disenchantment, to others. In the process of fulfilling the representational expectations of certain segments of the citizenry, therefore, Congress very well may be inadvertently sowing or watering the seeds of political discontent elsewhere.

Assessment

Several interesting themes concerning citizens' views toward Congress emerge from this data. The first is that despite the deep discontent with the institution and its performance recorded in most public opinion surveys, the people I interviewed clearly like the "idea" of Congress. As discussed earlier, several respondents spoke approvingly of the historic continuity of the institution and its place in our constitutional order, while many highlighted its contributions to the political process. Even while enumerating Congress's shortcomings, these citizens tended to relay an appreciation for representative government and the (at least potential) political strengths of the institution.

Participants also conveyed a sense of Congress at the center of our political process. The institution quite often was depicted as a driving political force, capable of framing the terms of political debate, setting national priorities, and providing national leadership. As one respondent expressed this, "they're responsible for a lot of our laws and getting things passed and getting things organized and hopefully getting things done. So, it's really the working force of our government. We depend on them for major things." Thus, rather than being perceived as weak and reactive, an inherently subordinate actor to the president, Congress is viewed by these citizens as a powerful and even indispensable institution whose primary duties include steering the national ship.[6]

Respondents cited a number of other important roles for the institution. Many subjects, as mentioned above, touched on its obvious legislative and budgetary responsibilities and powers. But there were other, more illuminating responses. As both the interview narratives and rank scales revealed, Congress is vital to these citizens as a forum for national political discourse, a place where the major issues of the day will be aired, debated, and hopefully addressed. Above all, perhaps, Congress is valued as a *representative* institution, as the body that best encompasses and expresses the nation's diverse groups, interests, and beliefs. In the succinct assessment provided by one respondent: "That's what Congress is; it's the people's voice being expressed." On an abstract, ideational level, then, being regarded as the "voice of the people" might be Congress's main calling card with the American citizenry. To the extent that *actual* Congress's are seen as deviating from this ideal, however, discontent with the institution may well be the practical result.

View of the Congressional Democratic Process

An unambiguous source of public discontent with Congress, according to some scholars who have recently studied the subject, is the legislative process itself. In their 1995 book *Congress as Public Enemy*, John P. Hibbing and Elizabeth Theiss-Morse set out to uncover the roots of public discontent with political institutions, especially Congress, which has been consistently recorded in opinion surveys over the past few decades. The authors arrive at some provocative and disheartening conclusions about the public's attitudes toward institutional representation and the larger democratic process.

Hibbing and Theiss-Morse maintain that Americans' dissatisfaction with the political system, and Congress in particular, stems in large part from their disdain for the procedures that define democratic governance and characterize institutional representation. They find that ordinary citizens are unfavorably disposed towards political conflict, competing interests, and the public airing of disagreements; prolonged debate and discussion; policy vacillation; and bargaining and compromise. These characteristics are, of course, most closely associated with legislative institutions. A slow, often conflictual, and relatively inefficient Congress simply does not sit well with a fast-paced society geared to immediate answers and quick action. In short, the democratic process is always on display, most clearly in Congress, and people do not like what they see.[7]

In fact, Congress is often viewed as the "enemy" precisely because it is *so public*; the relative openness of the legislative process, constant media scrutiny, and the increasingly partisan nature of congressional decision-making all combine to produce popular disdain for the institution. Thus, Hibbing and Theiss-Morse submit that institutional variables play a significant role in people's evaluations of Congress. Contrary to Fenno, they conclude that most people are able to think about Congress as a collectivity; citizens' ideas and expectations about the institution are not derived mainly from (the actions of) their representatives. But they also assert that on the whole Americans' conceptions of institutional representation are quite unrealistic and even undemocratic. What we expect from legislative bodies, and what those bodies can (and in some sense are designed to) deliver, are two separate things. Most critically, Congress's internal dynamics, especially those activities that fall under the rubric of deliberation, drive people's discontent with politics. And this does not bode well for the health of our political system. As Hibbing and Theiss-Morse acerbically conclude: "People profess a devotion to democracy in the abstract but have little or no appreciation for what a practicing democracy invariably brings with it" (p. 147).[8]

This contention, as the authors' note, was based largely on the data gleaned from a series of focus-group interviews. While rightly touting the value of focus-group research for revealing deeply held beliefs about political institutions, Hibbing and Theiss-Morse also assert that their study was designed to avoid one of the major pitfalls of such research: crafting questions and/or an interview environment that prompt people to respond in ways which validate the researchers' assumptions or hypotheses. In their words: "We knew we wanted to hear what people thought about political institutions and different parts of those institutions, but the moderator had no particular desire to induce damning, Congress-bashing statements . . ." (p. 87). Yet several of the questions asked during the focus-group sessions would seem to lead participants in precisely that direction. For example, the following is listed in the book's appendix as the second question asked of the focus-group participants:

> It seems as if people's dissatisfaction with government is heavily focused on Congress lately. What do you think? Are you dissatisfied specifically with Congress or are you dissatisfied more broadly with the national government?[9]

It is hardly surprising, then, that the citizens Hibbing and Theiss-Morse studied offered decidedly critical appraisals of institutional representation, since the focus groups they participated in basically steered them that way.

My study—which did not frame the institution in a negative light, but was designed to encourage people to think about the whole range of institutional roles—offers a somewhat different take on citizens attitudes toward the congressional democratic process. Although participants were not directly asked to comment upon or assess the legislative process, such remarks arose in over half of the interviews, either in response to the initial questions about Congress or follow-up probes.

These reflections often betrayed an appreciation for some aspect of the process of institutional representation. Several respondents, for example, highlighted the benefits gained from open discussion and debate. One mentioned how the "activities of Congress" help to educate the public ("things are aired in public and I think Congress serves as a forum where people can learn the facts about things"), while another touched on how they broaden members' outlooks: "I like to have them there discussing things with each other, not off someplace doing fundraising or whatever. It's important to have open debate where they can hear different viewpoints and things. You need to know what other people and areas want and are thinking to get a big picture of things, a bigger perspective." In much the same vein, a handful of participants approvingly noted that the legislative process is relatively transparent and open to public input and influence. (As one of them stated: "I really like that a lot of things are out in the open and you can see what's happening.") Most revealingly, as discussed earlier, the belief that Congress embodies and reflects the many groups, interests, and points of view in the country—a fact which several people acknowledged invariably entails conflict and "slows things down"— appeared to be a primary source of support for the institution.

The results from the rank scales only amplified this evidence from the interviews. Above all, the rankings bolster the conclusion that respondents value the representational and deliberative functions of Congress, its crucial role in providing a public arena for the articulation and resolution of important problems and issues. In short, the citizens I interviewed tended to endorse some of the very institutional activities, including the airing of diverse views/interests and open discussion and debate, that Hibbing and Theiss-Morse assert spur public dissatisfaction with government. One of my most interesting institutional findings is that many participants seemed to regard the expression of political and policy differences as one of Congress's strengths, not one of its major weaknesses.

This is not to say, however, that the subjects had no misgivings about the outcomes and methods of the congressional democratic process. The most common lament along these lines was that the institution moves too slowly and is inefficient. As one of the respondents put it: "What I don't like about Congress is . . . the length of time, uh, that things take."

A few people also ruefully noted that it is easier to block than to effect change in Congress. A young political activist touched on both of these concerns while asserting that the legislative process can warp the intent, and product, of legislative action:

> What I don't like is because of the way it's set up and the efforts to be so fair, things often get too, if this makes any sense, bureaucratic, and issues can get lost in like a maze of structures. Then by the time this one issue goes through the structure it comes out as something that looks completely different. And you don't remember exactly what happened to that original issue, and it gets distorted along the way and things get tagged on before a decision is made . . . that whole process is so costly. It's not effective in that it's not efficient enough, and it doesn't work quick enough.

Some of the more politically attentive subjects likewise assailed some of Congress's internal rules and procedures, especially those that they believed obstruct the "legitimate" exercise of majority rule or distort the representative process. The filibuster came in for criticism here, as did pork-barreling and vote trading. ("There's too much of this 'I'll vote for your bill if you promise to vote for mine, and I want to put something here in my district to keep it going.' They really sell their responsibility to the people by trading things back and forth.") A few people, as illustrated in the following quote, also expressed dismay with the amendment process:

> It always bothers me that they have a bill and then they tack on all these other things on the end of it, unrelated, *totally unrelated.* I just can't understand any kind of, uh, policy format that allows you to do that [*laughs*]. It doesn't make any sense to me . . . if we do this for you and you do this for us, I'm sure there's that kind of compromise, but to do it through the amendments to the bill or whatever method they use is wrong. (emphasis in original)[10]

What can we conclude from this disparate evidence? On the whole, I believe, that these citizens offered a fairly complex and balanced view of congressional democracy. Participants certainly had qualms with the way the legislative process plays out and highlighted what they believed were its drawbacks (as did the people in Hibbing and Theiss-Morse's focus groups), yet they also extolled the benefits of the process and the importance of Congress's institutional roles. Ultimately, there were few signs that the respondents hold the democratic process in contempt, even as they clearly expressed frustration with some of its procedures and outcomes. And, as the rank scales best illustrate, these citizens want Congress to engage in the type of democratic activities that naturally lend to slow-moving, deliberate, and even contentious decision making. The congressional process may take time, and generate substantial conflict, but that's part of the bargain, as a few of the respondents explicitly recognized. In the words of one of these individuals: "The process is bound to be slower because not everybody agrees on any topic. And there's resistance and it takes time to educate people. Most people have jobs and families and they can't devote much time to public affairs, so it takes time to reach them and convince them what the issues are."[11]

In sum, the participants' concerns about the limitations of institutional representation were matched by their appreciation of its blessings and strengths. This fairly nuanced perspective even surfaced in some of the individual interviews, as the following exchange indicates:

> RES: Well, I've got another gripe. It takes too much time [*pause*]. It's not really with Congress, it's the nature of the democratic process. It takes time to do something, it takes a while for something to get through Congress and through committees, voted on, etc. Sometimes that can be frustrating . . . the whole process itself is unwieldy.
>
> INT: Are there any good points to that?
>
> RES: Oh yeah, there are very good points to that. It allows for open debate, it allows for the representation, idealistically, of the everyday people to be brought up. On the positive side, Congress is the communication network for the individual citizen's ideas to be expressed.

Or, as one of the less sophisticated respondents phrased it while discussing how Congress makes decisions,

> RES: There's two sides to that, you know, a side that is the majority rules, but then again if there are votes against it they can bring the legislation down. And the time that it takes to pass certain things concerning health, and gun laws, and all that, I wish they would work a little faster sometimes . . .
>
> INT: Is that something that's just part of the system, or can that be changed?
>
> RES: That's what's good about it! It's good because it's democracy, that's the way it's supposed to run. People should have a say-so, and if you're opposed to a certain thing you should have a voice, and if as much people oppose it you should be able to kill an amendment or pass it on. . . . It's a slow process because you have so many differences of opinion.

Although it would be ill-advised to draw any definitive conclusions from this data, the participants in my study evinced an understanding of the congressional democratic process which seems both more realistic and favorable than that manifested in Hibbing and Theiss-Morse's focus groups. When given the opportunity to evaluate the institution as a whole, these citizens were sometimes critical but never summarily undemocratic. While they did not always like what they see in Congress, including conflict that they believe is generated solely for partisan purposes, neither were they blind to the benefits of an open, cacophonous, and often messy legislative process. Most importantly, they accepted the necessity of, or even actively endorsed, the same institutional processes that Hibbing and Theiss-Morse contend people disdain. Once again, in-depth individual interviews offer a perspective on people's political beliefs that does not, and perhaps cannot, surface in short opinion surveys or even certain types of focus-group studies.

The State of the Representative Process

A study of people's conceptions of the representative process would be incomplete without a look at their beliefs about the state of contemporary representation. Moving from the subjects' abstract ideas and expectations of the institution to their attitudes about today's representative process not only gives us a window into their views about how representation does work; it can also shed light on their core convictions about how representation *should* work. By exploring what these individuals see as impediments to effective institutional representation, as well as ways to improve it, we can gain better insight into their perspectives on politics today and underlying ideas about the nature of representation. Put another way, what ordinary citizens lament about the representative process helps to reveal what they long for.

Most of the participants voiced opinions about the health of the representative process while discussing the representative relationship and institutional representation. On the whole, respondents were not sanguine about the state of contemporary congressional representation. As was true of the initial critiques they offered (see chapter three), their pessimism appeared to stem from the belief that the representative process has been compromised or distorted in significant ways, to the detriment of both the represented and the larger political process. And one result was that they believed representatives increasingly lack the ability or willingness to make decisions as they ideally should, that is, in a non self-interested fashion.

The most widespread concern among subjects was the (growing) influence of money in the representative process. Members of Congress were repeatedly characterized as being captives of "big money" and overly responsive to lobbyists and special interests.[12] Nowhere did participants see this subservience better exemplified than in the power of campaign donors in the political process. Quite a few alluded to the idea that, because of their voracious need for cash, representatives are beholden more to campaign contributors than the citizens they serve. As one of these individuals put it, "I vote them in but I think it's important to know like who donated the most."[13] In the glum assessment of another, "It's all about their money. It's all about their dollar bill." And the belief that members are increasingly driven by financial considerations was not limited to the less or somewhat sophisticated subjects; all but one of the sophisticated respondents commented on the influence of money in the contemporary representative process. One of the political activists gave the following conflicted answer when probed about the effect of campaign contributions on members of Congress:

> I think it changes their behavior because the more money they get then [donors] come back and say, "we need you here on this." It influences their vote . . . and, you know, I think it's expected that you have to fund your campaign, and you have to fund your mail, and you have to get communications to the district, and you need money to do that, so you have to raise money . . . [but] if they're spending all of their time fundraising, and making calls and sucking up to people, and you've got to give me money for this and you're not going to the local people you're going to the corporations in Washington that are just giving you money left and right. It definitely disrupts the process.

This response also gives an inkling of what these citizens considered to be the deleterious effects of money on the representative process. Many of them, like the activist cited above, felt that members' issue stands, legislative priorities, and, perhaps most disturbingly, voting decisions are too often influenced and distorted by it. In their view, the endless pursuit of campaign funds absorbs too much of members' time and energy and ultimately compromises their integrity as political actors. Few subjects intimated that members are baldly on the take or out to become willing pawns of special interests. In fact, a handful noted that the importance of money in contemporary politics may stem largely from systemic pressures, especially the ever-rising cost of running a credible campaign: ". . . first of all, the amount of money it takes to be elected is important, so you've got to have fundraising, you've got to have money, and if so-and-so's lobby is willing to give you X amount of dollars for your campaign it's tough not to do that. Of course, along with that they have some expectations that you will follow their [position]."

But whatever the impetus, these citizens believe that the nexus between campaign contributions, elections, and governing is corroding the representative process and leading representatives to be, as one participant put it, "loyal to people other than their constituents." It also is propelling members into continual and contorted efforts to mask money's effect on the process, actions that only reinforce people's cynicism about their representatives and Congress as a whole. In the words of one of the respondents who touched on this, "you know that their next election depends on where the money is coming from, and they're going to be steered that way, and they're going to spin why they voted the way they did to make it appear they're doing it in our interest and hoping to get us to believe it."[14]

Participants were equally concerned about the impact of campaign finance on the political role of ordinary citizens. Several of them noted that because of the skyrocketing costs (both monetary and personal) of campaigns, the vast majority of American citizens cannot even aspire to run for higher office. Money "cuts a lot of people out," severely limiting the pool of potential candidates and therefore the possibility of better demographic and issue representation. "I just think it's difficult for the average person to run, and there are a lot of millionaires who are members of Congress, and that sometimes is what it takes. Do they accurately reflect their constituents? Probably not."[15] Above all, perhaps, subjects feared that the current electoral system mutes the political voice of ordinary citizens. As one person implored while discussing potential changes in Congress, "make it so that the average person can actually contribute and have a say, or not have it that the average person has to contribute money to get to talk to the congressman."

In sum, many of the participants in this study were highly skeptical about the ability of ordinary citizens to effectively compete, or even to make themselves heard, in the contemporary political environment. To these citizens, "money politics" is increasingly precluding true and equitable representation in Congress, as well as in other representative institutions. The following unsophisticated subject perhaps best articulated this view: "[Y]ou know, it's true when they say money talks. That is so true, and you're beginning to see that more and more and more. If you don't have money, you really don't have a say."[16]

Two other forces were presented as major impediments to effective (institutional) representation, albeit by a smaller number of respondents. One was the mass media. Six people discussed the political damage they thought was being wrought by today's media, including excessive scrutiny of politicians' private lives, a tendency to provide superficial coverage of issues and to focus on personal scandals and other "trivial" matters, and the erosion of public trust in the political process. A few of these individuals also observed that the media, especially television, has a profound influence on who is elected to Congress and their behavior in office. As one respondent put it: "I mean, all of these things that don't necessarily make for a good legislator make for good elections. . . . I think [representatives are] probably more photogenic, they're probably better at, you know, manipulating the media than people were a generation or two ago. . . . I think that because of the way the process works now you attract different kinds of people to play." In much the same way, another subject observed that "so much of politics now is based on sound bites and looking good, you know, and finding that little thing that gets you lots of publicity for free. . . . They're (elected officials) ignoring the real issues and going after the nonissues because that's what gets them on TV." This individual later outlined what he saw as the negative institutional effects of media coverage:

> I think it also affects Congress in that that kind of negative publicity makes it much harder to lead. The fact that more Americans now [*pause*] there are polls that show they have lost faith in Congress. A lot of that has to do with negative reporting by the press. . . . When we were looking for a way to do health care reform, the coverage tended to be very sensationalized and personalized, and it really didn't seem to allow much room to get things accomplished.

Secondly, a slightly larger number of respondents bemoaned the effect of party politics on the representative process. Political parties, and the two-party system in particular, were maligned for a number of reasons, from failing to stand for consistent ideas/principles or offer voters distinct choices to being creatures of special interests and impeding legislative action. Above all, these citizens were concerned that partisanship (and party pressures) produces members who are more attuned to the interests of their party than to those of their constituents or the nation. Party matters in the representative process, but by and large not in positive ways. The quote from the following subject reflects two of the variations on this theme:

> In essence you get ahead [in politics], whether it's the local or national level, by, you know, being a worker within your party. So that your frame of reference is party more than those folks that you might be representing. I think that's one thing that would lead it (the link between members and constituents) to break down. I think that's where you don't accomplish a lot in government because people vote the party. They are so concerned about getting elected that they have to, you know, if you got back to representing your district and the people and you really took a stand for [them] and not the party leadership you would accomplish so much more for the people.[17]

Finally, respondents also touched on the fundamental dilemmas that inhere in the representative process. This point was addressed in detail in previous chapters, but it is important to note that subjects appreciated some of the institutional aspects as well, such as reconciling responsiveness to local districts or the states with the constitutional injunction to promote the general welfare.

Improving the Representative Process

The corollary of exploring what people perceive as impediments to representation is documenting what they think might be done to improve it. Over the past two decades, numerous proposals and political initiatives have been advanced by elected officials, political organizations, and scholars seeking to revamp the representative process and Congress as an institution. Congress itself has engaged in its own series of internal reforms, most recently in 1995. Examining what individual citizens think can be done to improve Congress can help us to gain a better appreciation of the public's understanding and expectations of institutional representation. Accordingly, subjects were given the opportunity to offer their own counsel on how Congress could be improved. Each person was asked the following two questions (as well as appropriate follow-ups and probes):

- If you could give Congress some advice on how to do its job, what would you tell it to do?
- What changes would you like to see made in Congress to improve how it serves the American people?

Much of the advice that was tendered conformed to, and seemed to flow from, subjects' basic representational anxieties and desires. Thus, respondents suggested that Congress try to communicate better with the American people, think long-term (or set long-term priorities), resist special interest pressure, and focus on vital issues. The same held true for the disparate changes they recommended, ranging from reducing perks/special benefits for members and altering the length of representatives terms to speeding up the policy process and making congressional procedures more understandable to the public.

But the best illustration of this relationship proved to be the most popular prescription for change offered by respondents: campaign finance reform. Given their concern with the influence of money in politics and the rising costs of campaigns, and the fact that these issues have been on the national agenda for many years now, it is not surprising that over one-third of the subjects embraced changes in campaign finance as a key reform vehicle.[18] The percentage does, however, underscore what the respondents perceived as an integral connection between the current campaign system and the nature of representation. In their view, it is almost inconceivable that what members of Congress do in office—how (and how well) they serve their constituents—will not be critically influenced by what they have to do to get (re)elected. The way congressional campaigns are funded invariably colors the quality of representation that people receive. These citizens therefore see reform of the electoral process as necessary for rejuvenation of the representative process.

Respondents rallied around three main reform options, often in tandem with one another: contribution limits for campaign donors; public financing of congressional elections; and free radio/TV airtime for major candidates. The last option was a particularly revealing indicator of the participants' desire to open up and equalize the contemporary electoral process. In the view of one of these individuals, "I would like to see maybe TV and radio stations having a portion of their airtime be dedicated towards public announcements, instead of just having them [candidates] pay for commercials. A certain amount of free airtime to go on and say their peace. And then have paid commercials on top of that. So that the person with the most money can't get the most airtime." Or, as another participant argued, "[broadcasters] should be forced to give a certain amount of free time to all the candidates for election. It would help level the field, because then a man doesn't have to have so much money." A few people went a step further, advocating subsidized debates and even restrictions on paid political ads. To them, the increased competition and more informed citizenry they believed would result from such changes were worth the price of limiting candidates political speech. As one of these respondents put it, "I'd be very happy to pay a few bucks in my income taxes every year to see all the TV stations have debates. I think it's real important, it shows what they (candidates) [are] made of. . . . No TV commercials, no radio commercials, only debates, everybody is on the same footing. Then the incumbent doesn't really have an advantage except his or her bad name."[19]

A decline in the incumbency advantage was not the only boon subjects perceived in such changes. In fact, the most intriguing aspect of their advocacy of campaign reform was the diverse political benefits they thought it might bring, blessings that were closely tied to their representational worldviews. Campaign finance reform seemed to serve as a kind of political wish list for these citizens, who read into it a way to advance some of their most important representational goals and ideals. These included reducing the political dominance of major campaign contributors (to create "a system that would limit the ability of wealthy individuals to buy elections"), broadening the range of citizens who could conceivably be elected, elevating the quality of political debate, and reviving voters' confidence in elected officials and politics. Most of all, they hoped that finance reform might restore some of the influence of ordinary citizens in the representative process. As one individual somewhat ruefully concluded, "maybe [representatives] wouldn't do anything differently, but at least you would know that if you went down and sat with them that your voice had a little more weight in it because you didn't have to write them a ten thousand dollar check in order to be heard."

Whither Term Limits?

As a follow-up to the query about possible changes in Congress, each of the respondents was asked the following question:

- Some people believe that we should establish term limits for members of Congress. What do you think about this idea?

A question about term limits is particularly appropriate in a study of this kind. Term limits lie at the intersection of our electoral and governing processes. The term limitation movement was one of the most significant political forces of the 1990s, significantly reshaping legislative careers and institutions, especially at the state level.[20] The underlying impetus for the movement tells us much about public and elite attitudes toward political power, the professionalization of politics, and the performance of legislative institutions. Most importantly here, the notion of limiting representatives' terms in office goes to the heart of our beliefs about democratic politics. Term limits touch on some of our most basic concerns about representation—including who should serve, for how long, and to what ends. It also, as we shall see, taps into people's beliefs about incumbency and political careerism. Ultimately, people's views on these issues offer valuable insight into their core convictions about what the job of a representative ought to be, as well as their assessment of the contemporary representative process.

The participants were almost evenly divided in support or opposition of congressional term limits. Advocates recounted a variety of ways that limits would help revitalize the representative process and, equally important, serve as an antidote to what they saw as the damaging effects of professional politics. Several of them suggested that foreclosing "perpetual service" would reduce the time and attention members devoted to their own personal goals (especially reelection) and prompt them to focus on "getting the job done" and accomplishing their larger policy/ issue objectives. In essence, representatives would be freed from the electoral shackles that hamper both their political vision and decision making, and limited terms would channel members' energies away from satisfying their narrow personal ambitions toward achieving a lasting political legacy. As one individual expressed this, "You know what, if they didn't go for reelection, I think they could do great things, rather than just the expedient things. I think people would stand up and be honorable, because [they would say] 'this is it, this is all the time I get.'"[21] Limits might also move us closer to a political culture of true, time-bound public service: "You should see it as I did my job and served my people, and now someone else should come in and serve the people. I think it should be a natural changeover."

Supporters of limits seemed equally enthused about what they saw as two related benefits of mandatory retirement: a greater diversity of representatives and a continual infusion of new ideas and energy into the institution. For these respondents, regular turnover opens up the possibility of better demographic representation ("a chance for people that I want to see in office"), an at least partial revival of the citizen legislator, and a return to the classic Anti-Federalist tradition of requiring "politicians to get back into circulation and see what's going on and see what's working and what isn't." As one of them phrased it, term limits would end the "same old process of just doing things the same way, instead of bringing fresh new ideas with fresh different people." By breaking the grip of entrenched incumbency, these citizens were implying, limits would help prevent Congress and its members from becoming unaccountable, unresponsive, and stagnant. In sum, they would enhance both individual and institutional representation.

While those opposed to term limits might have agreed with parts of this assessment, most would dissent that the costs are too high. Most predictably, a number of these respondents argued that limits would restrict voters' freedom of choice, often noting that the electoral remedy is always available for wayward members. Beyond the issue that "people have the right to elect the person who they wish to represent them," many of the opponents broached another downside to term limits—the loss of effective advocates in Congress. Several people offered the most instrumental version of this argument, i.e. that local districts would lose their powerful congressional benefactors. As the following political activist put it, ". . . you get people who come in and learn the system, like in New York we've got people who move up because of seniority and you have more power and understanding of what goes on. So I don't think you should limit people's terms, *because I don't think it's in the best interests of the constituents*" (emphasis added).[22]

This quote also touches on a related and prominent theme of those opposed to term limits: the integral relationship between legislative experience and effective representation. Contrary to the (often implicit) assumption among proponents of limits that institutional seasoning is unnecessary for good representation, and may even subvert it, many of these respondents intimated that there is a kind of learning curve to becoming an effective representative. In their view, "on the job training" is an essential component of the representative process; it takes time, as several people phrased it, for representatives to "learn the ropes and how to get things done." Interestingly, a number of subjects surmised that this involves more than just becoming knowledgeable about issues; it also includes becoming familiar with one's colleagues, their interests and perspectives, and mastering the intricacies of the legislative process. One individual presented an almost Madisonian argument about the need for institutional experience:

> Well, you have to accumulate a body of knowledge and a better understanding of not just the process, and how you're going to go about it, but maybe going there to represent a state they have to have a better, broader knowledge of the whole country, and you don't get that overnight either. And even to understand exactly where the law is now on something, that can't be something you have when you get in.

An unsophisticated participant used a teaching analogy to express another side of this perspective: ". . . the more you do something the better you get at it. And it's like . . . in your classes, do you want them to keep changing teacher after teacher after teacher? First of all, he wouldn't know you guys, and you all wouldn't know him. It would be harder to relate." Finally, as a number of respondents emphasized, long-term service may beget both legislative proficiency and influence.

To these citizens, in short, term limits would rupture the vital link between legislative experience and representational effectiveness. They would make it difficult to produce (and impossible to retain) members of Congress with the requisite knowledge, skills, and expertise to be good representatives.[23] Congresses defined by term limits would invariably contain too many inexperienced members, with repercussions that would be felt at both the district and institutional levels. In the mixed metaphor offered by one respondent, "you would have people who were in training all the time, the whole Congress would be a bunch of sophomores, and I don't think that's ideal." The desire to preserve some measure of institutional stability and continuity even surfaced among some of the advocates of term limits, including this sophisticated subject:

> I think [limits] should be put in a way that all members of Congress don't have to leave at the same time. Structure it in a way that you don't have all your experienced, knowledgeable people leave the next year and then have all these new people coming in and they don't know what's going on. I think Congress has a unique history, and you have to know about this and you have to know how things work, and when you get elected to Congress you don't know what goes on. . . . I think there should be new ideas, up and coming, [but] yeah there's use for experience.

Concern about the effects of term limits *inside* the legislature, on institutional performance, was perhaps the most surprising aspect of discussions on the topic. It reflects, as do the other arguments given for and against, a general perception among the subjects that term limits would have a significant impact on both district-level and institutional representation. And the ambivalence many of them expressed about the idea points to a thoughtful recognition of the inherent trade-offs it would bring.

Incumbency and Careerism

Participants' views about incumbency and (for some) political careerism often bubbled up during the discussions of term limits.[24] These issues, of course, have been a primary focus of congressional scholars for the last few decades. The desire to divine the effects of political professionalization and incumbency—on democratic elections, political institutions, and the governing process—has often animated their research. Judging by the tenor of the respondents' comments, similar concerns resonate among ordinary citizens. Some of the subjects' views on the nature of contemporary representation found full expression in their attitudes toward incumbency.

Overall, the participants who touched on incumbency were as divided over its impact as they were about term limits. Some, like the following person, expressed personal ambivalence:

> Newcomers by far are more apt to listen to their constituents and look back, because that's where they're coming from. The distance hasn't been put between them yet, whether they're in Washington or in Albany away from their respective areas. But then again, you know, they don't know the system, they don't have the contacts that older representatives have, their time there is short, and it's difficult for them to work the system.

The notion that extended service brings "distance" from the district was a common refrain among participants. While most scholars and political analysts maintain that contemporary representatives go to great lengths to stay attuned to their constituents, and at times bemoan the fact that members (and the institution) are inadequately insulated from public pressures, respondents tended to express the conviction that representatives grow increasingly "out-of-touch" and unresponsive over time, more and more disconnected from the ever-changing interests and perspectives of their districts.[25] To them, the electoral security incumbency denotes seems to beget political independence of the worst kind: from the needs and wishes of the people back home. The following quote from one subject embodies this perspective: "I really believe that if they're in office for a very long time, and, of course, it's not everyone, but if they're in office for a long time many opponents don't run against them so they just get elected because no one else is there. And I think they lose touch with their community and what's going on around them."[26]

The belief that the bonds of the constituency connection become attenuated was the main lament about incumbency, as crystallized in this response from another respondent: "The main negative is, if they're going to constantly be reelected, who are they going to really listen to. That's the problem." Yet just as many subjects, including some who also expressed criticism, touted the individual and institutional advantages of incumbency. The value and necessity of inside experience was advanced once again, as was the position that (through the twin blessings of seniority and experience) representatives become more powerful and effective over time, better equipped to pursue and protect both their districts' and the nation's interests. Contrary to the presumption that ordinary citizens are overwhelmingly hostile towards incumbency, and blind to its benefits, the participants in this study were as likely to find significant representational advantages as disadvantages to extended service in Congress.

By contrast, political careerism came in for more consistent censure. Respondents basically leveled two charges on this count: one, that the emergence of a kind of careerist mentality among members leads them to place their personal goals above serving their constituents; and two, that the rise of the professional politician has heralded a concomitant and regrettable decline in a political culture based upon true public service. Underlying these arguments was a deep-seated suspicion about the motives of "lifelong politicians"; as one of the supporters of term limits questioned, "everybody who goes to Congress and wants to be there more than twelve years, what's he up to? Why does he need to be there?" These citizens often seemed to think mainly for the power and perks of office, especially when one factors in the demands and sacrifices representatives face in the contemporary political process. Unlike earlier generations of public officials, who "were like vying with each other to serve, to try to do something as an adjunct to their life," for today's members holding office *is* their life.[27] And this change in the fundamental impulse to serve ultimately works to the detriment of the representative process. As one participant concluded, ". . . who's left [in the system]? People who will put up with this nonsense. And that's exactly what you have. You have career people, and they don't care, they're going to stay here just to get the power."

The subjects' diverse representational ideals, sensitivity to the multiple dimensions of the representative process, and concerns about the quality of contemporary representation came to the fore in their discussions about term limits, incumbency, and political careerism. So did their underlying ambivalence about these ideas. Respondents touted the representational benefits of legislative experience in Congress, yet also bemoaned the deleterious effects of prolonged incumbency on both individual and institutional representation. Many of them would like to see better demographic representation in Congress, infuse new energy and ideas into the body, and restore a "lost" culture of true public service, but not at the expense of the institutional effectiveness and growing personal influence/skill associated with long-term membership in the institution. At heart, the dualities in the participants' views about term limits and incumbency reflect their own, and by extension the public's, complex and sometimes conflicting ideals and expectations for the representative process.

Conclusion: Conceptualizing Congress

As discussed in chapter two, the ability of citizens to think about Congress as a functioning institution rather than just a collection of discrete individuals forms a subtext to much of the research in the field, from the obvious (studies of people's evaluations of the institution and individual members) to the less expected (work such as Fenno's *Home Style*). The essential issue here might be framed like this: *how*, and *how well*, do people conceptualize Congress as an institution? My investigation of citizens' ideas about institutional representation offers insight on both counts. The first part of this question was addressed earlier in this chapter. The latter is the subject of this concluding section.

There were several distinguishing characteristics concerning the subjects' remarks about Congress. One was a definite degree of analytic uncertainty. Many of the respondents, including several who were otherwise politically knowledgeable and articulate, had some difficulty in defining and appraising the institution.[28] As mentioned earlier, the initial impressions of Congress tended to be vague and abstract, and at times even the more politically astute respondents struggled to describe what they liked and disliked about the institution or to specify its most important roles. On the whole, participants often seemed to possess a kind of nebulous or diffuse awareness and comprehension of Congress.

There was also a pronounced sophistication effect in the results. Far more than was true of representation in general or the representative relationship, the more unsophisticated subjects had trouble articulating substantive views about Congress.[29] They tended to have little awareness or sense of the institution and often had great difficulty specifying its roles in the political process, as the following excerpts from a number of these respondents suggest:

Oh. Unfortunately, it's not doing enough of what it should be doing, which is . . . reflecting what the people want. And now we're into what people want, and it's getting crazy. [*Pause*] Pose that to me again . . . most important things? I don't know, I really don't know.

RES: Congress, I mean, it's good that they make rules and all that [*pause*].

INT: How about anything you dislike about it?

RES: I can't think of anything, really.

INT: What do you think are the most important things that Congress does?

RES: . . . there's a lot of things the government can't do without Congress. They can't pass laws without Congress. [*Pause*] Most important things? [*Long pause*] I'm blank [*laughs*]. Most important things [*shakes head that he doesn't know*].

The same held true of their attempts to specify institutional changes or reforms. When these participants did offer advice, it was usually purely exhortational in nature; several of them stated that Congress should work harder or "do its best," while another suggested, "Try teamwork, and [*pause*] I don't know. . . . Communication. Teamwork, communication, you know, getting more involved with people." Based on the results of my study, then, Fenno's conjecture that people basically "cannot conceptualize Congress as a collectivity" would at least seem to apply to politically unsophisticated individuals.

This, of course, raises a larger issue: does the same also hold true for the majority of Americans? Or do most individuals possess some basic idea(s) of institutional representation? On balance, the evidence here suggests that although most people may find it hard to think about Congress as an institution, it is not impossible for them to do so; and while few possess well-defined or elaborate conceptions of institutional representation, most citizens probably do have some capacity to define, appraise, and evaluate institutional processes and functions. Congress does appear to have "independent standing in people's minds" (Dennis, 1981). More than that, Congress *matters* to the citizens I interviewed. It matters because it is seen as a powerful, indeed essential, force in our national political system. And it matters because of what the subjects believe the institution adds to the political process—particularly its' expressive, deliberative, and lawmaking capacities.

In essence, then, respondents tended to appreciate Congress in an *operational* as well as an *existential* sense. Yet even this does not adequately convey their overall perspective, for what this operational understanding meant is that the subjects (sometimes the same individuals) were often supportive of Congress and its political functions, critical of the contemporary representative process, and ambivalent about congressional democracy, term limits, and incumbency. Finally, as best exemplified in the discussions on term limits and the legislative process, many of the participants revealed a grasp of at least some of the conflicting imperatives and fundamental trade-offs embedded in the process of institutional representation. The ability of people to "consider Congress" may be limited, and certainly appears to be related to personal variables (including one's level of political sophistication) to a greater degree than is true of representation in general or the representative relationship. But when given the opportunity to reflect on Congress and its role in our political system, on the whole these citizens also demonstrated that there is more to the public's view of our national legislature than merely reflexive disdain.

Chapter Seven

The Public Side of Representation

The preceding chapters have, I hope, greatly added to our understanding of ordinary citizens' fundamental political beliefs. But there is one more facet to the public side of representation that must be further explored: the larger implications of people's representational perspectives. For the complexities and fault lines in the views of my respondents offer important lessons for the existing literature on representation; for our understanding of citizens' deepest political ideals; and perhaps most importantly, for the successful operation of our political process. Their convictions point toward what representatives and citizens might do to help revitalize the representative process—as well as some of the profound political quandaries and paradoxes built into people's representational expectations. Ultimately, the ideas articulated by the participants in this study offer a tantalizing and instructive blueprint for political change. They also present a set of formidable roadblocks to that end. In a very real sense, then, Pogo's old aphorism rings true with regard to the public side of representation: "We have met the enemy, and he is us."

Revisiting the Idea of Representation: Insights and Implications

In order to understand what ordinary citizens think about representation, one must begin with the idea of responsiveness. The notion of representation as responsiveness was virtually a common denominator in the participants' representational views. At the same time, their conceptions of responsive representation contained many of the same basic components: accessibility, attentiveness, involvement, education/persuasion, and, above all, communication. These form the essential building blocks in what one might call the respondents' "model" of the representative process. From their perspective, real and effective representation simply cannot be sustained in the absence of these processes. And while the particular criteria and mechanisms of responsiveness varied somewhat from individual to individual, the overriding desire was basically the same: to foster a vital and effective constituency connection, and thereby elevate the quality and tenor of the representative process.

But acknowledging the importance of responsiveness does not get us to the heart of the respondents' view of representation. To do so, we must dig deeper and consider some more fundamental questions: What are the basic purposes of representation? What else can responsiveness achieve? What, in short, is the representative process ultimately *for?* To the citizens in this study, responsiveness was generally seen less as an end in itself than a means to more vital political goals.

This crucial fact helps to put some of my most interesting findings about the subjects' global beliefs about representation into perspective. For instance, responsiveness was rarely defined by the provision of ombudsmen or constituent services. Instead, respondents tended to frame responsiveness in terms of the larger political objectives it could achieve: members who are more closely attuned to their districts and committed to their interests; citizens with greater understanding of key policy and political issues; legislative action that better reflects people's primary needs; enhanced public trust and support of government; and heightened constituent influence in the representative process. In other words, these citizens appeared more concerned about how the elements of responsiveness could promote better representation and democratic participation than how these elements can be used to satisfy the parochial wishes of constituents or interest groups.

The desire for citizens to play a more meaningful role in the representative relationship seemed of particular importance to many participants in my study. Although most of them clearly desired such qualities as honesty and integrity in their representatives, when asked about the ideal representative process subjects also appeared unwilling to rely upon personal trust as a surrogate for more direct forms of input and involvement. This helps to explain their advocacy of direct contact, issue access, and especially the various forms of two-way communication. Whether expressed as support for frequent and open town meetings, at-home contact with constituents, more informative and probing questionnaires, or ongoing education and persuasion about important issues, the underlying objectives were largely the same: to give citizens more opportunities to learn about elected officials' personal attributes and political views; to directly educate representatives about constituents' interests and preferences (and be educated and/or persuaded in turn); to expose members to the full panoply of interests and groups in their districts; and to some extent enable citizens to exert influence over members' positions and actions. In a variety of ways, then, participants relayed a wish to become more engaged in the representative process, partly in the service of securing a deeper kind of accountability from their representatives.

This is not to say, however, that they were motivated by the desire to dictate their representatives' preferences, behavior or decision making. Even as many respondents expressed the desire for a more participatory representative process, they did not evince a longing to do away with that process. On the whole I was struck by how deeply the representative impulse was ingrained among these citizens. Several voiced apprehension about various forms of direct popular rule, including initiative and referendum, or touched on what they believed to be the blessings of representative government.[1] Most of all, as the yearning for members of Congress who display political courage, pursue the national interest, use their informed judgment, and "say no the people" when necessary indicates, few subjects wanted representatives to march in lock-step with their constituents or serve as unthinking agents of their wishes (even if that were somehow possible).[2]

What these citizens seemed to crave instead was the *opportunity* for real input, the chance to capture representatives' attention as needed and perhaps influence them in ways that they do not feel they are able to now—and therefore to balance the power of other forces, especially major campaign contributors, lobbyists, and interest groups, that they believe have "captured" members and drowned out constituents' voices. Many of the respondents appeared to think that a lack or decline of citizen input and influence has distorted the political process and tempted representatives into self-serving actions and derelictions of power. I often sensed dissatisfaction on their part with being only spectators to, and passive consumers of, the representative process—something that they perceived as an ominous trend in contemporary political life.[3]

These ideas and expectations are perhaps best exemplified in the participants' view of the "ideal" representational voting process. The following sketch is drawn mainly from answers to the (admittedly highly stylized) hypothetical voting questions. A composite portrait that inevitably blurs some key details and differing emphases, it nevertheless reveals the core elements and common features in the subjects' conceptions of representational decision making—views shaped in no small measure by their perceptions of what they do not get from their own representatives. The portrait tells us, in short, how these citizens think the voting process *should* unfold. As such, it provides valuable insight into their core ideas about responsiveness, the essential roles of both representatives and citizens in the political process, and the ultimate ends of that process.

Overall, the subjects' prototypical decision-making process would include the following:

1. Thorough *explanation* of a representative's position on a major issue, which often included justifying that position. Clear communication of the member's opinion and intentions was often deemed essential.

2. *Education* of the constituency so that people have the information and perspective they need to truly understand the issue involved (or to see the "big picture"). This could entail laying out all the relevant sides or dimensions of a policy debate, providing citizens with alternative perspectives about an issue, and clearly specifying the probable impact of a bill on the district. Ultimately, all of this is in the service of helping constituents make informed opinions about policy issues and participate knowledgeably in the representative process. And as was true of explanation, many people seemed to think · that this kind of education should be a more common part of the process.

3. Full and open *discussion/debate* about a bill, which includes hearing from "both sides" on the issue.

4. Attempts to *persuade* citizens to change their viewpoints or preferences, if necessary. Under certain circumstances members were expected to present their case before constituents and demonstrate leadership by trying to convince people to "see it their way." A number of respondents also emphasized that such persuasion should occur before final decisions are made or votes are cast.

5. Solicitation of informed constituent *input* or *"feedback,"* through surveys, town meetings, and other forms of contact and communication. For some people this was embodied in advocacy of two-way education. Subjects generally wanted representatives to engage constituents in a kind of decision-making dialogue and to be open to constituent opinion and even persuasion. The underlying belief was that citizens should have a clear say, or "voice," in the process and that members have an obligation to (seriously) consider their perspective.

6. Further explanation and perhaps persuasion after the member's vote choice. At heart, most subjects felt that representatives have a fundamental responsibility to *fully* and *honestly* report back about their legislative and political actions and the rationales behind them. Besides the representational advantages to be gained some people thought that members could reap political benefits from doing this.

In distilled form the process would look something like this:

Initial Explanation → Proactive Education-Persuasion → Discussion/Debate/Constituent Input → Vote Choice → Reactive Explanation-Persuasion → Decreased Public Cynicism and Greater Trust/Satisfaction/Participation

Several things immediately stand out about this version of the ideal representational decision-making process. Perhaps the most striking is its unavoidably two-way cast. In the subjects' depiction of the process, both representatives and constituents have vital roles to perform, parts that depend on the involvement and commitment of the other side to properly play out. In this way the decision-making process acts as a kind of bridge between representatives and the people they serve, binding them together through a set of mutually dependent political roles and responsibilities. Another intriguing feature is the evident link between representatives' actions and constituents' attitudes. What these citizens are offering, in effect, is a series of behavioral recommendations for members that they (explicitly or implicitly) believed would not only improve the representative process, but also alter people's political attitudes and engagement—and perhaps even their long-run expectations for that process. Finally, one should recognize the deliberative nature of this view of decision making. The representative process here is complex, layered, and quite involved. It would appear to require a great deal of time, energy, openness, and commitment, particularly on the part of representatives. Such a process also hinges on having members with the willingness and political courage to put themselves on the line in support of it.

This, of course, raises a fundamental question: how plausible is this vision of representation?[4] Most of the participants favored at least some elements of this decision-making model, and several hoped that something like it would become a regular part of the representative relationship. But *could* or *would* representatives regularly engage in such a process? And even if they did, would constituents be there to fulfill their side of the bargain? It would, after all, require significant and sustained involvement on the part of citizens as well. A strong case can be made that this decision-making model does not fit very well with what we know about the dynamics of contemporary politics, the legislative process, and the state of political participation. Yet many respondents seemed to feel that citizens might be energized by such a development, that, to borrow a line from the movie *Field of Dreams*, "if you build it, they will come."[5] From their perspective, one of the main problems with the current representative process is that it seems so far *removed* from this paradigm. Decision making that conformed more closely to it would bring tangible representational and political benefits to representatives and citizens alike. Arguably the most intriguing would be its promise to at least partially reconcile two of the most fundamental, widely shared, yet seemingly conflicting representational ideals expressed by participants: for greater citizen involvement and influence in the representative process and for more independent, politically courageous representatives.[6]

In crucial respects, then, these citizens held remarkably similar beliefs about the nature and ends of the representative process. Within this general consensus, however, some striking and important divergences emerged over the *means* necessary to achieve these ends. In some cases this could be traced to a difference in emphasis, such as the particular importance placed on issue accessibility by the political activists. More often, though, the participants' responses exposed significant rifts over how true responsiveness can and should be achieved. Involvement in the district, for example, proved to be a contentious "pillar" of representation. Respondents were sharply divided over the necessity and importance of visibility and direct contact; what were defining elements of responsive representation to some people were superfluous, and even counterproductive, to others.

But there were other major areas of disagreement. As both the interview narratives and rank scales revealed, subjects were quite polarized over the representational value and impact of district and constituency services. There was also a discernible lack of agreement about the most important roles for members of Congress and the institution, with respondents particularly split over the relative value of lawmaking and constituent service for members and lawmaking/deliberation and communication/district service for Congress. And lurking beneath all these differences was the fundamental question about the constituency connection: should it be paramount or partial? Should the district be the end-all of a representative's decision making, or only one of several imperatives that she must weigh and balance? Participants varied greatly in their perspectives on this fundamental issue.

In short, this study suggests that citizens are far from one mind about the best way(s) to ensure responsive representation. One person's representation pudding, in a manner of speaking, could be another's representational poison. Equally important, as the rank scales perhaps best illustrated, these differences frequently appeared to be related to an individual's level of political sophistication, implying that different people and perhaps segments of the citizenry hold qualitatively different job expectations for representatives and may subscribe to distinct "models" of congressional representation.

The political implications of this are sobering. No matter how members of Congress present and try to implement their vision of the representative relationship, they are bound to incur the dissatisfaction or even wrath of a good portion of their constituents.[7] Unlike what Fenno asserts, "everything homestyle" *does not* work to enhance representation in the public eye. In practice, members of Congress may face significant trade-offs in their personal support, and more broadly in public assessments of the representative process, by simultaneously pursuing the multiple avenues of responsiveness. Some degree of political discontent among citizens may simply be built into the operation of the representative relationship.

My exploration of the demand side of representation also has important implications for the existing representational literature. Most clearly, the findings generally bolster the idea that the basic elements of responsiveness delineated by Fenno and others have become a vital part of the representative relationship. In particular, Fenno's assertion about the overriding importance of two-way communication is validated here: citizens, too, see it as a defining characteristic of the representative process. To some degree, then, what citizens expect from the representative process appears to match what representatives believe they want (and what members generally offer to them). With the notable exception of district and constituency service, the people I interviewed clearly value the types of responsiveness that the literature indicates representatives bestow on their constituents.[8] This finding suggests, of course, that there is an integral connection between individuals' abstract ideas about the representative relationship and the larger political universe. Citizens' views about representation are not set in stone or hermetically sealed from the political process. Indeed, the evidence here strongly suggests that (changes in) the political environment influences their representational beliefs. A lifetime of exposure to, and experiences with, members of Congress and our national legislature, as well as with other representative actors and institutions, serves to mold and remold citizens' basic convictions about the representative process.[9]

Yet there is more to this story, for my research suggests that the arrow actually runs *both* ways: people's general ideas and expectations about representation also influence their assessments of real representatives and the actual representative process. To illustrate, did certain subjects portray Senator Daniel Patrick Moynihan so favorably because he fit their model of a good representative, or because their paradigm of the good representative is derived from what they see in him? Probably both. Those individuals evidently saw in Moynihan many of the qualities they associate with a good political representative. By the same token, however, Moynihan's personal attributes and handling of the office likely shaped their expectations of what members of Congress should be like and what they should do. To some extent, at least, his "ideal type" may have served (and may still serve) as a benchmark against which other representatives are judged.

More importantly, the apparent symmetry between the abstract representational ideals of citizens and members, and between those beliefs and the dynamics of the representative process, is not reflected in participants' assessments of the representation they receive. Many believed that they are shut out of any meaningful role in the representative process, either because they lack the means to consistently and effectively make themselves heard or because representatives are using the tools of responsiveness mainly for their own political benefit. In fact, respondents' dissatisfaction with the process often appeared to stem from their appraisal of the absence, superficiality, or distortion of the primary mechanisms of responsiveness—and the deleterious impact this has on the kind of representational accountability and citizen participation they consider essential for truly meaningful representation.

Thus, we encounter what might be dubbed the "paradox of the representative process." Despite the abundant evidence indicating that members of Congress are plugged in to their constituencies and doggedly proffer responsiveness through their home styles and constituent service, many of the people I interviewed feel profoundly *disconnected* from their representatives. The actual representative process does not measure up to these citizens (often lofty) expectations for it, expectations that owe much to the political environment they inhabit and the ways in which members of Congress and other elected officials actually portray and provide representation. Ironically, the underlying perception is of an increasingly hollow representative process, or even the absence of true responsiveness, in what many scholars depict as a highly responsive political climate.[10] Combined with the inherent differences in the ways the citizens I studied believe responsive representation should be achieved, this is clearly a recipe for political disenchantment.

Institutional Representation

This study also offers some important lessons for our understanding of public attitudes towards Congress. Taken as a whole, the respondents' view of the institution might best be described as this: an "essential abstraction." On the one hand, many of the participants evinced a rather limited understanding of Congress as a collectivity. While most did possess some capacity to define and appraise the institution, they tended to have difficulty thinking about Congress as a discrete body with its own internal dynamics, incentives, and pressures as opposed to basically just a collection of individuals.

Congress is, in short, something of a mystery to many of these citizens. Certain political concepts appear to be firmly embedded in people's minds and readily accessible to them. Subjects across the range of political sophistication typically had little trouble defining how the representative process should work or the essential ingredients in the representative relationship, but they often struggled in conceptualizing Congress as an institutional entity. The apparent lack of a strong grasp of the "institutional Congress" in the public at large seems especially important in an era when congressional parties have become more disciplined and ideologically coherent, congressional elections have become more national in focus (1994, 1998, 2002, and 2006), and Congress has (fitfully) reasserted its policy and political leverage. Thus, although the representative process has in some respects become more nationalized—and Congress has had an increasingly important impact on their social, economic, and political lives—most citizens may have only a nebulous understanding of the institution and its essential dynamics.

Yet this fact should not lead one to conclude that participants failed to recognize the importance of Congress, or to appreciate its role(s) in the political process. They often did. And this appreciation extended well beyond abstract and somewhat predictable expressions of support for the basic idea of Congress or its place in our constitutional order. Many of the subjects depicted the institution as a vital, even preeminent, force in our political system, and in some way emphasized the significance of its legislative powers and duties. More tellingly, they provided a view of the congressional democratic process both more realistic and favorable than the one portrayed in the work of scholars like Hibbing and Theiss-Morse. As both the interview narratives and (especially) the rank scales indicated, the citizens I surveyed value Congress for its deliberative, representational, and legislative functions—precisely the kind of activities that some studies assert drive people's discontent with the institution and the political process more generally.

One direct consequence of this finding is that the "paradox of congressional support" may be as much an artifact of certain research techniques as it is of deep-seated public attitudes. At a minimum, it certainly appears less formidable when people have the opportunity to reflect upon and evaluate the institution and its roles. The participants in this study could be, as I have shown, quite critical of the contemporary representative process. But these assessments seemed to stem more from their perception of deviations in the way the process works, such as the inordinate influence wielded by "big money", than from fundamental flaws in its nature, as the respondents appreciation of the operational as well as existential features of Congress underscores. Congress matters—a great deal—to these citizens, and not only for negative reasons or its failures. And this revelation points us toward another important lesson to be drawn from this project: of the tangible benefits of a research strategy predicated upon thorough explication of people's core political beliefs.

Surprising Sensitivity—and Blind Spots

The institutional findings highlighted above are just one example of the unexpected and valuable insights gained from having citizens ponder their representational assumptions and beliefs. As the prior chapters illustrate, in-depth interviews reveal what would otherwise remain hidden concerning people's views about the representative process and provide an alternative perspective on their attitudes toward representational actors and institutions. Above all, having citizens think broadly and deeply about representation hints at what may be a critical political duality in the public at large: an unexpectedly rich and nuanced grasp of the representative process that challenges prevailing assumptions about people's political convictions and capacity to think about public affairs; *and* the existence of profound obstacles for those seeking to revitalize public trust in politics, impediments that are closely related to ordinary citizens fundamental ideas and expectations about representation. We turn now to the first part of this duality.

A primary contribution of this study is the finding that while citizens may generally think of representation as responsiveness, their conceptions of it are more complex than commonly assumed. Beyond this, however, lies an even more intriguing discovery: of a surprisingly subtle and realistic understanding of the dynamics of the representative process. This understanding was evident in the participants' frequent recognition of the numerous and often conflicting obligations faced by members of Congress (short versus long-term priorities, district versus national interests, constituency demands versus personal beliefs, etc.). It was evident in their acknowledgment of diverse institutional imperatives and outlook on the congressional democratic process, best reflected in their institutional role preferences. It was evident in respondents' awareness of, and surprising sympathy toward, representatives' political dilemmas and job demands. And it was perhaps most evident in their grasp of the many levels of the representative process.

The last point proves particularly illuminating. My work suggests that citizens recognize that the set of gestures members make and the behaviors they engage in have many motivations and, potentially at least, many representational and political benefits. Participants felt, for example, that going back to the district, being receptive to constituent input, facilitating town meetings, and engaging in explanation/persuasion—the myriad features of representational contact and communication—can simultaneously advance constituents' larger representational aims and help representatives satisfy their electoral goals. More broadly, subjects often believed that responsiveness, properly understood and pursued, can serve both members' instrumental political interests and the democratic process writ large.

Now this outlook did not preclude criticism of contemporary representation or representatives. But these critiques were rarely unreflective or patently untenable. Both individually and as a whole, respondents often fused pessimism about politics and sharp critiques of members and their behavior with an appreciation of the inherent problems, conflicting demands, and real (or potential) blessings of the representative process. Three-quarters of the participants who expressed discontent with the representative process, for instance, also recognized the political dilemmas and occupational hazards embedded within it. Such a perspective on the process reveals a side of people's political views—as well as a capacity for nuanced political thought—which one simply does not glean from most other research or public opinion surveys.[11]

It also challenges some conventional stereotypes about public opinion, especially the presumption of a reflexive and almost total disdain of representatives and the representative process, part of a larger "subculture of cynicism" about politics and government in the United States. This subculture is arguably the by-product of a contemporary political nexus, comprised of the mass media, political candidates, interest groups, activists, and commentators, that has a vested interest in delineating and decrying the failings of representative institutions, actors, and processes. The proliferation of electoral attack ads, caustic talk radio, and highly critical (and often intrusive) media coverage over the past two decades are symptomatic of this political environment, and have added more virulently negative dimensions to it. Incumbents themselves are a product of, and even contributors to, this subculture, as Fenno perceived long ago with the phenomenon of "running against Congress." These political elites often bemoan the public's antipathy toward, and apparent ignorance of, the representative process, yet do little to counteract such attitudes—and much to reinforce them. In fact, given our current political universe, one would almost be surprised if citizens held anything *but* simplistic and critical views about the representative process.

To some extent, then, the stock cynicism that appears so prevalent among ordinary citizens may be a kind of public echo of a worldview that exists all around them and is continually hammered home by many parts of the political establishment. Put another way, the dismay people routinely express about politics may be as much a reflection of the political milieu in which they find themselves (as well as research techniques that tap into their cursory attitudes) as it is of their deep-seated beliefs.[12] The more complex and often realistic view of the representative process documented in this study suggests that this is so.[13] In important respects, the superficial characterizations of people's representational beliefs and the reality of these views do not match up. My work tends to bolster the thesis, proffered in the work of scholars such as Robert E. Lane and William A. Gamson, that people demonstrate a greater awareness of and sensitivity toward political matters when given the opportunity to freely and fully delve into them. Thus, the approach I took to explore political beliefs and expectations, while harder than the survey method, ultimately proves more rewarding for revealing how people really think about representative actors and institutions.

In sum, this study suggests that ordinary citizens possess a deeper understanding of the dynamics of representation than is commonly depicted. At the same time, however, my research indicates that there are serious blind spots in people's conceptions of the representative process. One of the most significant of these revolves around the kind of responsiveness widely favored by the participants. While a few respondents were cognizant of the impact that frequent constituent input and pressure, serious explanatory and educational efforts, and continuous contact/communication (among other things) can have on representatives and the representative process, many of them overlooked or were oblivious to the repercussions that a strong constituent connection might have, including on their own representational ideals and expectations.

There was also little awareness of the institutional consequences of members' devotion to constituency. Subjects generally did not appear to see any significant conflicts between pursuing responsiveness at home and fulfilling responsibilities in Washington (or Albany). In fact, the few who touched on this issue were more likely to express irritation, or even outright amazement, that members of Congress would miss, say, legislative votes or committee meetings than to ponder the reasons why they would do so. And even as participants recognized the multitude of job demands representatives face, the former did not seem to fully appreciate the amount of time that would be required to undertake the kind of public communication and explanation/education they envisioned. Perhaps most of all, these citizens often seemed unaware of the larger implications of their abundant, and at times competing, ideas and expectations about the representative process.

For example, many of the respondents were equally adamant about having representatives reflect constituents' needs and preferences *and* live up to their own campaign promises, political principles, or judgment/conscience. Few considered how members should resolve the conflicts that inevitably arise. Similarly, participants often opined that representatives should maintain fidelity to district interests and preferences yet also adopt a long-term, nationally centered approach to their job.[14] Some offered facile solutions to these competing imperatives: that better responsiveness to individual districts, for instance, would invariably result in better legislation and a more harmonious political process rather than greater political conflict and more contentious legislative outcomes. In short, the central dilemma of how to say both yes and no (or perhaps *when* to say yes *or* no) to constituents may increasingly bedevil members of Congress, but the larger ramifications of this predicament did not preoccupy too many of my respondents.

I do not want to overstate this point. It is certainly true that many of the subjects wrestled with some of the individual and systemic-level representational dilemmas posed by these conflicts, particularly during the hypothetical voting scenarios. And as discussed above, many also had a fairly nuanced grasp of the dynamics of the representative process, and sensed the potential for representational processes such as two-way communication and education to reconcile some of their divergent beliefs. But the underlying representational quandary here should not be discounted. In a variety of different ways, these citizens expressed a desire for more "authoritative representation" from members of Congress—for a politically independent, more courageous, trustee-style approach to the representative process. Yet they also tended to embrace a very personal and constituency-centered, symbiotic, almost therapeutic view of the representative relationship, one that seems very much in keeping with contemporary social trends. It is in the gap between these two distinct visions of representation that one can locate some of our most enduring and vexing political conflicts. The age-old issues of whether representatives should primarily serve as agents or independent actors, what members of Congress must do to truly represent the people they serve, and how legislators should balance parochial and more universal political obligations still resonate in our political culture—and may have become even more acute given the nature of contemporary politics and people's prevailing beliefs about representation.

Public Beliefs and the Representative Process

The previous section directs us toward one of the most important lessons to be drawn from my study: that there are both real opportunities for and profound obstacles to revitalizing the contemporary representative process. Equally important, both opportunities and obstacles appear to have deep roots in people's central ideas and expectations about representation. We turn now to the first part of this equation.

In the eyes of ordinary citizens, what could members of Congress do to improve representation and counter public cynicism about politics? What recommendations might people offer to enhance the representative process? The following constitutes one possible "Menu for Reform," based upon the views articulated by the participants in this study. Like the ideal decision-making process outlined earlier, it consists of advice and admonitions from constituents to legislators—a kind of blueprint of exemplary behavior—that these citizens believe might energize the representative process and change people's perspectives about it.

1. Demonstrate, both in words and deeds, a tangible commitment to constituents through the process of responsive representation.
2. Truly know your district—become and stay intimately familiar with constituents' needs, interests, concerns, and beliefs.

3. Use the elements of responsiveness to promote larger democratic ends rather than simply parochial electoral goals.
4. Give priority to forms of contact/communication that foster a two-way representative relationship.
   - presume the importance of an ongoing and reciprocal flow of information, ideas, viewpoints, and preferences between representative and represented;
   - *properly* utilize town meetings, newsletters, surveys, polls, and other forms of communication and observation to enhance democratic education and participation;
   - more superficial, one-way attempts to foster constituency connection (like visibility) are as likely to elicit unfavorable as favorable appraisals.
5. Conform as much as possible to the "ideal" representational decision-making model. (see pp.)
6. Fervently attempt to fulfill campaign pledges (but also refrain from making excessive or unattainable promises).
7. Strive to balance constituency needs and preferences with other vital representational responsibilities.
   - be willing to subsume constituency interests when necessary, and adopt a long-term representational perspective whenever possible.
8. Exhibit political courage: be willing to oppose district opinion when it contradicts your judgment, and take political risks when you believe they are in the best interests of the district/state/nation, fulfill your political commitments, or conform to your political principles.
   - what you instinctively perceive as politically deadly behavior may actually work in your favor (can have representational and political benefits).
9. Engage in direct contact at home; aim for a truly *experiential* connection with citizens.
10. Finally, don't underestimate your constituents' capabilities as citizens.
    - constituents are more capable of appreciating the many demands and conflicting imperatives of the representative process then is commonly believed; build on this in order to improve the quality of the representation you provide and people's understanding of the process.

Most of the respondents would likely endorse the preceding as practical and effective steps to address some of the most important defects in the contemporary representative process. Yet trying to implement these recommendations, as one can imagine, would be far from easy, and in ways that participants did not always appreciate. Doing so would also produce a host of unforeseen consequences. The political dilemmas and paradoxes rooted in people's basic representational ideas and expectations are a major reason why. What ordinary citizens believe about representation, in short, may very well set the boundaries for what representatives can plausibly hope to achieve in terms of reducing public discontent with government.

For example, one of the knottiest challenges members of Congress face is that of combining responsiveness to the district with other crucial representational functions. Many of the respondents not only believed that representatives must do right by their districts, their own principles, and/or the national interest; they *passionately* held to these divergent expectations, without often defining how members should choose between competing priorities or resolve the conflicts that inevitably arise among them. When faced with the task of doing so, as they were during the hypothetical questions, subjects typically struggled to arrive at workable solutions. In fact, as each of the preceding four chapters demonstrates, it is clear that members of Congress and the institution are confronted not only with potentially conflicting representational expectations but an *abundance* of such expectations.[15] Given the nature of the perspectives of the citizens in this study, it may not be too much to say that representatives today are expected to be "all things to all people."

The views articulated by participants also raise important practical implications for the representative process. For one, what effect would the pursuit of "true" responsiveness to the constituency have on members' ability to discharge their other obligations? Respondents did not often appreciate the representational consequences of the kind of intimate and continual connection they favored. For example, frequent and unmediated contact at home would require members of Congress to assume responsibilities normally handled by their staffers, take time away from legislative business, and perhaps make them more vulnerable to the charges, both of which surfaced in these interviews, that they are shirking their primary duties and are more interested in currying favor with voters than serving their districts.[16] By the same token, a significant increase in "two-way" communication and public explanation/education would require a substantial commitment of time, energy, and resources, such as expanded franking privileges and electronic town meetings, on the part of congressional representatives. As a result, members would have less time to devote to the other essential obligations that participants enumerated, and perhaps become even more susceptible to constituent demands, yet still remain vulnerable to the political indictments outlined above.[17]

Representatives may face a real bind not only in deciding how to ensure responsiveness, but also *when* to do so. For a variety of reasons, members need to establish a strong bond with their districts. Doing so requires in part that they make themselves widely known and accessible to their constituents. Therein lies the rub. The findings here accentuate that efforts to reach out to citizens, establish communication, make direct contact, and otherwise connect with people during *election season* can arouse their ire and bolster their negative images of members. When constituents are most likely to be attentive to the representative relationship, in other words, is when they may be most likely to perceive the elements of responsiveness as self-serving, purely electoral gambits.

The political implications of this are clear. Representatives have to establish the basic building blocks of responsiveness, but doing so during the campaign process only seems to exacerbate people's cynicism about politics. Yet this is, of course, one of the best times for members to try to reach out and reduce their relative invisibility among constituents, when many citizens are most likely to be paying attention to, and perhaps even expecting, such activities. In a very real sense, then, representatives are damned if they do and damned if they don't. Members of Congress and other representative institutions face the daunting task of combating people's selective attention to the political process and their frequently skeptical attitudes—especially the penchant to interpret representatives' efforts at responsiveness solely as evidence of political expediency.[18]

Lastly, one cannot underestimate the political perils that representatives would perceive in the kind of explanation, education, and persuasion advocated by these citizens. While a significant number of respondents touched on the benefits they believed members might reap through these processes, representatives themselves would likely see political dynamite scattered across this type of representational landscape, even as some recent research suggests that such educational efforts can enhance understanding of members legislative actions and voting decisions and may even redound to their electoral benefit.[19] Abstract expressions of support for members who are willing to continually inform and educate constituents (especially on highly controversial issues), challenge and even resist constituent opinion, and commit to an open and demanding "two-way" representative relationship are one thing; the impact of these actions in the voting booth is something else entirely. To most representatives, the short-term political costs of such activities are abundantly clear and potentially catastrophic; the long-term benefits (for both themselves and constituents) hazy and uncertain. Better instead to rely on visibility, name recognition, and constituent services. So, too, with efforts to increase people's understanding of the legislative process and Congress's strengths as an institution, even as my work suggests that citizens *do* appreciate Congress and might be amenable to such instruction. As Fenno observed in *Home Style*, representational processes like education usually entail the willingness to spend political capital and make a political leap of faith in the interest of enlightening constituents and altering their preferences. As Fenno also noted, those preconditions help explain why you don't see much of these activities.

What does all this finally tell us? Quite simply, significant obstacles stand in the way of attempts to strengthen the representative process and revitalize public support for representative actors and institutions—obstacles that come from both citizens and their representatives. Equally important, these impediments can be linked to the fundamental beliefs and expectations that people hold about representation.

Let's take this argument a step further. The evidence from my study suggests that responsiveness may have debilitating effects on the public's view of members of Congress and Congress as an institution, in part because of people's conflicting beliefs about what representation should entail. Most of the participants, for example, conveyed that effective representation requires that representatives continually cultivate their constituencies and reflect their interests/wishes, but many of the same individuals also bemoaned what they saw as parochial decision making and the absence of political courage on the part of members of Congress. The way many of the citizens I interviewed believe the representative process actually unfolds reinforces their suspicion that members are political toadies, too willing to curry favor with certain voters or interest groups at the expense of the "real" needs of their districts and/or the public good. Yet these same citizens also stressed the vital importance of a strong constituency connection. Similarly, participants often disparaged the political behaviors and institutional outcomes that suggest representatives are captives of parochial interests and electoral impulses, yet they also presented a take on the representative relationship that would tend to keep members beholden to these demands.[20]

In effect, many of the respondents look at Congress and see a coterie of individuals willing to place their own, their party's, pressure groups, or even their districts' interests above those of the nation as a whole, and are led to question the legitimacy of the political process. But what they generally fail to perceive is that *citizens'* fundamental expectations for the representative process place significant pressure on members to act in ways that fortify both people's core representational beliefs *and* their negative impressions of elected officials and contemporary politics. This is really the heart of the problem, and extraordinarily difficult to resolve . . . yet public attitudes toward members of Congress and the institution are at stake.

Clearly, then, representatives and representative institutions face an uphill battle in trying to reduce public cynicism about politics and rehabilitate the public image and standing of elected officials. There appear to be significant limits to the restoration of citizens' faith in members of Congress, Congress as an institution, and the representative process in general, boundaries that my research indicates are related, and perhaps intimately so, to people's central assumptions and expectations about representation.[21] The ultimate irony is that while there may be far more to people's representational views than the superficial cynicism recorded in public opinion surveys, their deeper and more enduring representational ideals and expectations could pose even more intractable problems for the rejuvenation of the contemporary political process. In essence, a revival of public trust in political institutions and actors may be circumscribed in large part by ordinary citizens' fundamental political beliefs.

Some Final Thoughts

At heart, this study tells us that people's representational beliefs are richer and more complex than conventionally assumed—and that they have very real consequences for the democratic process. What citizens think about representation has both individual and systemic political ramifications. People's representational viewpoints are part and parcel of their political being, and therefore serve to influence their civic attitudes and assessments, yet they also bear directly upon the direction and success of the political process.

This relationship between individual political beliefs and systemic outcomes is particularly evident in the issue of "hyper-responsiveness." To some students and practitioners of American politics, one of the dark sides of contemporary representation is excessive obeisance to public opinion. From this perspective, the modern representative process places a premium on catering to individual constituencies and interest groups at the expense of larger political needs, including a coherent and effective legislative process, policy making with a long-term national focus, and members' willingness to make tough policy decisions. But how (and where) do representatives and representative institutions draw the line between being truly responsive—and engaging in the types of activities that most citizens believe are absolutely indispensable to good representation—and simply pandering to constituents while undermining their other essential responsibilities in the representative process? The findings in this book emphasize that there is no easy answer to this question. They also reveal how deeply, and in how many ways, the dilemma of hyper-responsiveness is intertwined with people's representational belief systems.

In much the same way, we need to further consider the implications of the evidence of a dynamic relationship between people's general representational beliefs and their specific expectations/evaluations of the representative process, as well as between this constellation of beliefs and the political environment.[22] These relationships highlight the value of documenting and evaluating the array of people's political views. But they also underscore the importance of getting citizens to consider the systemic consequences of their representational viewpoints and judgments. And this includes not only those views that tend to bolster their negative preconceptions about politics and intensify the inherent dilemmas in the representative process, but also those, such as the subjects' sensitivity toward a member's "tough job," that could result in more realistic and even favorable political appraisals and expectations.

My work certainly suggests that citizens have the capacity to do so. The conflicts and dilemmas about representation that students and practitioners of politics grapple with are not beyond the ken of ordinary Americans. It may be fairer to say, in fact, that many individuals possess a largely unappreciated and untapped "representational consciousness," an awareness that in-depth interviews helped bring to the surface for the citizens in this study. It is equally true, however, that the participants' representational consciousness was marked by blind spots, simplistic assumptions, and unrecognized side effects. Above all, perhaps, few of these citizens were willing (or in some cases able) to fully weigh the political and policy implications of having public officials and institutions try to create the kind of representative process that they envisioned.

There are, in short, both real possibilities and pitfalls for those who would look to citizens' political ideas and ideals for guidance as to how to strengthen contemporary representation. Like politics itself, people's representational perspectives tend to be messy, complex, contingent, and conflicted. The key may lie in encouraging them to think about these beliefs and the political process with this reality in mind—and to adjust their attitudes and expectations accordingly. If my research tells us anything, it is that any bid to reduce public misunderstanding and discontent with politics *must* be "two-way." Part of the effort must come from citizens themselves.

The issue then becomes how political elites—congressional representatives, other legislators and elected officials, political activists and reformers, scholars and analysts—can provide avenues, opportunities, and incentives for people to reevaluate their political assumptions, deepen their understanding of the representative process, and examine the larger implications of their representational ideas and expectations. But equally important would be the development of political mechanisms to nourish and advance the richer conceptions of representational accountability and public participation in the representative process which emerged so clearly in my interviews. Of particular value would seem to be forms of direct citizen access and involvement that encourage members of Congress and other representatives to engage constituents in "deliberative communication," and thereby foster two-way political education/persuasion, while preserving their freedom to act with discretion and informed judgment.[23] The potential gains from doing so, for both individual representative relationships and the representative process writ large, would certainly seem to be worth the costs.

It may well be, as I have intimated, that there is a ceiling to how much the representative process, and citizens faith in it, can be revitalized. Grounded in both people's abstract beliefs and their sundry real-world expectations, a certain degree of public cynicism and dissatisfaction appears endemic to this process. The dispiriting evidence (both real and contrived) of representatives' individual and institutional malfeasance, subservience to powerful and entrenched interests, and devotion to electoral imperatives over the good of constituents and the nation only serves to deepen this disillusionment. But these facts do not signify that there is no room, or hope, for improvement. Ordinary citizens, I have found, are not oblivious to the problems and predicaments inherent in the representative process, as epitomized in the subjects' general recognition and acceptance (if only partial and grudging) that representation is often a balancing act. On some level most of them understood that representatives must balance philosophical and state or national commitments with their responsibilities to their districts. Yet this realization did not entail an acceptance that the contemporary representative process has approached its democratic potential. Navigating from the disheartening shores of what representation *currently is*, through the turbulent waters toward what it *might be*, is arguably one of the central dilemmas in our politics today. Humanistic scholarly enterprises like this study can provide valuable beacons, warning signs, and fruitful paths for efforts to move in that direction.

Appendix A
Research Instruments

Survey Questionnaire

The Idea of Representation

- Political leaders often like to say that they are elected to represent us. What does it mean to you when you hear them say something like this?
- In your view, what would be the ideal kind of relationship between elected officials and the people they serve?
- In general, what do you think are the most important responsibilities of elected officials?

  Follow-ups: Anything else? Ideally, how do you think they should divide their time among these responsibilities?

- Overall, then, who would you say best represents you?

  Probe: Why did you pick _____?

The Representative Relationship

- What is your definition of a good congressperson?

  Probes: What would you say you value the most in a congressperson?

  What (qualities) do you look for in a member of Congress?

- When you vote for a candidate to Congress, what do you expect that person to do in office?

  Follow-ups: Anything else? Of all the things you mentioned, which one do you consider to be the most important? How do you think representatives should balance between their work in Washington and time at home with their constituents?

Appendix A

Institutional Representation

- In general, what do you like about Congress? What do you dislike about it?
- Congress does many things in our political system. What do you think are the most important things that Congress does?
- If you could give Congress some advice on how to do its job, what would you tell it to do?
- What changes would you like to see made in Congress to improve how it serves the American people?

    Probe: Some people believe that we should establish term limits for members of Congress. What do you think about this idea?

    (time permitting)

- Do you believe that the people we elect to Congress today are different from the people who used to serve in Washington?

    If so: How are they different?

Hypotheticals

- Suppose a bill to increase environmental regulations on business was being considered by Congress. Congresswoman Y thinks the bill will hurt the the economy, but the people she represents support environmental regulation and are in favor of the bill. What do you think she should do in this situation?
- Now let's say Congressman Z believes it is important for the country to reduce government spending to balance the budget. A bill to do this has come up for a final vote in Congress. However, some government programs will have to be cut under the bill, including a program that supports the _____ (ex. Watervliet Arsenal) in the congressman's home district. What do you think he should do when faced with this kind of voting choice?

Rank Scales:
Congress and Your Representative

A. The following is a list of responsibilities that a representative in Congress can have. Please rank them in order of importance from 1 to 6, with 1 being the most important to you and 6 being the least important.

_____ Helping people back home when they have problems with the government

_____ Discussing and debating important or controversial issues

_____ Bringing federal money and projects back to the district

_____ Spending time in the district meeting with constituents

_____ Keeping people informed about what's going on in Washington

_____ Passing bills that deal with important national problems

Please describe any other responsibility not listed above that you think a representative in Congress should have.

_____

B. The following is a list of responsibilities that Congress can have. Please rank them in order of importance from 1 to 6, with 1 being the most important to you and 6 being the least important.

_____ Representing the different groups and interests in America

_____ Discussing and debating important or controversial issues

_____ Keeping people informed about what's going on in Washington

_____ Preventing the president from becoming too powerful

_____ Providing federal money and projects to local districts

_____ Passing bills that deal with important national problems

Please describe any other responsibility not listed above that you think Congress should have.

_____

Sophistication Survey

1. *Background Information*

   Age: (circle one)   18–25   26–40   41–55   over 55

   Education: (circle the highest level completed)

          Grade school   High school   Some college

          College (BA/BS)   Master's/PhD

   Occupation:

   Political Affiliation: (circle one)

          Democrat   Republican   Independent

2. Can you name each of the following elected officials?

   U.S. President   _____

   Speaker of the House   _____

   Your U.S. Representative   _____

   NYS Governor   _____

   Your NYS Assemblyman   _____

3. How long are the terms in office for each of the following elected officials?

   U.S. President   _____ years

   U.S. Senator   _____ years

   U.S. Representative   _____ years

   NYS Governor   _____ years

   NYS Assemblyman   _____ years

4. Did you vote in the 1996 presidential election?   YES   NO

   Did you vote in the 1992 presidential election?   YES   NO

5. How often would you say that you vote in congressional elections?

   Always   Usually   Occasionally   Never

6. Please tell me if you have ever done any of the following:

Attended a town meeting held by an elected official	YES	NO
Contacted an elected official about a problem/issue	YES	NO
Participated in a political rally or demonstration	YES	NO
Been involved in a politically active organization	YES	NO
Contributed money to a candidate or political party	YES	NO
Worked for a candidate running for public office	YES	NO
Been involved in a local community organization	YES	NO

7. Please rank your top *three* sources of political information, with 1 being the most useful source.

    _____ Nightly network news (ABC, CBS, NBC, PBS, CNN)

    _____ C-SPAN

    _____ Weekday talk shows (Nightline, Crossfire, Rush Limbaugh, Larry King Live, etc.)

    _____ Weekend news shows (Meet the Press, This Week, Washington Week in Review, etc.)

    _____ Local newspaper

    _____ National newspaper (New York Times, Washington Post, etc.)

    _____ News magazines (Time, Newsweek, New Republic, etc.)

    _____ Radio news

    _____ Internet

    _____ Direct mail from elected officials, political parties, interest groups, etc.

    _____ Other _____

8. How much interest would you say you have in political issues and events?

    A lot   Some   Not much   None

9. Can you identify a major bill passed by Congress and the president in 1997?

_____

Appendix B
Interview Excerpts

Note: The following excerpts are drawn from three of the participants' answers to the hypothetical voting questions for members of Congress. Set A includes two respondents—one sophisticated, the other relatively unsophisticated—similar "solutions" to the first hypothetical quandary. Set B illustrates another person's attempt to reconcile his divergent representational expectations over the course of both questions. Both selections well represent the subjects' often thoughtful appreciation of these representational voting dilemmas, their struggles in attempting to resolve them, and the emphasis they placed on explanation and education/persuasion in the decision-making process. The most important passages are highlighted in **bold**.

SET A

First Respondent

INT: The last questions I had were a couple of hypotheticals but they are sort of true to life in the dilemmas that a representative faces. (Environmental Regulations Question).

RES: **I feel for her, because I would probably be in a dilemma myself** [*laughs*], **because I can see both points of view in that.** [*Pause*] **I think if I was her, she really has to think whether or not it helps her district, not only in the short run but in the long run. I mean, and she has to make that decision, but what I would do if I were her with every decision I made I would make sure I had a lot of stuff to back up my decision, to try to persuade the other side that this is the best thing, and what I would do is some kind of PR thing to make sure everyone knew that. A lot of them do that.**

INT: Do you think that is an important part of what they do?

RES: **To a certain extent they have to educate the constituents on what's going on, and constituents sometimes look at the short-term,** the local, and, of course, they say all politics is local, but like with the environmental issues are you cutting off your nose to spite your face? I mean, down the road are we going to have a terrible quality of life? Stuff like that. So **I think they should do a certain PR thing, or they make sure they appease whatever group is voting the opposite direction of with some other legislation. That's the other trick. "I can't vote with you on this, but I'll vote with you on that."**

INT: Okay, let's say she has done that, she's tried to persuade them and she's said, "I'll vote for this," but still there's a majority that favors the bill and she's opposed to it and the vote comes up. What do you think she should do?

RES: Okay. But she's leaning against it. **I think to a certain extent she has to vote what she thinks is best for the district, and let the chips fall. But the reality she may vote, some people may vote that way, and then other people just count the numbers and say "I may face a primary [challenge] if I don't vote for this."**

INT: What do you think she should do? What would you like her to do?

RES: **I think first of all it would depend on how important that bill is to my leadership in the House, and what am I going to get as a trade-off for my district if I vote for it. And that's the game that's played. And that's how I would look at it, and this way you can deliver, you've got to make it a win-win for everyone, even for those who vote against you on the other side of the issue.**

INT: **But what if there wasn't [*laughter*]. You're thinking of all the things that can soften the impact—**

RES: **Well, I think that's what goes on. I think she's just going to have to vote her conscience . . . it all depends on what as a candidate I had promised my constituents. If I had said that I was the environmental candidate, I would have to vote for it.** It depends on what I'm doing if people . . . and then you can always say, "you helped elect me but I always said this is how I viewed the issue."

Second Respondent

INT: Okay, the last couple of questions are just a pair of hypothetical questions, but they deal with sort of real-life issues. You can put yourself in the position of the congressman or the congresswoman. (Environmental Regulations Question) What do you think she should do in that kind of situation?

RES: **Okay, there are always ways to handle something. There are always ways to have a win-win situation.** Number one, you want the economy? What is one of the fastest growing economies in the world, especially in this country—tourism. You want a dirty river, you want a dirty lake, how many people do you think are going to come into your community. When people break away now they want to go to either fantasy-land, where everything is all man-made but lots of pretty landscaping, or they like to get away to nature. Even just riding people say, "Oh, what a lovely village or isn't the river beautiful." **It's an investment; a very wise investment. Okay, it might hurt the economy in the short haul, but in the long haul, absolutely not. Besides, even businesses want to be, even caring businesses want to be . . . they like to do it themselves, it's good PR, you might be able to say how would you like to blah blah blah. But it's a win-win situation. For good things, there's always a win-win situation.**

INT: But what if, using this example or thinking or another one, where they are at odds in the sense that people favor one position and the representative doesn't. In that kind of case, if it comes down to that kind of conflict, what do you think she should do? What would you expect that representative to do?

RES: Who am I? Am I the voter? Am I pro-business or pro-environment? [*laughs*]

INT: Let's say you are one of the people in the district who support this environmental bill, and she opposes it. When it comes to a vote, what do you think she's going to have to do? Is she going to have to go with what she thinks, or do you think she's got to go with her—

RES: **Okay, number one she should definitely have had a little town meeting. Uh, she should've definitely been reading her mail from her constituents, not from the corporations down in Albany, Georgia. I think she should do a lot of reading and a lot of studying. I think that's really important . . . when you're doing something with an impact like that.** Come on, who can be against the environment? I can't stand it. Well, so then she has to vote, **she has to vote her heart. Even if it's against what I believe. As long as it's not as long as somebody is doing her a little favor. If it's from her heart, that's the way I expect her to vote, and I've got to respect her for that. I may not like it, but I'll respect her for it. If she explains it.**

INT: **So it makes a difference if she goes to the effort to try to explain and educate as opposed to saying, "well I—"**

RES: **Well, but should she really go with—I don't know, that's tough, it's really tough, you know? I suppose it depends on the situation, the environment, well . . .**

INT: There's no way that you could say she either goes with the people or with her judgment?

RES: **I guess sometimes you have to go with your heart, and sometimes you have to go with your people, and sometimes if you go with your heart you have to alternately be thinking what is the best for my constituents, what is the best for them, because the way it should be is like the Indians, think of the seventh generation. What is not good for you, what is good for the children of the children of my children. That's what it comes down to. That's the way it should be, that's not the way they think. They think right now, here now now NOW NOW. Wrong.**

INT: Do you think they are the only ones like that, or do you think most people or voters are really like that?

RES: Oh, it's terrible, terrible. My friends I can't believe it, it's like right now, yeah, but what about? Never mind that. But I think in some ways people are softening up.

SET B

INT: Okay, here are some hypothetical questions—well, they are somewhat hypothetical, but they're also true to life. (Balanced Budget Question).

RES: **I guess . . . the thing he has to do is work to make sure that what's also included in that bill are things that will help people who lose their jobs transition into new jobs,** and not just people in his district but all the people who are affected. But **if that's really the best thing for the country, and that's what he feels, and that's for his district in the long run, then maybe what he should do is show leadership with the local people by getting on television and being up front and honest. If he feels that's what's best explaining why he feels it's the best, and explaining how he knows it will hurt people, and show how he's worked to make sure those people are taken care of, not that he's heartless and all that, but there are tough decisions that politicians have to make, that leaders in any position have to make, and you just have to stand up and do it.**

INT: And try, being in that position, to educate his constituents or at least inform them about the reasons for making that decision—

RES: **And show leadership. Not too many guys are willing to do that. I know I would tend to vote for a guy like that, but I know if I lost my job I'd probably vote against a guy who did that. So you have to count on losing those votes, and you have to be pretty secure in your position to do that. But, you know, that's the ideal thing to do.** I think the thing you also have to be willing to do—

INT: Or is that part of what being a politician should be?

RES: **What being a politician should be is you should be able to take the heat. To say, look, part of the reason you voted for me is because you felt I was the kind of leader to lead us,** and I've got to show leadership, and if you don't support my opinions and don't think I've shown any leadership then you'll vote me out, as long as I really believe in what it is then it's okay to be voted out. **And not too many people can do this, to say I was voted out of office because I supported something I really believed in, but that's the kind of leadership that you're looking for.**

INT: It's kind of interesting the way you've put it, they really have to be concerned about both the interests of their constituents and the interests of the nation as a whole. Thinking about the hypothetical, if they come into conflict like that, which do you think should be the top priority for a member of Congress? Or just in general—

RES: **I think in general a congressman has to support his district. You know, if you're going to shut down the major employer in your district (*A*) it's political suicide to do anything else and (*B*) you're not represent-ing your district and you are there to represent the people in your dis-trict.** So I would say as a politician I don't think I'd vote to shut down the major employer in my district, you just couldn't do it. Even if I believed in the bill in general, I couldn't do it.

INT: **Where does that place you when you said the ideal would be to show that kind of leadership?**

RES: **The ideal would be to do that, but the reality is different. Maybe the best you could do is you could abstain, but I can't see that . . . unless you were just conceding not being reelected, or were just tired of trying to be reelected and said, I'm just not going up for reelection this year so I'm going to vote the way I feel, but I would still want to feel that I was representing my district and I don't think I'd go against what more than two-thirds of the people in my district would not agree with. I mean, if it were 55 percent to 45 percent, I would feel comfortable. But if was 80 percent to 20 percent, an overwhelming majority, I would have to go with what my constituents said rather than what I believed in.**

INT: There was another hypothetical I had along these lines: (Environ-mental Regulations Question).

RES: **Again, it depends on. . . . Politics plays in gray areas. Eventually when it comes time to vote you have to vote yes or no on a specific bill, but certainly before that you can work behind the scenes to tailor a bill so that it's more acceptable to your individual constituents, maybe you can make some compromises** where you reduce some of the really onerous regulations that are really limiting and really expensive, or you can try to incorporate that into a multilateral thing with other nations where at least we're not competing with other people who are not interested in those issues at all.

INT: But what if it comes down to that kind of choice—

RES: If it comes down to a black or white—

INT: Let's say it's not even black or white, let's say you made some of these changes but you still support the bill, you've worked to modify some things but still it's clear a majority of your constituents . . .

RES: Again, I think it depends on what's the level of the majority in the district. You have to look at your own personal beliefs on the bill and how effective it's going to be. **Now, if it's one of those things where I re-ally think people will be helped even if they don't believe in it, and in** the long term help them, I might vote for it. A personal conviction thing, if I really, really felt it's for the best interests I'd just work hard to sell it. But if clearly again I'm just not representing my district, I would feel uncomfortable.

INT: So it's a natural kind of conflict, a fine line they have to walk?

RES: It's something that requires a lot of discretion. And that's why you need to elect people who are highly intelligent and have high personal integrity.

Appendix C
Coding Tables

Overview: The coding tables found on pp. 158–164 are based upon the comprehensive set of note cards derived from my analysis of the interview transcripts. The tables show, in graphic form, how (and whether) each participant responded in each of the approximately fifty content codes developed for the three major topic areas explored in this study: the *Idea of Representation*, the *Representative Relationship*, and *Institutional Representation*. The tables thus provide a kind of capsule summary of the participants' responses under the content codes and subcodes that served as the foundation for the descriptions and assessments presented in this book. They also show how many subjects made observations about a particular issue—in effect, how much that issue resonated with them. Overall, the tables allow the reader to evaluate many of the substantive categorizations and conclusions I have made, including those based upon the sophistication level of the respondents.

A brief explanation of how the tables should be read is necessary. Participants' transcript notations and level of sophistication are presented across the top of each page. The primary subject codes under each overarching representational topic are listed in the left-hand column. For each code, a respondent could receive a 1, 2, or 3 rating in the appropriate box (an empty box indicates that there was no response for that code). A 2 rating signifies that the respondent made a reference to the subject, however brief or cursory. A 1 rating denotes either of two things: a strong or fairly detailed response about a particular subject; or that the participant supports or agrees with the idea. For example, a 1 in the category "Constituency Focus" means that the respondent clearly expects this from her representatives and/or discussed the concept at some length. The same rating for the category "TL: Supports" indicates that the participant backs congressional term limits. A 3 rating, by contrast, represents an opposing or dissenting position. Thus, a 3 in the category "Direct Contact" means that the respondent does not favor such contact by representatives, while a 3 for "Benefits of Term Limits" signifies that the respondent expressed reservations about or enumerated drawbacks to the idea. A box containing two numbers indicates that a respondent acknowledged both sides of an issue, vacillated in his position, or endorsed divergent opinions. A letter in parentheses following a number specifies which aspect of a code category the respondent was discussing; for "JO: Agenda/Beliefs," a 1(A) indicates that that person expects members of Congress to try to fulfill their campaign agendas while in office. Finally, a "*" after any number refers to a particularly thoughtful, illuminating, pointed, or representative statement—one that merited quotation in the text.

A reference list of terms and acronyms appearing in the table is provided below:

Idea of Representation: (IR)—Initial Response; (IA)—Issue Access; I—Involvement; C—Communication; C: Obstacles To; (S)—Structural; (P)—Political; (B)—Both; TM—Town Meetings; Res.—Responsiveness; H1—Hypothetical Question 1; H2—Hypothetical Question 2; EX—Explanation; EP—Education/Persuasion

Representative Relationship: PQ—Personal Qualities; PoQ—Political Qualities; JO—Job Obligations; Reps: Role Models: (M)—Moynihan, (Ng)—Negative model

Institutional Representation: GW—General Welfare; DP—Democratic Process; CFR—Campaign Finance Reform; TL—Term Limits; Defining Congress: H—Hard, SC—Some Capacity

Coding Table
General Beliefs

	SOPHISTICATED									
	AA	C	F	G	I	M	O	P	Q	R
Idea of Represent.										
Discontent w/Process	1	2		1(IR)	2	3		1(IR)	2	3
Constituency Focus	2/3	1*	1		1*	2	1	3	1*	2
Long-Term View		1	2					2		
National Interest	2	2		2	1		2	1*		1
Attentiveness	2	*1*	1		2		2		1*	2
Oppenness/Access		2	1(IA)			2(IA)	1(IA)	1	2(IA)	
I: Visibility		2			1*					
I: Direct Contact		2			1		2	3	1	1
I: Benefits Of			1		1					2
C: Inform Constituents	2	1	2	2	1	1*	1	1	2	
C: "Two-Way"	1	*1*	1	2	2		1*		1*	2
C: Benefits to Member			2		1		1*	2		1
C: Benefits to Process	2	1		2	2		1*		2	2
C: Obstacles To (S/P)		1(P)			1(S)	2(B)	1(B)	1(B)	2(B)	
TM (Benefits Of)		2	1(2)	1(1/3)		1(1)*	1(1)		1*(2)	1
Res: Sham/Self-Serving	2	1		2		2		1		
H1: Delegate Position	3	1	3	1/3	1*	3	3	3	1	1
H1: Compromise Pos.	1		1		1					
H1: Qualified Position	1		1	1		1		1	1	
H2: Vote Beliefs	1/3	1	3	1	1	3	1	1	3	1
H2: Qualified Position	1	2	3		1*	1	1		2	
Sympathy: Reps. Dilem.	2	1	1		2	1		2/3		2
EX: Voting Decision	1	1*	2		1	1*	2	1	1	
EX: Benefits Member			2		1*		1			
EX: Benefits Constit.		1			2	1				
EP: Importance Of		1*	1	1	2	1*	1*	1	1*	2
EP: Benefits Members		1	1				2			
EP: Benefits Constit.		2	1	2		1	1	2	1	
EX/EP: Failure Of		1*		2				1*	2	
Responsive: Absence		1	3	1*		1/3	3/1	1	2	3
Citizen Input/Influence	2	1*	2		1	2	1*		2	2

(*continued*)

Coding Table
General Beliefs (*continued*)

	BB	A	B	D	E	H	K	L	N	X	CC
	SOMEWHAT SOPHISTICATED										
Idea of Represent.											
Discontent w/Process	1	1(IR)	1(IR)	1	2	1	2	1(IR)	1(IR)	1(IR)	
Constituency Focus	1	2	1		1*	1*	1*		2	1	2
Long-Term View		1*	1					2	2	1*	
National Interest			2	2	1					1	2
Attentiveness	1	1	2		2	1			1		1
Oppenness/Access	1	1	1*		1	1*		2		2	
I: Visibility	1*		3		1*	3	2				
I: Direct Contact	1	3	1*	3	3	1	3/1		2		1
I: Benefits Of	1		2	3		2	3				2
C: Inform Constituents	1	1	1	2		1	1		1	1*	2
C: "Two-Way"	1*	1	1		2	1*	1	2	2		
C: Benefits to Member		1	1						2		
C: Benefits to Process	1		2			1		1	1		2
C: Obstacles To (S/P)		2(B)	1(S)		2(S)		1(B)	1(S)	2(P)		2(P)
TM (Benefits Of)	2/3		1(1)					1(1)*	2	1(2)	
Res: Sham/Self-Serving	1*	1*		1	1		1	2	1	1	
H1: Delegate Position	3	1	3/1	1/3	1	1*	1	3	1	1	1/3
H1: Compromise Pos.			1*	1		1		1		2	2
H1: Qualified Position	1	2			1			1			
H2: Vote Beliefs		1	1	1	3	3	3*		1	1	3
H2: Qualified Position		2			1	2				2	2
Sympathy: Reps. Dilem.		1		2	1			2	2		
EX: Voting Decision	1	1*	2	1*		1	1	1	2	1	1
EX: Benefits Member	2	1	1	1*			2	1	2		
EX: Benefits Constit.		2	1	2			2			1	2
EP: Importance Of		1			1*	2	1*		1	2	
EP: Benefits Members						1	2		1	2	
EP: Benefits Constit.		1			1	2			1		
EX/EP: Failure Of		2				2			1	1	
Responsive: Absence		2		1	1	3/2	2		1	1	
Citizen Input/Influence	1	1	2		2	1	1		2	1	

(*continued*)

Coding Table
General Beliefs (*continued*)

	J	S	T	U	V	W	DD
UNSOPHISTICATED							
Idea of Represent.							
Discontent w/Process	2(IR)			1(IR)	1(IR)	1/3	2
Constituency Focus	2	1	2	1		2	1
Long-Term View		1					
National Interest	2	1			2		2
Attentiveness				2		2	
Oppenness/Access		1*				1*	
I: Visibility	3	2			2		1
I: Direct Contact		1*	1*	1*	2	3	2
I: Benefits Of		1		1			2
C: Inform Constituents		1	2			1	
C: "Two-Way"	1	1*		2	2		
C: Benefits to Member	2	1		2			
C: Benefits to Process	1	1*		1			
C: Obstacles To (S/P)					1(P)		2(S)
TM (Benefits Of)	1(1)	1(1)		1(2)	1		
Res: Sham/Self-Serving	2			1	1		
H1: Delegate Position	1	3	1	1		1*	
H1: Compromise Pos.							2
H1: Qualified Position	1						
H2: Vote Beliefs		1	1	3/1	1	3	
H2: Qualified Position	1		2		2	3	2
Sympathy: Reps. Dilem.	1	2			2		
EX: Voting Decision	1*	1			1	1	2
EX: Benefits Member		1			1	2	2
EX: Benefits Constit.					2	2	1
EP: Importance Of	1		2			1	
EP: Benefits Members			2				
EP: Benefits Constit.	1					2	
EX/EP: Failure Of					2	1	
Responsive: Absence	2			2	1	2	2
Citizen Input/Influence	3	1		2			

Coding Table
Job Responsibility

	SOPHISTICATED									
	AA	C	F	G	I	M	O	P	Q	R
Representative Relat.										
PQ: Honesty/Integrity	1	2	1	3		2(I)	1	1(H)*	1	1
PQ: Role Model										
PQ: Flex/Thoughtful		2	2			1	2			
PoQ: Intelligence/Leader	1(B)*	2	2	1*		2		1		2
PoQ: Courage/Indep.	1		1	3(I)	1	2	2	2		
JO: Agenda/Beliefs		3	1(A)	1(A)*	1(A)*				2	
JO: Judg./Conscience	1			1	2	1	1	1	1	
JO: Responsiveness		1	2		1	1				
JO: Constit/District Serv.	1(D)			1(C)		3(C)	1(C)	3(D)*	1(D)	
JO: Institutional (Laws)	2	1(L)	1(L)*	1			1		1	1
Reps: Role Models	1(M)*	2/3		3		1(Ng)	1*	1(Ng)		1(M)
Reps: Criticism Of	2	1*		1			2	1*	2	3
Reps: "Tough Job"	1*	1*	1		1	1	2	3		1
Dilemmas of Represent.	1*	2		2	1	2	1*	1		1
Institutional Repres.										
Expressive Role: Posit.		2	2		1			3	1	
Leadership/GW	1		2		2	1	1	2		
DP: Appreciation		1*	1/3			2	2			1
DP: Procedural Imped.		1	2		2	3	3	1		
DP: Ambiv./Balanced		1	1		1					1
Money: Influence	1	2	1/3	1	1(3)	1	1		1	2
Money: Quality of Rep.	1		1	2	1*	1*/3	1		2	
CFR: Mention Of	1*		1*	1*	1	1	1			1
CFR: Benefits Of	2		1	1*	1*	1	2			
TL: Support	1	3	3	3	1	3	3	3	3	1(A)
TL: Benefits Of	1*	3	3*/1	3	1*	3*(1)	3		3(1)	1/3
Incumbency: Positive	3(1)	2	1/3		3/1*	1(3)	1*		1*	1/3
Careerism: Positive	3	3*					2	3		
Defining Congress: H						2			1	
Definina Congress: SC	1	2	1	1	2	1	1	1		1
Media/Party Pol.: Impact	1(B)		1(P)	1(P)*	1(P)		1(P)		1(M)	

(*continued*)

	SOMEWHAT SOPHISTICATED										
	BB	**A**	**B**	**D**	**E**	**H**	**K**	**L**	**N**	**X**	**CC**
Representative Relat.											
PQ: Honesty/Integrity		2		1	1	1	2	1	1	1	2
PQ: Role Model			1*	2			3*	2		1	
PQ: Flex/Thoughtful		1*	2				2		1	2	
PoQ: Intelligence/Leader	1(B)	1				2		2	2		1
PoQ: Courage/Indep.		1	1	2/1	3	1(C)		1(I)			2
JO: Agenda/Beliefs	1		2	1(A)*	2		1(A)	2	1(A)	1(A)	
JO: Judg./Conscience	1		1	1	3			2	1	2	
JO: Responsiveness	1	2				1	1				
JO: Constit/District Serv.	3(D)		1(D)	3(D)						3(D)	1(C)3(D)
JO: Institutional (Laws)		2				2	1				
Reps: Role Models	2(M)	1(M)/3		1	3	3/1		1(M+)			
Reps: Criticism Of	1/3	1	1	1/3	2	1	3/1	1*	1*(3)	1*	
Reps: "Tough Job"	2	1		1	3			3/1	1		
Dilemmas of Represent.	2	2	1*	2	1		2		2		
Institutional Repres.											
Expressive Role: Posit.	1*			2	1*	1	2				
Leadership/GW		1*	2		1		2	1		2	1
DP: Appreciation	1(3)			1	1	3		2		3	2
DP: Procedural Imped.	2	1*				1			2		
DP: Ambiv./Balanced	1		2								2
Money: Influence	1/3	2		1	1			1	2	2	
Money: Quality of Rep.	2		2		1*			2		1	
CFR: Mention Of		2					1	2			2
CFR: Benefits Of							1	2			
TL: Support		1(3)	1	1*	1/3	1	3/1	3	1	1*	1
TL: Benefits Of		3		1*	1/3	2	3/1			1	1/3
Incumbency: Positive	3	1*	1/3*	3	3/1	3	1		3		
Careerism: Positive			3	3*					3*		3
Defining Congress: H		2			2		2	2	1	1	
Definina Congress: SC		1	2	2		1	1	2			2
Media/Party Pol.: Impact	3(P)		1/3(P)	3(P)1(M)	2(M)	1(P)*	1(M)		2(M)		1(P)

(*continued*)

Coding Table
Job Responsibility (*continued*)

	UNSOPHISTICATED						
	J	S	T	U	V	W	DD
Representative Relat.							
PQ: Honesty/Integrity	1*	1	2	2	1		2
PQ: Role Model	1*			3	3	3	
PQ: Flex/Thoughtful							
PoQ: Intelligence/Leader	2					1	
PoQ: Courage/Indep.		2					2
JO: Agenda/Beliefs	1(B)	1(B)*		1(A)*	1(A)	3	2
JO: Judg./Conscience		2					
JO: Responsiveness				1			
JO: Constit/District Serv.		3(D)				1(C)	1(D)
JO: Institutional (Laws)	2		2			2	
Reps: Role Models		2		2(Ng)			
Reps: Criticism Of		1(3)	2	1	1	2	3(1)
Reps: "Tough Job"				1	1		2
Dilemmas of Represent.	2	1		2	1		
Institutional Repres.							
Expressive Role: Posit.	2				2	1	
Leadership/GW				2			2
DP: Appreciation	2	1*/3				3/1	
DP: Procedural Imped.		2					
DP: Ambiv./Balanced		1				1*	
Money: Influence		1		2	1		1
Money: Quality of Rep.				2	1		2
CFR: Mention Of							
CFR: Benefits Of							
TL: Support	3	1	3	1/3	3	1	1
TL: Benefits Of		1/3				1	2
Incumbency: Positive	1	3			1	3*	
Careerism: Positive						2	
Defining Congress: H	1	2	1*	1	1	2	2
Definina Congress: SC		1				2	
Media/Party Pol.: Impact							

Notes

Chapter One: Introduction and Overview

1. This "may be because people perceive Congress as a more powerful institution" (Bowman and Ladd 1994, p. 53). If so, it would be interesting to know whether people's perceptions of the balance of power between Congress and the president have changed markedly since 9/11 and its aftermath, and the subsequent aggressive efforts of the Bush administration to expand the authority of the executive branch.

2. Academic studies have generally mirrored this result. See Dennis (1981) and Parker (1989).

3. In March 1994, just 8 percent of the respondents in a Gallup poll expressed a good deal of confidence in Congress. In May 2005 the comparable figure was 22 percent, the lowest confidence rating for Congress in eight years. And support for the national legislature continues to erode. By comparison, although confidence in the other two branches of the national government has also fluctuated and waned over the past thirty years (especially in the last decade), the decline has been less pronounced, with each institution receiving higher levels of peak support and lower levels of dissatisfaction. This is particularly true for the Supreme Court, whose job approval rating has remained comparatively stable over this period (see Kritzer 2005).

4. For a thoughtful and thorough review of contemporary public attitudes toward government, see *Deconstructing Distrust: How Americans View Government* (Pew Research Center, 1998).

5. A 1991 Kettering Foundation study suggests that Americans place great stock in their relationship with elected officials. It also indicates that much of the public's dissatisfaction with politics today stems from the belief that the representative process has been compromised in a political system dominated by lobbyists, interest groups, and the media. "People

believe two forces have corrupted democracy. The first is that lobbyists have replaced representatives as the primary political actors . . ." (p. v.) As one participant in the study put it, "'The original concept was for elected representatives to represent your interests. That is no longer true'" (Ibid.).

6. The most notable research in this vein has been conducted by Glenn Parker (1979, 1989). Several important conclusions can be drawn from Parker's work. One is that in order to explain differences in approval ratings for Congress and individual members, it is necessary to distinguish between people's conceptions of individual and institutional representation. Citizens simply use different criteria when they are trying to assess Congress versus their own representatives. Second, district and constituent service are now the primary duties people expect of their representatives, and perhaps even the predominant components in people's understanding of the representative process. Third, citizens fail to appreciate or even grasp the internal dynamics of Congress. In Parker's words: "As for the legislative process, when have citizens praised Congress for delaying legislative action or for being a deliberative assembly?" (1989, p. 56). Finally, and in line with many other contemporary scholars, Congress is portrayed as something of an "incumbent protection society" (Ehrenhalt 1991), where individual members generally have been able to insulate themselves from negative evaluations of the institution. To Parker, this is because people evaluate individual representatives and the institution on different grounds, incumbents are adept at favorably exploiting the criteria used to judge them, and negative perceptions of Congress don't seem to have much of a "spillover effect" on members themselves.

A number of scholars have challenged this last conclusion. Richard Born (1990), for example, finds that evaluations of the institution are a strong predictor of feelings toward individual representatives. At the same time, however, these feelings appear to be tied closely to the attentiveness component of evaluations. In his view this underscores the importance to constituents of the "representational function." Randall B. Ripley, Samuel Patterson, Lynn Maurer, and Stephen Quinlan (1992) contend that perceptions of individual members are influenced most by constituency attentiveness, partisanship, and evaluations of the institution. Herb Asher and Mike Barr (1994) stake out a similar position in their survey of public support for Congress. Pointing to the decrease in victory margins for House incumbents, as well as the parallel decline in public approval for Congress and individual members in the early 1990s, they insist that there is "some limitation in the public's ability to keep judgments of the members separate from judgments of the institution" (p. 18). Most recently, Monika L. McDermott and David Jones (2005) assert that public evaluations of Congress have a significant impact on voting within individual U.S. Senate races across a variety of electoral contexts.

A common thread in this group of studies is that while *individual-level* responsiveness is a key factor in people's evaluations of legislators, it is by no means the only one. As important is their discovery of a link between institutional assessments and perceptions of individual representatives. Citizens' evaluations of Congress may have a distinct impact on their attitudes toward their own member. This suggests that conceptions of individual and institutional representation are related, if not completely intertwined. *To some degree,* therefore, people perceive their own members as part of a larger institutional process, expect them to perform certain institutionally based representative duties, and hold them accountable for Congress's performance as a whole.

7. For example, Carl D. McMurray and Malcolm B. Parsons (1965) discovered that modern voters prefer representatives who act as "instructed delegates," although a study of Iowa constituents by Samuel C. Patterson, Ronald D. Hedlund, and G. Robert Boynton (1975) indicated that a large majority wanted legislators to exercise their own judgment even as they furthered district and state interests. The classic work on representational role theory and its applications can be found in John C. Wahlke, et al. (1962).

8. The bulk of this literature is a product of the behavioral tradition. Although this approach has unquestionably enriched our understanding of the representative process, it has predisposed scholars to define representation mainly as a series of functional responsibilities that legislators should fulfill, to consider the representative process from the perspective of representatives, and, perhaps most importantly, to virtually ignore ordinary citizens' conceptions of representation.

9. Political culture can be defined as the set of collective perceptions—beliefs, symbols, feelings, and values—that people draw upon to help understand and explain their society's political institutions and processes (see Cantori and Ziegler 1988, p. 159). It is important for political scientists to know how political belief systems work to support or weaken the institutions of democracy. The reverse is also true: we need to better understand how (the actions of) political institutions shape democratic values and attitudes.

10. In their 1995 review of major studies of public opinion formation, James H. Kuklinski and Gary Segura conclude that individual policy preferences are largely endogenous to politics. That is, citizens tend to form policy views on the basis of cues from elected representatives, and particularly from the most visible and influential leaders. Thus, people may look more to prominent members of Congress than to their own representatives for policy guidance. I wanted to know if a similar process occurs with regard to citizens' conceptions of representation. Do people's expectations for the congressional representative process appear to be influenced by elected officials? If so, are their beliefs affected by the personal attributes, actions, or

institutional position of their own members of Congress, or are individuals' ideas about what representatives should be like based more on the models provided by congressional "elites"?

11. This perspective is in keeping with most academic studies. Much of the extant research on public evaluations of Congress and its members, for instance, has been guided by the notion that "images of major institutional structures have independent standing in people's minds" (Dennis 1981, p. 321).

12. As is true concerning their beliefs about representation in general, the test is not whether people hold well-defined or elaborate "theories" of institutional representation. It is whether they possess some kind of congressional "orientation" that is not totally dependent on current political events, issues, and figures and that may have on impact on their attitudes toward, and evaluations of, the institution.

Chapter Two: Research Methodology

1. People's beliefs about representatives' roles were examined for the first and to date only time in the 1978 NES, when participants were asked to rank order a list of "activities that occupy members of the U.S. House of Representatives as part of their job." The activities were "helping people" (constituency service); "keeping in touch" (communication); "protecting the district" (district service); administrative oversight; and working on policy. Respondents ranked communication as the most important activity, followed by policy making, oversight and district service (tied), and constituent service. The survey also indicated that delegate roles and communication are closely related; those who felt that policy making was the most valuable representational activity were less likely to favor a delegate orientation than those who believed keeping in touch was most important.

Besides the low ranking given to district and constituency service, what I find most interesting about these results is the importance people seem to place on having members of Congress keep them abreast of what government is doing. This suggests not only that citizens may be less apathetic about public affairs than is commonly assumed, but that they also consider their representatives to be one of their most vital and reliable connections to the political process. Unfortunately, the survey gives us no inkling as to *why* people clearly value communication with their member, or how this might relate to their larger conceptions of representation. Addressing these kinds of gaps in the existing literature was a driving force behind this project.

2. For example, if first asked how they would rate the current members of Congress, and then Congress as an institution, respondents are cued to think of Congress *apart* from its members. This could lead to the

judgment that Americans remain supportive of Congress even when they are disdainful of incumbents. The viability of the institution therefore remains intact (see Asher and Barr, pp. 16–17). The point is not that this interpretation of congressional attitudes is necessarily wrong. Rather, it is that we might reach a different conclusion if the subject was broached in a slightly different way (say, if the survey questions *encouraged* people to link their representatives to the institution).

3. I believe this holds true even if, or *especially* if, these views are fragmentary, composed of bits and pieces of divergent ideas and expectations that do not coalesce into a coherent whole but nevertheless reveal much about a person's mind-set and our political culture. It is quite possible that people borrow from a number of different and even contradictory belief systems in developing their views about representation. The objectives are (1) to find out exactly *what* they think about representation; and (2) to discover (as much as possible) *why* they think that way.

4. William A. Gamson, in *Talking Politics* (1992), relies on focus group conversations rather than individual interviews. Because I was interested in recording the beliefs that individuals brought *to* the table, and not the collective product of "sociable public discourse," one-on-one interviews were more appropriate for my needs. But the underlying principle behind both approaches is essentially the same: to let people discuss political issues in their own way, with the researcher keeping his or her eye on how the discussion reflects certain values or beliefs central to their political identity. It is also important to note that the use of in-depth interviews and focus groups to investigate people's political beliefs has become increasingly widespread in both academic and political circles.

5. Yet because the interview process was semistructured, I was also able to give direction to the conversations, to focus on the issues I deemed important, and to keep the process from turning into a current events discussion about Congress or individual members. In short, respondents were able to speak "in their own voice," but in a setting explicitly designed to reveal their understanding and expectations of the representative process.

6. These factors include the congressional districts people were from and their levels of political "sophistication." The latter variable is discussed in greater detail later in this chapter.

7. The idea that the political/representational environment may have a significant bearing on citizen's beliefs about representation underlies this project and was the impetus behind examining such contextual factors as the congressional district.

8. Of course, spontaneous probes present their own set of problems. The biggest dangers are that these questions may lead subjects, especially the most inarticulate and reticent ones, to respond in certain ways or react to (and perhaps endorse) the researcher's assessment of their initial

replies. Probes can also result in repetitive answers and excessive involvement on the part of the interviewer. Although each of these concerns did crop up at times, on balance the quality of material gained from the probes far outweighed these negative side effects.

9. There are at least two versions to the thesis that House members themselves have an impact on people's attitudes about representation. The "weaker" one, evident in Parker's work, is that public evaluations of representatives are related to the behavior and home styles of incumbents. The "stronger" version, embodied in Richard F. Fenno's *Home Style*, holds that people's basic expectations of the representative process may be profoundly shaped by their own representatives. Note: Although Gerald Solomon no longer represents NY's 22nd congressional district, he was in office the entire time the interviews were conducted.

10. A handful of interviews were conducted after this time period in order to fill certain shortcomings in my sample population. Thirty people were formally interviewed, but I was unable to use two of the interviews. One of these subjects took the session as an invitation to launch into a rambling discourse on American society, and failed to answer more than one or two of the questions. This was the only such occurrence in the entire interview process.

11. A detailed example should help to clarify this process. Under the broad rubric of "The Idea of Representation," nearly twenty codes were developed, such as "Visibility/Direct Contact," "Communication," "Town Meetings," and the "Representative as Delegate." Some of these were split into subcodes because of their importance and multiple dimensions. For example, the code "Communication" was divided into four categories: "Importance Of," "Benefits Of," "Obstacles To," and "Problems When Absent." Each of these became the heading on one side of an index card. A group of subheadings for each subcode then emerged based upon close reading of the transcripts; for "Communication (Importance Of)," the subheadings included "Informing constituents" and "Soliciting feedback." By the end of the review process, these subheadings were followed by a number of notations indicating the particular transcript and page number of a passage. Each subheading line on a code card thus looked something like this:

Enhanced by modern technology: *J–5*; K–2; X–4; *C–12*; BB–34

The same process was used for the two other major topic areas ("The Representative Relationship" and "Institutional Representation"). It is important to note that these codes and subcodes were driven more by subjects' responses than my analytic constructs; the task then became to marry what people had said to the research questions I was trying to address. Tables categorizing each of the participants' responses for the key content codes and subcodes—those at the heart of this book—are presented in appendix C.

12. In the course of my analysis, therefore, I decided to take up the following issues: Do politically knowledgeable and attentive citizens perceive the representative relationship differently than their more apolitical brethren? In what ways? Do politically active people hold distinctive views about how the representative process should work? Or when given the chance to discuss representation at length (and in their own words), do citizens tend to express similar ideas about it regardless of their level of political knowledge or involvement?

13. Within this category is a subset of people who I call "political activists."

Chapter Three: The Idea of Representation

1. The analytic categories here instead emerged from respondents' own views about representation, but are still clearly related to previous research in the field. There are two important benefits to this. Because the analytic distinctions in this chapter are based upon what people said, they embody the subjects' understanding of the representative process. The categories reveal both the broad contours and specific dimensions of subjects' conceptions of the representative process—and thus made it possible for me to develop a kind of "model" of the public's view of representation. Yet in developing these categories I also relied on related research, especially Fenno's work. My findings thus can be readily compared with, even incorporated into, the existing literature. In this sense, my project can be seen as the application of Fenno's and others ideas about representation to the realm of the ordinary citizen.

2. For example, the subject who opined that representatives will do whatever they feel will get them reelected quickly modified his position by stating that "I'm sure, you know, what gets them reelected is generally what we want to see done, but I think there are a lot of processes where they keep track of for themselves and not finding out what the people would like to hear." And the person who said that expressions of responsiveness from representatives are "just a lie" shortly thereafter touched on the difficulty of fulfilling representational obligations: "Well, I think it would be kind of hard just to please everybody across the board, to meet each and every person's needs, you know what I'm saying?"

3. It should be noted that not every respondent explicitly mentioned all these concerns. What is true, however, is that they seemed to form a subtext for most of the respondents' specific representational ideas or expectations.

4. In its broadest sense the term "representatives" can denote elected officials in both legislative and executive offices and at any level of government. The first set of questions was consequently designed to avoid linking the concept of representation to specific government officials or

institutions. Interestingly, however, respondents typically understood references in these questions to "elected officials" or "to represent" to mean *legislators* of some kind. While some statements were made about major executives, the *idea* of representation seemed to be most closely associated with (members of) legislative institutions in people's minds. This result would suggest that the representative process is still considered to be the special province of legislators. Thus, unless specified otherwise, the terms representatives or elected officials henceforth refer to members of legislative bodies.

5. Ironically, as will be discussed in chapter five, many respondents also expressed the desire that representatives stick to their policy commitments, keep their campaign promises, and fulfill their stated political "agenda." Admiration ran high for politicians who try to live up to their pledges. In other words, most subjects hoped that elected officials *won't* be easily swayed or willing to shift their positions or priorities, particularly if such changes appear to be made for electoral reasons. Some people did sense the potential conflicts between having representatives who, as one person put it, "stick to their guns" and having representatives who are open to political change and constituency influence.

6. Some of the impediments to attentiveness and openness mentioned by respondents included "bureaucracy," legislative staff, and representatives lack of time or interest.

7. A few people additionally thought that such contact gives representatives a better sense of the range of views in their constituencies. ("Like if they come to a community center, they're getting a . . . whole bunch of people's views on what's in the inner city and what people think.")

8. Although most of the participants did not clearly differentiate between the kind or degree of visibility/direct contact they expected from different representatives, several did contend that local and state officials have a greater opportunity and obligation to attend to their districts than do members of Congress. In the words of the same person who posited a link between visibility and trust, "I don't expect my Washington representatives to be as visible. If my Washington reps. were as busy as this guy (a state assemblyman) I'd really worry, because then I don't think they are attending to business in Washington. At the local level, state level, politicians need to be more involved in the local community, and more visible, like showing up at the banquet and consistently submitting articles to the local paper." In this view our federal system influences the nature of the representative process; to some degree the representation we get from national officials should be different than what we receive at the state and local level.

9. A few respondents similarly implied that the absence of direct contact can result in misguided policies and poor representation. In the view of one of these subjects, "these welfare [reform] bills were passed by peo-

ple that have never had any contact with poor people. They don't understand that there are a lot of people that are never going to make it on their own or are going to have to be dependent on government all their lives."

10. This outlook may be as much a reflection of their professional position as their personal beliefs. Ultimately, it may be impossible to determine whether these views flow from their role in the political process or deeply held preferences they brought to the job. It was true, however, that among all politically sophisticated respondents, activists were more likely to stress the importance of issue-based access.

11. Fenno goes further to make a strong case for including communication with constituents as a primary element of political representation. To him, communication itself has several facets: presentation of self; explanation of Washington activity; "feeling out" constituency opinion; and ensuring access. Fenno's perspective has greatly influenced other students of the representative process. For example, Malcolm E. Jewell, in *Representation in State Legislatures* (1982), includes communication with constituents as one of his four essential components of representation.

12. As another subject put it, "I think that whether they (representatives) are happy with the outcomes of their meetings, they still have a responsibility to report back. I think that's a great medium. If people don't want to go, then they're failing their duties as citizens."

13. Having meetings that are truly accessible to more than just political elites was an important consideration to some respondents. After spending a lot of time listing various impediments to public access to elected officials, one participant insisted that representatives should make sure that they have "town meetings and stuff like that open to the public and not just to reporters and high-quality officials, locally and what-not."

Chapter Four: Representation in Practice

1. It was at least somewhat surprising to me, given the (usually very) low assessment of people's knowledge about representatives and the political process in many studies. I was particularly struck by the complexity and ambivalence in many of the respondents' answers; they often seemed to grasp the difficult and at times conflicting problems elected officials may encounter in trying to communicate often and effectively with their constituents. These problems include trying to handle their legislative responsibilities in Albany/Washington, an issue that will be taken up in the following chapter.

2. Compare this with Fenno's assertion in *Home Style* that "[t]he more one observes members of Congress at work in their districts, the more one is impressed by the simple fact that people are hard to find.

Members (and their staffs) expend incredible amounts of time and energy just trying to locate people to present themselves to" (p. 234). Some of my subjects might counter that this is because representatives aren't trying hard enough, are looking in the wrong places, or are searching to simply "present themselves" (create visibility) rather than to establish meaningful contact. But those people who touched on the size and growing diversity of legislative districts would probably acknowledge Fenno's point that "the more kinetic and fragmented American society becomes, the more difficult it will be for House members to reach people" (p. 236). As already discussed, many of the more politically engaged respondents were aware of the difficulty in opening and maintaining good lines of communication in the contemporary political environment.

3. In a handful of interviews, either the content of the first question was altered because of the political orientation of the individual or one of the questions was dropped if the respondent had dealt with the dilemma earlier in the interview. For example, the congresswoman's position in the first question was switched for two respondents who had revealed that they were active on environmental issues, in order to heighten the voting dilemma for them. In two other interviews, the issue in this question was changed to make it more compelling to the respondent; thus, one person who had made repeated references to immigration issues and helping minorities received a "help to immigrants" version of the question.

4. Although these questions dealt specifically with members of Congress, the way some respondents discussed how members should act during the decision-making process indicated they meant their ideas to apply to all legislators. Their answers were framed in terms of providing general "rules of thumb" for political representatives.

5. Both of these subjects also agonized about the proper course for the representative to take, and both finally arrived at a kind of modified trustee position. Because their responses were so emblematic of the representational conflicts people struggled with, but from different points on the "sophistication scale," extended excerpts of both are included in appendix B.

6. This result was consistent with some of the most commonly expressed expectations of representatives: that they should stick to their campaign platform/commitments, make what they believe is the right decision, and demonstrate political honesty or courage. These expectations will be discussed in the next chapter. In addition, since the question did have a long-term angle to it (i.e., the member believes that a balanced budget is necessary for the future good of the country), the result may also reflect the weight that several respondents placed on having representatives who possess a "long-term" vision for society and/or a commitment to the nation's future.

7. One subject explicitly recognized the institutional factors that would affect the member's ability to protect his district: "That's where his own individual influence comes into play, how much power that individual congressman has. Is he able to influence the leaders in Congress to keep funding for that certain project? That's where the freshman congressman is at a big disadvantage, whereas the guy who has been in Congress for many years has more influence, more power, and it depends on what party he is. If it's the minority party, his influence obviously isn't going to be as great as if he's in the majority party."

8. An extended excerpt from perhaps the best example of this is included in appendix B.

9. In fact, a number of subjects appeared to adopt a kind of representational calculus which resembles the one Thomas E. Cavanaugh (1982) contends representatives' use in their own decision making. Cavanaugh found that members consider the nature of the issue involved, the intensity of constituency preferences, personal opinion, and their view of the national welfare in making voting decisions. As several of the quotes here indicate, the subjects often wanted representatives to consider similar kinds of factors (although they differed, of course, on the specific factors cited or the weight assigned to each). The underlying point is that respondents typically did not offer simple, ironclad rules for congressional decision making. Many acknowledged the need for, and sometimes explicitly endorsed, fairly complex and politically sensitive approaches to the voting process. In other words, it was not unusual, broadly speaking, for subjects to envision members acting as "politicos," either by design or necessity.

10. I could not identify any major distinctions between how sophisticated and unsophisticated respondents resolved the hypothetical voting dilemmas, nor did I find any significant differences in the incidence of discussions about explanation. However, sophisticated respondents were more likely to mention and stress the importance of education-persuasion. In addition, they tended to provide more involved and articulate answers, as could be expected, and politically active subjects often fleshed out their responses with personal illustrations and examples. These individuals were also more prone to recognize the conflicting political and representational imperatives in these voting situations and to offer complex (and perhaps more politically realistic) solutions to them. What was most striking, though, was the basic similarity in approaches to the problems and the widespread appeal of such processes as explanation and education. What emerged from the interviews, then, was almost a set of "common denominators" about the key components of the representational decision-making process.

11. The advantage of focusing on the long-term benefits of difficult decisions proved to be a recurring theme; another subject likewise argued

that "if people know what's going on even if they don't like it in the short-term perhaps they'll be able to get an idea of what's trying to be done in the long-term."

12. The respondent just cited in the text also emphasized that representatives can capitalize on the advantages derived from their institutional position to further the educational process: "I would say [education] would work well, only because she probably has more insight into what is going on, uh, and has more knowledge as to what's going on than the people. And she can explain it in layman's terms, you know . . . [and say] 'Think about it and then come back tomorrow and tell me what you think.'"

13. Or, in the trenchant words of another participant, "instead of coming back to do fundraising, it would be much more interesting to see a congressman coming back and really try to find out what the core issues of concern to the constituents are and what the solutions are to them. Town meetings that really had an educational value, stuff like that, would be good."

14. For a few people such education-persuasion was intimately related to the desire for representatives to serve as guardians of their constituents and/or the nation's long-term interests. In the words of one subject, "To a certain extent they have to educate the constituents on what's going on, and constituents sometimes look at the short-term, local [interests], but like with environmental issues are you cutting your nose off to spite your face? I mean, down the road are we going to have a terrible quality of life? Stuff like that."

15. Or the other way around. In responding to the first hypothetical, one person contended that the representative should vote her judgment unless persuaded otherwise during the communication process. "Yeah, I would vote for the bill, if I believe it's a good bill. I realize that you don't like it, you may not think it's good, but I think we should do it. Unless somewhere along the line one of you showed me things about it that I didn't realize, then I think she should be honest enough to say, 'I didn't understand this, I didn't realize it. Now I see what your problem is and I'm opposed to the bill.'" Although here the education is coming from the other side, notice the underlying desire in all these cases for constituents to play an important role in the decision-making process.

16. For a few participants, explanation/education/persuasion seemed to take on particular importance given their dim view of the public and its opinions. Consider the following Lippmannesque observation from one subject: "I think it (explanation and persuasion) would be a major part of her job. People are stupid, you know. People have very, very little knowledge about what's going on around them and really don't pay attention to a lot of things. So if attention is given to something and somebody says, 'Well, I don't think you know all the facts,' let them know

all the facts and say make that decision again. . . . If it's a different decision [from what the representative prefers], then at least you know you've given them all the facts." (Of course, this perspective is only Lippmannesque up to a point. Lippmann would likely have been less sanguine about the impact of such educational "attention" on ordinary citizens, and would surely have been alarmed at the prospect of letting the public make the final decision!).

17. The varied and dogged ways representatives try to cultivate this can partly be attributed to the electoral imperative. But in Fenno's eyes responsiveness goes deeper than that; it is part and parcel of a members' everyday behavior. Meaningful representation is a product of 'everything homestyle': "nearly everything he does to win and hold support—allocating, reaching, presenting, responding, communicating, explaining, assuring—involves representation" (p. 240). These "extrapolicy" activities, perhaps even more than issue or policy congruence, are the standards by which to gauge effective representation. In this way *Home Style* can be read as an unabashed defense of representation as responsiveness. Fenno's fairly benign view of individual-level responsiveness contrasts sharply with the perspective of other congressional scholars who have been deeply concerned about its systemic implications. To give just two examples, Morris P. Fiorina (1989) depicts the emergence of a malignant "Washington Establishment" predicated on members' hyper-responsiveness to constituents, while Gary C. Jacobsen (1987) warns about the dangers of a system characterized by "individual responsiveness and collective irresponsibility."

18. *Home Style* suggests that a number of factors—individualized home styles, members' own ideas about representation, and the perennial strategy of "running against Congress"—ultimately affect not only how representation occurs, but also people's attitudes toward the representative process. Indeed, on an even deeper level, the way people *think* about representation may be a function of their representative's behavior. And this has important implications for views about what I call "institutional representation." Fenno contends that ordinary citizens have a very limited understanding of the representative process as a whole, in large part because home styles effectively condition people to "think only about their relationship with their member" (Ibid., p. 246). In this milieu Congress cannot be conceived as a collectivity; there is little grasp of representation as a "public, institutionalized arrangement." Representatives thus have the power to shape, reshape, and perhaps even define our understanding of the representative process. And this understanding apparently does not include any conceptions of institutional representation. The extent to which constituents' ideas about representation are affected by home styles is, of course, open to question. One of the limitations of *Home Style* is that it does not investigate constituents' beliefs

about the representative process and their perceptions of members' behavior, even while making definite assertions about their perspectives. Addressing this deficiency was one of the main rationales for my study.

19. Respondents differed to some degree on how to achieve this. Some, particularly the most politically active and sophisticated, emphasized the importance of having representatives provide an "open door," issue accessibility, interactive newsletters, and the like. Others, especially the more unsophisticated subjects, focused on direct contact with constituents in their own communities. And respondents endorsed various forms of two-way communication that enable constituents to clearly make their voices heard. In sum, although they shared the goal of constituent influence in the representative process, the participants in this study offered diverse paths on how to get there.

20. But there is another issue to consider here: *which* constituents are most likely to benefit from these processes? For example, one could argue that the kinds of two-way responsiveness endorsed by most respondents (such as direct issue access, frequent town meetings, interactive newsletters, and the like) would tend to enhance the representative relationship for—and further skew the relationship toward—those individuals and groups who are already advantaged in it. In other words, those citizens with the "right" personal and institutional resources (the political experience, knowledge, access, commitment, and connections) are better able, and most likely, to capitalize upon these avenues of representational participation. These mechanisms are geared toward the politically savvy and articulate. On the surface, the representative process may appear highly accessible and responsive, but mainly for those segments of the constituency already benefiting from it. Put another way, the inner rings of Fenno's "concentric circles" of represented are most likely to prosper in this kind of representative process. This may help to explain the emphasis placed on direct contact by many of the more unsophisticated respondents; perhaps they felt (or sensed) that their influence in the representative process in practice depends upon alternative forms of engagement with their representatives.

21. Some of the politically active participants did not share this viewpoint. In fact, those subjects were the ones most likely to think that representatives are fairly responsive, as well as to believe that the representative process is open to citizen influence. This relative optimism seemed to flow from their personal experiences in the political arena. Respondents lacking such direct contact with members, or what might be called a "privileged position" in the political process, were less likely to share these views. The results here therefore suggest that access to elected officials and active participation in politics tend to produce more favorable assessments of the quality of contemporary representation.

22. Once again, some of the politically active respondents had a different perspective. Several relayed personal anecdotes about how the threat of electoral defeat had induced greater attentiveness from representatives; one even concluded that the electoral connection is the primary reason members "do make an effort to reach out and talk to constituents." In short, these subjects (sometimes grudgingly) noted that the electoral process may promote greater responsiveness, rather than hindering it.

Chapter Five: The Representative Relationship

1. By contrast, several people, including three of the unsophisticated respondents, emphasized that personal morality was distinctly secondary or irrelevant to the discharge of a representative's duties. The following subject expressed this position most forcefully: "To me they (character issues) are not even in the running. Some of our best presidents have had lousy characters. I don't think it's important, I don't think that they're necessarily role models. I think that if they can get the job done it doesn't really matter to me who they sleep with." (Int: Do you think there is a difference between your private character and your public character?) "I do. I absolutely do. I think if people can carry out a job competently and . . . ethically, while still making mistakes personally. We all do." Such attitudes, while in the minority, were strongly held, and may hint at a significant disjunction in the public mind over the cardinal virtue of "private character" in political life.

2. Other respondents lamented the absence of honesty among today's politicians. As one of them stated: "I think the worst thing about politics now is you can't trust anybody." Interestingly, subjects of varying political stripes held up Jimmy Carter as the embodiment of political integrity. The person just cited also remarked, "You know, it's funny, I voted for Jimmy Carter years ago, and he's pretty liberal . . . but if he were running today I would have voted for him out of pure honor. I could trust him, right down the line. Weak as he was, you could trust him. (Int: Is that something you wished other politicians had?) Yeah. Absolute clarity and trust." This veneration of Carter's personal qualities is perhaps not surprising given the dynamics of the later Clinton years.

3. As one participant stated, "the number one thing is personal integrity. There is just so much power associated with, so many opportunities for someone who doesn't have an unusual level of personal integrity. I think that's the number one thing you have to look for. You can't be somebody who can be bought." Intriguingly, though, this person shortly thereafter touched on the dilemma such virtue poses for representatives in the contemporary political process: "You know . . . that's a very difficult thing given how expensive campaigns and things are. You basically

have to allow yourself to be bought a little bit, but there are some people who are able to rise above that."

4. One respondent believed that the ossification of this trait was one of the main drawbacks of incumbency: "You know, once the incumbents are in they usually, at least from my perspective, get set in their ways. So then it's difficult for them to keep an open mind."

5. Of course, breaking from party ranks when the district's interests are on the line is arguably the easiest and most politically acceptable form of political courage.

6. Another subject expressed admiration for Harlem representative Charles Rangel because "he always has something to say, he's opposed to a lot of stuff that your streamlined Republicans and Democrats go for."

7. As one unsophisticated respondent exhorted: "Don't make all of these promises that you know within your heart that you really can't keep, you know what I'm saying? Don't just say that to get in there. . . . The way they make it sound, they make it sound like, woo, we're going to get miracles. And the whole world's going to be different. That's how they make it sound. [How about] 'I will do my best when I get in there to do this and this and this.' I think that would make it better than saying, 'Oh, I promise I'll do all of this.'"

8. It also may reflect the respondents' desire to see a stronger connection between the electoral and governing processes. In other words, these citizens seemed to want elections to have a more meaningful impact on the policy and political decisions made by their representatives, even as some of them insisted that they want candidates to scale back the scope of their agendas. The sense that campaigns have become increasingly divorced from the governing process appeared to be a source of political disenchantment for several of the participants.

9. Many of the same respondents also ruefully noted that representatives are often not willing to do this, or that "it's very difficult for them to do this."

10. Several respondents advanced the thesis that exhibiting political courage is both the right thing to do (ethically and/or on the grounds of policy effectiveness) and can be politically beneficial (rewarded at the polls). That is, voters might respond favorably to representatives who are willing to stand up for what they believe in, even if it isn't popular, especially at a time when the conventional wisdom is that politicians govern by watching the polls. As one of these subjects stated: "I think more officials would get elected more often if they worried about getting the job done and not about getting elected." In short, taking political risks would not necessarily be to members' political detriment.

11. These results also broadly correspond with Patterson et al.'s (1975) finding that people expect representatives to exercise their own judgment even as they further both district and state/national inter-

ests. This suggests that many (most?) citizens want representatives who can juggle district imperatives with larger concerns, who can effectively combine responsiveness to the constituency with independent thought and action.

12. On the whole, the respondents who emphasized constituent-centered job responsibilities were not the same people who advocated more trustee-oriented obligations (making the right decision, using one's own judgment, etc.). This suggests that citizens may subscribe to differing and to some degree competing "models" of effective congressional representation. In one model, constituency is the centerpiece of a member's job obligations and the foremost influence upon her decision making. In the other, constituency must be balanced with (and in some cases subsumed under) other representational imperatives, such as the long-term public interest or a member's political vows. From this latter perspective, constituent needs and preferences are just one, and not necessarily the most compelling, factor in a member's representational calculus. These are different visions of how congressional representatives should approach their job—and they lead to different expectations of what members should do in office, how they should make decisions, and what it means for them to be responsive. In sum, there appear to be important distinctions in people's expectations for the representative relationship, with attendant implications for how members (and perhaps even the institution) will be evaluated. And, as will be more fully explored in the concluding chapter, if the fundamental requirements for the job vary from citizen to citizen, there may be real limits to how well members can represent their constituencies or the "public"—as well as to people's overall level of satisfaction with the representation they receive.

13. Several people alluded to the importance of attending legislative sessions and, especially, being there to vote. As one of these individuals inveighed, "One of the things that drive me nuts is when, it comes out about once a year, you see in the paper how many votes so and so actually attended, and they don't attend, that irritates me when I think about that . . . obviously they are going to miss some, but if I missed as many days of work as they did I'd lose my job." These subjects did not appear to think that representatives might be missing these votes to attend to other legislative business, or to serve their constituents in some way; more importantly, they did not ponder the impact that their general preference for a devotion to constituency might have on members' institutional obligations. As the respondent just quoted replied to a follow-up probe, "I think a lot of the missing votes they are not back home with their constituents. If they were back home . . . I think someone in that position should be able to budget their time well enough to make a majority of the votes as well as spend time with their constituents and still get in eighteen holes of golf once a week, without really killing

themselves." This was one, and not the only, instance of respondents failing to recognize the larger implications of their preference for a strong constituency connection.

14. J. Tobin Grant and Thomas J. Rudolph (2004) find that constituents' job expectations condition the effects of members' legislative activities on their job approval ratings.

15. The ranking scales thus were broadly consistent with the interview narratives. There was also a good deal of internal consistency; respondents who touted communication, lawmaking, the need to serve constituents, or other relevant duties in their discussions of member's responsibilities tended to rank the same duties highly.

16. The respondents, then, did not universally embrace the role of lawmaker. In part this may stem from the recognition that their representative is only one of many, and that his or her legislative power is therefore inherently limited. Still, it is noteworthy that a significant number of people discounted this most basic of representational roles.

17. Its relevance in the voting booth, however, may be another matter!

18. The perception of Congress as an august body for discussion, persuasion, and oratory goes back to the founding of the Republic, and may be the most enduring (if inaccurate) public image of the institution and its members. The view of Congress as a place for stirring debate also resonates in modern popular culture; one has to think only of the climactic, archetypal speech by Jimmy Stewart in *Mr. Smith Goes to Washington*. Even today, debate on the floor is one of the most common and arguably appealing images of representatives at work. The advent of C-SPAN has brought this image directly into the homes of millions of Americans. It is worth noting here that a number of respondents made direct, and positive, references to C-SPAN in their interviews.

19. While discussing and debating issues is clearly not a precise match for policy making, my deliberative category does have policy making overtones or elements to it.

20. Some studies, for instance, indicate that members of Congress gain a positive "multiplier effect" from constituency service. That is, someone who receives assistance from his representative may tell his family, friends, and associates about the experience, who in turn may relay it to others, which potentially boosts the member's political standing in all their eyes. Helping one citizen, then, may mean a better image among many. Such research would seem to validate members' belief that they do little but gain from the provision of constituency service, and the conclusion that people at heart value such assistance. But it also brings home in yet another way the impact that political understanding and communication—in this case from *citizen* to *citizen*—can have on people's conceptions and evaluations of the representative process.

21. This person's dissatisfaction with Solomon thus appears to stem partly from the latter's "betrayal" of conservative principles in his posi-

tion as chair of the House Rules Committee. That is, as a member with significant internal responsibilities and power, Solomon was positioned (and perhaps compelled) to act in ways that run counter to the conservative faith. In his institutional role, then, Solomon was undercutting his standing as a "truly" conservative representative, at least in the eyes of this subject. Obviously, given Solomon's overwhelming reelection margins before his retirement, the critical perspectives cited here are not representative of his home constituency.

22. Another important caveat should be added here. It is possible that members of Congress as a whole have a more diffuse, but still significant, impact on people's representational attitudes, especially over the long-run. As is true of their general views of the representative process, the "representational environment" ordinary citizens are immersed in, as well as the store of political memories they carry, may subtly shape or alter their congressional expectations over time. Thus, to some degree what people want from members of Congress may reflect both the examples provided by admired (or disliked) individual members and the larger congressional universe.

23. Another conservative respondent also voiced respect for Moynihan's willingness to take stands "which are contrary to positions you might expect him to take," but he added that "at the same time, [Moynihan] doesn't fight for these positions. He makes pronouncements. He doesn't stand up and say I won't vote for this or I will vote for that."

24. Approximately one-third of the respondents chose a local or state official when asked "who best represents you today." These subjects offered a host of reasons why they favored such officials, all of which seemed connected to their fundamental ideals about the representative process. For example, local representatives were believed to be more attuned to and interested in constituent opinion; more likely to share the same views and interests as the people they serve; more accessible and open to citizen influence; and better able to get things done.

A smattering of participants went a step further. Like the following individual, they hinted that because local officials are easier to contact, observe, judge, and perhaps influence, they may be the only representatives who can truly reflect the individual: ". . . my alderman, you know, I know personally, and I know he's very interested in what people in the neighborhood want and has worked very hard to take care of that kind of stuff, and I don't know if *I can name another person* that *represents me, my wants and needs*" (emphasis added). To these citizens, local representatives offer the best fit of attachment, perspective, and interests. Based on their comments, one might add a corollary to the old adage that all politics is local: the best representation takes place close to home.

25. It is worth noting that many subjects struggled or hesitated before arriving at a choice. In the succinct assessment of one of these individuals: "Oh, man, that's a hard one [*laughter*]."

26. At least some of this appreciation can probably be attributed to the respondents' relative penchant for politics. The "tough job" references came mainly from somewhat and very sophisticated subjects, and the latter were most likely to provide the most discerning remarks about members' personal and professional concerns. To some degree, therefore, the sympathetic view that emerged in these interviews may be an artifact of the sample population. Involvement in or exposure to politics may deepen people's understanding of the representative relationship, and perhaps soften their attitudes about it. Still, it is noteworthy that this perspective on the modern representative's job surfaced among people from diverse political orientations and at different levels of political sophistication.

27. Quite a few participants, as discussed in chapter four, were highly critical of the impact of the electoral connection on representatives' behavior. Occasionally, however, respondents detected a paradox at the heart of the representative process that inescapably involves the reelection motive: the necessity of being reelected to achieve long-term goals/ambitions or to continue "doing good." As one subject who declared that the "the system itself right now is broken" later advised, "[I would] tell them to do their job and stop worrying about being reelected [*laughs*]. Except I know that doesn't work for them, because if they don't worry about being elected they can't do their jobs, because they won't be there in two years."

Chapter Six: Institutional Representation

1. On the other hand, many respondents also touched on ways in which they think the contemporary institution falls short in its duties. In the estimation of one person, "You know, I like the idea that I actually have a voice on the largest political platform of the nation. I dislike the fact that doesn't actually carry out in practice necessarily." Participants offered a host of reasons for this gap between theory and practice. These included the inordinate power of special interests and lobbyists, excessive partisanship ("party politics"), the corrupting influence of members' perks/special privileges, and overly expansive government. In most of these cases, the underlying theme was that in its actual operation Congress is either inattentive to, or distorting, the preferences and interests of the public. In short, *mis*representing the people.

2. Unlike lawmaking, which was alluded to by a variety of subjects, almost all the references to the budget/taxes/spending were made by sophisticated respondents.

3. There appears to be an institutional dimension to people's conceptions of representational communication. Congress is expected to engage in explanatory and educational efforts almost as much as individual

members. On the other hand, the provision of district services by and large was not considered to be a key part of institutional representation (eighteen of the subjects ranked it from 4–6). This result conforms to the generally critical treatment "pork barreling" received in the interviews.

4. The phrase normal political circumstances must be emphasized. It is quite possible that the events of 9/11 and its aftermath would have had a tangible effect on the rank scales (and perhaps the interviews themselves). In this case, given the contentiousness of both the foreign and domestic policies of the Bush administration, it is quite likely that the checks and balances role would fare differently now than it did at the time of my interviews.

5. All but one of the unsophisticated respondents ranked institutional communication 1 or 2 and district service from 1–3.

6. This perspective, it should be noted, runs against the grain of media coverage of how the political process works, which (explicitly or implicitly) tends to define the presidency as the locus of government action and bolster perceptions of its strength and importance. Research indicates that the chief executive receives far more, and generally more favorable, coverage than does the national legislature. One study of network news programs found that, depending on the year, the programs devoted three to thirteen times as much attention to the president as to Congress (see Farnsworth and Lichter 2005). In other words, people's views about the systemic importance of Congress are neither a product of media coverage, nor are they strongly reinforced by it. While the media dwells on the presidency, Congress somehow retains its hold on people's political imaginations.

7. It is also worth noting that the authors found a clear relationship between political knowledge/involvement and views about Congress. Highly educated and politically active respondents ("experts") were more appreciative of the institution and of democratic procedures (such as debate and compromise) than were political "novices," but the experts in turn proved less tolerant of political professionals and interest-group representation than more apolitical citizens. At the same time, increasing knowledge of politics was *inversely* related to support for particular members of Congress; well-educated and politically active citizens were less likely to be satisfied with the performance of individual representatives and the ongoing professionalization of politics.

8. Robert H. Durr, John B. Gilmour, and Christina Wolbrecht (1997) arrive at similar judgments in their analysis of congressional approval. They too find evidence "that public opinion toward Congress is in some substantial measure determined by the activities of Congress itself" (p. 199). Yet this link between institutional behavior and approval rates does not bode well for the institution. The authors found that when Congress acts in its constitutionally prescribed role—by debating issues and passing legislation—it is rewarded with declining rates of approval. In

essence, falling public approval rates result from Congress simply doing its job. Like John R. Hibbing and Elizabeth Theiss-Morse, Durr et al. conclude that Americans harbor unrealistic expectations about Congress's lawmaking and deliberative functions. The thesis that ordinary Americans disdain the democratic process of open debate and compromise and are generally averse to any involvement in politics is further developed by Hibbing and Theiss-Morse in their 2002 book, *Stealth Democracy*.

9. Such queries are likely to elicit a "negative valence" in people's responses. Moreover, since the focus group setting is designed to mimic "sociable public discourse"—what people would say to one another in informal discussions about politics—questions like this may foster a group dynamic that inhibits the expression of more balanced or favorable views on the subject. Put another way, one is unlikely to speak up in defense of Congress, or even to consider the positive aspects of the legislative process, when exposed to questions like "What could Congress do if it were working really well? What's gone wrong? That is, why isn't Congress doing what we expect from it? Have you been upset about Congress for a long time or is this a recent thing?" (another set of questions posed by Hibbing and Theiss-Morse). This is particularly true if those around you are offering consistently negative appraisals. Given the tenor of the questions asked and the nature of group discussions, more positive views of Congress and the legislative process were unlikely to surface in these focus-group sessions. They were more apt to evoke collective cynicism and dissatisfaction, which they did. In a sense, participants did not appear to be given the "space" needed to advance alternative opinions about institutional representation.

10. As this quote suggests, these subjects were disenchanted with, even bewildered by, some of Congress's basic legislative conventions and rules. The filibuster, vote trading, and riders were perceived as corruptions of the legislative process, rather than as key political stratagems, the grease that keeps the legislative wheels moving, or at least part of the normal operation of the institution, as they are usually seen by academic observers. To use another example, logrolling was considered a perversion of how decisions should be made or how support for a bill should be generated (on the merits of the issue) instead of as an essential mechanism for neutralizing political opposition, building majorities, or solving "collective action" problems. In the view of these citizens, such practices subvert how the representative process *should* work, the way in which members should represent the people. As another participant described the use of riders, "I think they should stick to the issue they are dealing with; adding these other things to it distorts the whole process. Pretty soon they're not really dealing with the issue anymore but all those unrelated things."

11. As the respondent, cited earlier in the text, who complained about the length of time things take in Congress later remarked: "I mean, for the number of constituents and the number of people, actually the time that it takes is not that bad [*laughs*]. You know, for the number of issues and the number of various things that come into that institution that have to be brought down to a decision on one side or the other, there's no like sliding half of it by. That can become very difficult. So I probably wouldn't tell it to do anything differently."

12. Several respondents also pointed a finger at the privileged position of business and the wealthy in American politics. In the words of the most vehement of these individuals, "Actually, I don't believe that our government runs things anymore, let's face it, it's big business which runs everything. . . . I think they have total control of the politicians one way or another." Although other participants offered less strident perspectives on the balance of power in the representative process, the sense that government is increasingly "by the rich, for the rich" was a definite undercurrent in a number of the interviews.

13. Another respondent put a slightly different, and more nuanced, twist on this theme: "No, they're still accessible, I guess the question is whether they're responsive . . . if GE gives them a ten thousand dollar campaign contribution if that has an effect. I guess it's an integrity call."

14. This quote also hints at what participants identified as the negative institutional effects of the current electoral process: a legislative system skewed toward "whoever has the biggest group or the most money to spend," and policies that fail to reflect the needs, interests, and preferences of ordinary citizens.

15. As another subject asserted, "Well, there are probably a lot of well-educated university professors who could do an excellent job in the legislature, but they don't have the money."

16. A different respondent relayed a similar sentiment in a more sophisticated fashion: "I think the relationship on the surface works well. The part that doesn't work well is the part we don't see, which is how he goes about raising $10,000 bucks a week in order to run for re-election. You know, he'll respond to my letters, he'll sit down and meet with us when we call to make an appointment, but that's not what sways the issue."

17. The laments about party came predominantly from the politically sophisticated respondents. Indeed, nearly all of the political activists (including the subject cited here) expressed qualms about the effects of partisanship and party line voting. Citizens today are often taken—by political commentators, party operatives, and academics alike—to have an almost inveterate disdain for party politics. "Excessive" partisanship is believed to be one of the public's stock criticisms of the political process. In

this study, however, those subjects directly involved in the political process or with members of Congress, who might be thought to have the greatest understanding and appreciation of the role of party in politics, were most likely to express reservations about it. Now the fact that they did so may stem mainly from negative political experiences they had with certain representatives, or even from their greater political articulateness. Still, it is revealing that those citizens with the best firsthand knowledge of politics harbor such doubts about party's impact on the representative process. Instead of being perceived by them as a necessary vehicle for effective representation, as it is by most political scientists, party was seen more often as an obstacle to it.

18. Most of these participants were politically sophisticated. This suggests that interest and involvement in, as well as exposure to, public affairs affect the saliency of campaign finance reform as an issue. On the other hand, the fact that it was mentioned mainly by this group of subjects may reflect nothing more than superior ability to "talk politics." In other words, campaign finance reform lies at the top of their more accessible political consciousness. If specifically asked to comment on it, many of the other respondents might have endorsed it as well.

19. Another subject, skeptical of free airtime, felt that this approach would help elevate the level of political discourse during campaigns: "I would say that the only time a congressman's face appears on TV is in a debate organized by an outside organization. I don't think that free time on TV is going to get away from the sound bites and superficiality. It doesn't help people understand what's going on, what the issues are. I think they should have to answer questions, debate each other, and that's the only time their mugs would show up on TV when they campaign."

20. Based on the results of their 2002 survey of state legislators, John M. Carey et al. (2005) conclude that term limits have had a tangible impact on the balance of power between state governing institutions and on certain behaviors and priorities among legislators. Above all they discern a "Burkean shift" among term-limited representatives, who become less beholden to the constituents in their districts and more attentive to other interests.

21. This respondent, among several others, also believed that term limits would reduce the likelihood of corruption among members, or the corrupting effects associated with lasting power.

22. The sophisticated respondents were consistently opposed to term limits; only two of them expressed support for the idea.

23. As one of the supporters of term limits conceded: "Well, I think it is a problem to always have fresh blood, because then everyone is getting to learn the ropes and by the time they learn the ropes they're out." In the acerbic commentary of another participant, "they wouldn't have a clue about what the hell is going on, and the country would be run by staff."

24. Respondents' attitudes about term limits often seemed to be integrally related to, and in some cases a product of, their beliefs about the impact of incumbency and careerism on the representative process.

25. As one subject expressed it, ". . . the longer you are in Congress the less you are in touch with the real world, since you become a Beltway kind of guy. It's a cliche, but it's also true."

26. Like this person, a few others opined that the power of incumbency produces members who are reelected more by default than on the strength of their accomplishments, not to mention increasingly apathetic voters. As one of these individuals said: "I think that some congressmen, in their glory of getting elected and what have you, after a few terms of that some people just like forget, don't care, they look at the ballot and say, 'oh yeah, I remember him.' And he just stays there."

27. As another participant contended, "I think they might see it less as public service and more as a career. I think that has changed. They get into it and think, 'this is my job,' as opposed to 'I'm here because I'm representing my constituents.'"

28. As one of the somewhat sophisticated subjects professed off the bat, "I don't think I know enough about Congress to answer your question."

29. The rank scales also indicated that there were significant differences in the institutional expectations of unsophisticated and sophisticated respondents. Above all, unsophisticated individuals were much more likely to consider communication and the provision of district services to be important responsibilities of Congress.

Chapter Seven: The Public Side of Representation

1. This raises an important issue: is this belief about the blessings of representation widely shared across the country? Would the results be much the same if the interviews were conducted in states, such as California, Oregon, and Montana, which have long histories of direct popular rule and where mechanisms such as initiative and referendum are available to (and fairly popular with) the citizenry? Is the representative impulse as deeply ingrained among the citizens of these states, or do their political cultures and processes tend to make people more skeptical of representative government and supportive of constituent control over representatives? Is there, in short, a distinct "geographic bias" to people's representational views? Such questions underscore the importance of further inquiry into people's attitudes and expectations about the representative process.

2. One of the most important issues for any democratic polity—which some participants recognized and wrestled with, others seemed unaware of, and a few blissfully ignored—is how to reconcile democratic participation with representative government. Respondents struggled

to find a solution where they might have it both ways: where voters might have politically courageous and independent representatives *plus* fidelity to district interests and constituent preferences, where constituents could exert real influence over members without turning them into "pure" delegates and sacrificing the benefits of representative governance. Ultimately, these citizens too seemed somewhat bedeviled by the fundamental dilemma of how to blend what Heinz Eulau described as responsive versus responsible governing.

3. Taken at face value, this finding challenges the presumption that Americans are essentially apolitical creatures who lack the time, energy, or inclination to become politically engaged as more than just voters (if as that). The classic "liberal tradition" holds that the private sphere trumps the public in America; that people want to focus solely on their personal lives at the expense of their responsibilities as citizens. The evidence here suggests that at least some citizens hanker for something more, for a public sphere that does not shortchange their desire to become *meaningfully* involved; that is, for a politics where their involvement is perceived as making a difference (as it tends to be at the local level) rather than simply as window dressing for the self-serving needs of others, especially their representatives. Americans are a practical people. They have little desire to participate just for the sake of doing so, and certainly don't want to be involved all the time. But they do want the chance to become engaged when necessary—and to make it count when they do, and thus to provide a counterweight (or corrective) to the influence of more privileged interests and elites. What one might call a "practical participatory democratic" perspective.

4. It should be noted here that participants were not explicitly questioned along these lines, and their frequent recognition of the complexities of the representative process suggests that at least some of them would have acknowledged this issue. It is also true that the issues posed in the hypothetical questions were quite substantial. They were not presented, or taken, as run of the mill issues, and respondents' conceptions of the voting process should be considered in that context. Finally, one should recall that this is an *idealized* version of the decision-making process.

5. Of course, interviews cannot accurately gauge how much time and effort these (or any other) citizens really would be willing to invest. Would they, in other words, actually "walk the walk"? If pressed, many of the subjects would probably concede that such a taxing and complex process could not be undertaken all, or even most, of the time. But their response might be that it is still something to shoot for. The more actual decision making approximated this model, especially for major issues, and the more real representatives aspired to it, the better the representative process would be. Even if many citizens failed to capitalize on it, at

least the *opportunity* for better representation and more meaningful participation would be there for the taking.

6. In particular, explanation and education-persuasion were seen as tools to simultaneously increase constituent understanding of representational decision making *and* build support for and trust in members of Congress themselves (which, as Fenno astutely noted, in turn provides members with the leeway necessary to act with political daring and discretion). In the subjects' view, well-informed, engaged constituents who truly understand the dynamics of major issues—what the problems are, what's really at stake, what options are available, and why a member acted as she did or wants to act as she does—are more likely to recognize the need for making tough decisions, to (en)trust a representative to make those decisions, and to be more accepting of the outcomes (even if they seem contrary to constituents' immediate interests or preferences). Representatives who genuinely and consistently make the effort to engage in these processes therefore are more likely to fare well, or at least get the electoral benefit of the doubt, than those who do not. Put another way, regular explanation and education-persuasion would enhance, rather than undermine, members' political standing and ability to safely and effectively serve as trustees. It would provide the political foundation for them to act with the political courage and informed judgment that many political elites, as well as citizens in this study, believe is so vitally needed—and often missing—in Washington today.

7. And since representatives adopt a variety of home styles, present a host of different visions of the good representative/representative process, and offer divergent perspectives about the nature of institutional representation, citizens over time are exposed to an array of cross-cutting cues about the representative process and the proper roles of members of Congress and the institution in it.

8. The quality of this responsiveness is another matter, of course. Critics of the current representative process might argue that what representatives really want to give constituents is just enough contact and communication—enough "face time"—to keep them appeased. As discussed in the previous chapters, more than a few respondents also appeared to believe this, a perspective which clearly contributed to their political disenchantment and cynicism.

9. Nowhere is this better illustrated than in the prevalence of the belief in representation as responsiveness. Beginning with *Home Style,* much of the representational literature has documented and explored the myriad ways in which representatives try to ensure responsive representation. Immersed in a political world that accentuates the importance of responsiveness to constituents, it is not surprising that this would come to be a centerpiece of ordinary citizens' representational belief systems.

People of varying political stripes and at various levels of political sophistication may think of representation in terms of individual-level responsiveness because this is how the relationship generally unfolds and because they receive innumerable cues that this is how it *should* be. Citizens' abstract views about representation are formed within a particular political context—and continually buffeted and (re)shaped by it.

10. This outcome might be partly attributed to the diverse and at times conflicting expectations citizens have for representatives and the representative process. As I asserted at the end of chapter four, people's representational expectations may have grown considerably over the same period that their faith in government institutions and actors has sharply declined. Perhaps this illustrates the law of inflated expectations: the more that people are offered and receive, the more they expect; and when these burgeoning expectations inevitably go unfulfilled, the greater is their discontent. In any event, what is clear is that subjects' judgments about what they are (not) getting out of the representative process may be a prime source of their political discontent and cynicism.

11. Was this outlook an idiosyncratic result of the people I spoke with, who overall were more politically knowledgeable, active, and interested than is typical? Was it an outgrowth of the interview process, where participants were induced to think about representation in an unusually thoughtful way? Or does it reflect a depth and complexity in people's political beliefs that is not otherwise revealed? I believe a little of each. On the whole the convictions expressed by the citizens in this study likely are somewhat atypical, although it is important to recognize that subjects at *all* levels of political sophistication expressed interesting views about representation and had some grasp of its inherent problems. It is also true that the research method adopted here tells us more about what people *can* think about representation than the attitudes they carry at the top of their heads. That is one of its singular virtues. Other studies that use in-depth interviews or discussion groups to examine people's political beliefs, such as Gamson's *Talking Politics*, have found that "ordinary" citizens have the capacity to form reasoned opinions about political issues and may hold fairly complex political views. My results suggest much the same thing. But unlike focus group studies, my work offers a window into people's underlying beliefs and political capacities solely as individuals. In-depth interviews thus permit us to tap into the deeper layers of a person's "representational consciousness" in a way that other research methods do not, a consciousness that I find to be an amalgam of thoughtful perspectives and "blind spots." And both dimensions, as we shall see, have important implications for the democratic process.

12. Given the importance to many respondents that ordinary citizens have a significant impact on the representative process, and their

expressed desire for the opportunity to become more meaningfully involved, part of this cynicism might also be a natural response to being effectively shut out of any meaningful role in the contemporary process. Whether they really are or not is, of course, a matter of debate and perception. But in an important sense perception *is* reality—particularly when it comes to people's political attitudes and assessments.

13. My research, in fact, offered ample evidence of both this surface cynicism and people's capacity to go deeper, as the reflexively skeptical attitudes expressed early in many of the interviews often gave way to more thoughtful and balanced perspectives. Of course, it is certainly not mutually exclusive to possess a nuanced understanding of the representative process and be highly critical or even cynical, as the results of my interviews attest (some wags might even say they go hand in hand!). But the findings here do suggest that there is more to citizens' representational views than merely "jaded ignorance."

14. The prevalence of such Federalist-style ideals and expectations testifies to their deep roots and enduring resonance in our political culture. But part of the appeal of these ideas might also be traced to the behavior of political actors. Some elected officials, particularly members of the representational "elite"—the president, senators, House leaders, other well-known members of Congress—like to present themselves as guardians of the public weal, framing their positions and actions in the language of the national interest, the long-term good of the country, and so on. While citizens may be (understandably) skeptical of these stances, it is also possible that they filter down to have a subtle yet important impact on their representational belief systems. Whether purely instrumental or not, such appeals may encourage people to think, "yes, representatives are not just supposed to take care of their own districts; they must also look out for the common good and act accordingly." To the extent that ordinary citizens are most aware of, and influenced by, the political cues/models provided by highly visible and influential public officials (which several studies, including mine, suggest), this "commonwealth-centered" view of the representative process is likely to have a tangible impact on citizens' representational expectations.

15. And this holds true for people at all levels of political sophistication. Indeed, the most politically active and knowledgeable respondents were among the staunchest advocates of a strong constituent connection, two-way communication, public education, and citizen influence in the representative process—*and* the need for representatives to exhibit political courage, vote their judgment or convictions, and pursue the national interest. At the same time, they were also most likely to discuss the inherent dilemmas of representation and the "tough job" that members face. These individuals therefore exemplify one of the more intriguing

findings of my research: of citizens who both recognize the complexity of the representative relationship yet still hold diverse and often conflicting expectations for it.

16. A brief note about district and constituency services should also be made here. Given the participants' representational expectations, their assessments of the representative process, and the challenges faced in combining this assistance with other key responsibilities, the provision of these services appears to be at best a mixed blessing for members of Congress.

17. The same holds true for the other dimensions of what David R. Mayhew called advertising, especially newsletters and the like. While traditionally perceived as almost cost-free political tools, I found that these techniques sometimes bolster people's cynicism about the shallowness of contemporary representation. Efforts to create representational familiarity, it seems, can breed contempt—especially when they are seen as being patently self-serving.

18. Some of this belief about representatives' lack of commitment to ensuring responsiveness may be the product of selective memory on the part of the participants. The perception that members are only attentive during election time thus may be more a reflection of citizens' sporadic attention to politics than a mark of members' actual behavior. It certainly does not jibe with the level of responsiveness that the literature indicates representatives provide. A similar critique could be made about the belief that citizens do not have a meaningful role to play in the representative process; maybe this is more a convenient excuse for the apathetic and uninvolved than a fair assessment of contemporary representation. In some cases perhaps both are true!

19. This research indicates that citizens do become better informed about representatives' issue positions when members make the effort to instruct them. Daniel Lipinski (2001), for example, found that constituents whose representatives made a concerted attempt to publicize their voting positions, through newsletters and the like, were significantly better able to correctly identify members' positions and more likely to have favorable impressions of them. In effect, representatives can successfully communicate policy priorities and decision-making choices to constituents through educational efforts. See also Kim Fridkin-Kahn and Patrick J. Kenney (2001) for the effect of issue messages on citizens' political knowledge and engagement.

20. Put another way, they don't see the representational and political demands made by other constituencies—only legislators (and legislatures) responses to those demands. Or, if they do perceive these demands, they tend to regard them as excessive or illegitimate.

21. Expectations that, lest we forget, come not only from civics lessons and people's abstract ideals, but also from the way representatives

and political institutions portray and undertake the representative process. The dance of discontent about representation ineluctably takes at least two partners.

22. One intriguing issue, beyond the scope of this study, is the influence of these forces on the most basic component of political behavior: the *vote* choice. What effect do citizens' underlying representational ideas and expectations have on their voting decisions? Do voters even implicitly match up candidates against their internal conceptions of the good representative? Do they judge an incumbent by how well he or she has lived up to their personal and job expectations for members of Congress? In the same way, what impact do views about the representative process have on whether, how, and how much people participate in politics? The relationship between people's underlying representational beliefs and their political behavior certainly merits further investigation.

The results of this study raise a number of other interesting research questions. Above all, as mentioned in note number 1 regarding views on the representative impulse, would they be replicated on a national scale? Are my findings essentially an artifact of a particular survey population in a particular part of the country, or are they generally representative of the nation as a whole (as I believe likely)? What, if any, regional differences exist in citizens' representational beliefs and expectations? Similarly, are there discernible partisan variations in these views (in particular, do self-professed Independents hold qualitatively different views on the representative process than either Republicans or Democrats)? What would the results of a nationwide survey on representational roles, based on questions like those asked in the 1978 NES or my interviews, reveal today? Finally, does political sophistication have a significant impact on people's representational worldviews, as suggested here? These and related questions highlight the importance and research potential of further inquiry into the "public side of representation."

23. Such vehicles to help citizens become more politically informed and engaged, educate (and be educated by) elected officials, and gain a greater voice in representatives decision making include electronic town hall meetings, citizens' assemblies, and "deliberative polls." See for example Robert C. Luskin et al. (2002) and Ned Crosby (2003). These mechanisms closely fit, and would certainly advance, the representational ideals and objectives offered by the citizens in this study. And this could include enhancing the ability of representatives to serve as "trusted trustees." As discussed earlier in this chapter, explanation and education-persuasion were often perceived as vital tools (and prerequisites) for representatives to effectively act with political courage and independence. Precisely what many respondents said they expect, even hunger for, from their representatives . . . and precisely what many believe is sorely lacking in today's political climate.

Bibliography

Achen, Christopher H. "Measuring Representation." *American Journal of Political Science* 22 (August 1978): 475–510.

Alpert, Eugene J. "A Reconceptualization of Representational Role Theory." *Legislative Studies Quarterly* 4 (November 1979): 587–603.

Arnold, Douglas. "Can Inattentive Citizens Control Their Elected Officials." In *Congress Reconsidered*. Edited by Lawrence C. Dodd and Bruce Oppenheimer, 401–416. Washington, DC: CQ Press, 1993.

———. *The Logic of Congressional Action*. New Haven, CT: Yale University Press, 1990.

Asher, Herb, and Mike Barr. "Popular Support for Congress and Its Members." In *Congress, The Press, and The Public*. Edited by Thomas Mann and Norman Ornstein, 15–43. Washington, DC: American Enterprise Institute and the Brookings Institution, 1994.

Backstom, Charles H. "Congress and the Public: How Representative is the One of the Other?" *American Politics Quarterly* 5 (October 1977): 411–435.

Bartels, Larry. "Constituency Opinion and Congressional Policymaking: The Reagan Defense Buildup." *American Political Science Review* 85 (June 1991): 457–474.

Bianco, William T. *Trust: Representatives and Constituents*. Ann Arbor: University of Michigan Press, 1994.

Born, Richard. "The Shared Fortunes of Congress and Congressmen: Members May Run from Congress, but They Can't Hide." *Journal of Politics* 52 (November 1990): 1223–1241.

Bowman, Karlyn, and Everett Carll Ladd. "Public Opinion toward Congress: A Historical Look." In *Congress, The Press, and The Public*. Edited by Thomas Mann and Norman Ornstein, 45–58. Washington, DC: American Enterprise Institute and the Brookings Institution, 1994.

Cain, Bruce, John Ferejohn, and Morris P. Fiorina. *The Personal Vote.* Cambridge, MA: Harvard University Press, 1987.

Cantori, Lewis J., and Andrew H. Ziegler. "Introduction: Political Culture and Political Socialization." In *Comparative Politics in the Post-Behavioral Era.* Edited by Louis J. Cantori and Andrew H. Ziegler, 159–162. Boulder, CO: Lynne Rienner Publishers, 1988.

Carey, John M., Richard Niemi, Lynda Powell, and Gary Moncrief. "The Effects of Term Limits on State Legislatures: A New Survey of the 50 States." *Legislative Studies Quarterly* 31 (February 2006): 105–134.

Cavanaugh, Thomas E. "The Calculus of Representation: A Congressional Perspective." *Western Political Quarterly* 35 (March 1982): 120–129.

Chanley, Virginia, Thomas Rudolph, and Wendy Rahn. "The Origins and Consequences of Public Trust in Government: A Time Series Analysis." *Public Opinion Quarterly* 64 (Autumn 2000): 239–256.

Chong, Dennis. "How People Think, Reason, and Feel about Rights and Liberties." *American Journal of Political Science* 37 (August 1993): 867–899.

Cnudd, C. F., and David McCrone. "The Linkage Between Constituency Attitudes and Congressional Voting: A Causal Model." *American Political Science Review* 60 (March 1966): 66–72.

Cook, Timothy E. "Legislature v. Legislator: A Note on the Paradox of Congressional Support." *Legislative Studies Quarterly* 4 (February, 1979): 43–52.

Crosby, Ned. *Healthy Democracy: Empowering a Clear and Informed Voice of the People.* Edina, MN: Beaver's Pond Press, 2003.

Davidson, Roger H. *The Role of the Congressman.* New York: Pegasus, 1969.

Dennis, Jack. "Public Support for Congress." *Political Behavior* 3 (December 1981): 319–350.

Durr, Robert H., John B. Gilmour, and Christina Wolbrecht. "Explaining Congressional Approval." *American Journal of Political Science* 41 (January 1997): 175–207.

Ehrenhalt, Alan. *The United States of Ambition: Politicians, Power, and the Pursuit of Office.* New York: Times Books, 1991.

Erikson, Robert S. "Constituency Opinion and Congressional Behavior: A Reexamination of the Miller-Stokes Representation Data." *American Journal of Political Science* 22 (August 1978): 511–535.

Erikson, Robert S., and Gerald C. Wright. "Representation of Constituent Ideology in Congress." In *Continuity and Change in Congressional Elections.* Edited by David Brady, John Cogan, and Morris Fiorina, chap. 8. Stanford, CA: Stanford University Press, 2000.

Erikson, Robert S., Norman R. Luttbeg, and William Holloway. "Knowing One's District: How Legislators Predict Referendum Voting." *American Journal of Political Science* 19 (May 1975): 231–246.

Eulau, Heinz. "Changing Views of Representation." In *The Politics of Representation*. Edited by Heinz Eulau and John C. Wahlke, 31–53. London: Sage Publications, 1978.

Eulau, Heinz, and Paul Karps. "The Puzzle of Representation: Specifying Components of Responsiveness." In *The Politics of Representation*. Edited by Heinz Eulau and John C. Wahlke, 55–71. London: Sage Publications, 1978.

Eulau, Heinz, John C. Wahlke, William Buchanan, and LeRoy C. Ferguson. "The Role of the Representative: Some Empirical Observations on the Theory of Edmund Burke." In *The Politics of Representation*. Edited by Heinz Eulau and John C. Wahlke, 111–126. London: Sage Publications, 1978.

Farnsworth, Stephen, and S. Robert Lichter. *The Mediated Presidency: Television News & Presidential Governance*. Lanham, MD: Rowman and Littlefield Publishers, 2005.

Fenno, Richard F. Jr. *Home Style: House Members in Their Districts*. Glenview, IL: Scott, Foresman and Company, 1978.

———. "If, as Ralph Nader Says, Congress is 'The Broken Branch,' How Come We Love Our Congressmen So Much?" In *Congress in Change: Evolution and Reform*. Edited by Norman Ornstein. New York: Praeger, 1975.

Fiorina, Morris P. *Congress: Keystone of the Washington Establishment*. New Haven, CT: Yale University Press, 1989.

Fridkin-Kahn, Kim, and Patrick J. Kenney. "The Importance of Issues in Senate Campaigns: Citizens' Reception of Issue Messages." *Legislative Studies Quarterly* 26 (November 2001): 573–597

Gamson, William A. *Talking Politics*. New York: Cambridge University Press, 1992.

Grant, J. Tobin, and Thomas J. Rudolph. "The Job of Representation in Congress: Public Expectations and Representative Approval." *Legislative Studies Quarterly* 29 (August 2004): 431–445

Griffin, John D., and Brian Newman. "Are Voters Better Represented?" *Journal of Politics* 67 (November 2005): 1206–1227.

Gross, Donald A. "Representative Styles and Legislative Behavior." *Western Political Quarterly* 31 (September 1978): 359–371.

Herrera, Cheryl Lyn, Richard Herrera, and Eric Smith. "Public Opinion and Congressional Representation." *Public Opinion Quarterly* 56 (Summer 1992): 185–205.

Hibbing, John R., and Elizabeth Theiss-Morse. *Congress as Public Enemy: Public Attitudes toward American Political Institutions*. New York: Cambridge University Press, 1995.

———. *Stealth Democracy: Americans' Beliefs about How Government Should Work*. New York: Cambridge University Press, 2002.

Hurley, Patricia A. "Collective Representation Reappraised." *Legislative Studies Quarterly* 7 (February 1982): 119–136.

Hurley, Patricia A., and Kim Quaile Hill. "Beyond the Demand-Input Model: A Theory of Representational Linkages." *Journal of Politics* 65 (May 2003): 304–326

Jacobson, Gary C. *The Politics of Congressional Elections.* Glenville, IL: Scott, Foresman and Company, 1987.

Jewell, Malcolm E. "Legislators and Constituents in the Representative Process." In *Handbook of Legislative Research.* Edited by Gerhard Loewenburg et al., 97–131. Cambridge, MA: Harvard University Press, 1985.

———. *Representation in State Legislatures.* Lexington: University of Kentucky Press, 1982.

Jewell, Malcolm E., and Gerhard Loewenburg. "Toward a New Model of Legislative Representation." *Legislative Studies Quarterly* 4 (November 1979): 485–499.

Karps, Paul D., and Heinz Eulau. "Policy Representation as an Emergent: Toward a Situational Analysis." In *The Politics of Representation.* Edited by Heinz Eulau and John C. Wahlke, 207–227. London: Sage Publications, 1978.

Kettering Foundation. *Citizens and Politics: A View from Main Street America.* Dayton, OH: Kettering Foundation, 1991.

Kimball, David C. "Priming Partisan Evaluations of Congress." *Legislative Studies Quarterly* 30 (February 2005): 63–84.

Kingdon, John W. *Congressmen's Voting Decisions.* New York: Harper & Row, 1981.

Kritzer, Herbert M. "The American Public's Assessment of the Rehnquist Court." *Judicature* 89 (November–December 2005): 168–176.

Kuklinski, James H. "Representatives and Elections: A Policy Analysis." *American Political Science Review* 72 (March 1978): 165–177.

———. "Representative-Constituency Linkages: A Review Article." *Legislative Studies Quarterly* 4 (February 1979): 121–140.

Kuklinski, James H., and Gary Segura. "Endogeneity, Exogeneity, Time, and Space in Political Representation." *Legislative Studies Quarterly* 20 (February 1995): 3–21.

Kuklinski, James H., and Richard Elling. "Representational Role, Constituency Opinion, and Legislative Roll-Call Behavior." *American Journal of Political Science* 2 (February 1977): 135–147.

Lane, Robert E. *Political Ideology.* New York: The Free Press, 1962.

Lipinski, Daniel. "The Effect of Messages Communicated by Members of Congress: The Impact of Publicizing Votes." *Legislative Studies Quarterly* 26 (February 2001): 81–100

Lipinski, Daniel, William T. Bianco, and Ryan Work. "What Happens When House Members 'Run with Congress'? The Electoral Consequences of Institutional Loyalty." *Legislative Studies Quarterly* 28 (August 2003): 413–429

Luskin, Robert C., James S. Fishkin, and Roger Jowell. "Considered Opinions: Deliberative Polling in Britain." *British Journal of Political Science* 32 (2002): 455–487.

Mansbridge, Jane. "Representation Revisited: Introduction to the Case Against Electoral Accountability." *Democracy and Society* 1 (Fall 2004).

———. "Rethinking Representation." *American Political Science Review* 97 (November 2003): 515–528.

Mayhew, David R. *Congress: The Electoral Connection*. New Haven, CT: Yale University Press, 1974.

McCrone, Donald J., and James Kuklinski. "The Delegate Theory of Representation." *American Journal of Political Science* 23 (May 1979): 278–300.

McDermott, Monika L., and David Jones. "Congressional Performance, Incumbent Behavior, and Voting in Senate Elections." *Legislative Studies Quarterly* 30 (May 2005): 235–257.

McMurray, Carl D., and Malcolm B. Parsons. "Public Attitudes toward the Representational Role of Legislators and Judges." *Midwest Journal of Political Science* 8 (1965): 167–192.

Miller, Arthur H., Martin Wattenberg, and Oksana Malanchuk. "Schematic Assessments of Presidential Candidates." *American Political Science Review* 80 (June 1986): 521–540.

Miller, Warren E., and Donald Stokes. "Constituency Influence in Congress." *American Political Science Review* 57 (March 1963): 45–56.

Oppenheimer, Bruce. "The Representational Experience: The Effect of State Population on Senator-Constituency Linkages." *American Journal of Political Science* 40 (November 1996): 1280–1299.

Page, Benjamin I., and Robert Y. Shapiro. "Effects of Public Opinion on Policy." *American Political Science Review* 77 (March 1983): 175–190.

———. *The Rational Public: Fifty Years of Trends in Americans' Policy Preferences*. Chicago: University of Chicago Press, 1992.

Parker, Glenn R. *Characteristics of Congress: Patterns in Congressional Behavior*. Englewood Cliffs, NJ: Prentice-Hall, 1989.

———. "The Role of Constituent Trust in Congressional Elections." *Public Opinion Quarterly* 53 (Summer 1989): 175–191

Parker, Glenn R., and Roger H. Davidson. "Why Do Americans Love Their Congressman So Much More Than Their Congress?" *Legislative Studies Quarterly* 4 (February 1979): 52–61.

Parker, Suzanne L., and Glenn Parker. "Why Do We Trust Our Congressman?" *Journal of Politics* 55 (May 1993): 442–453.

Patterson, Samuel C., Randall B. Ripley, and Stephen Quinlan. "Citizens' Orientations toward Legislatures: Congress and the State Legislature." *Western Political Quarterly* 45 (June 1992): 315–338.

Patterson, Samuel C., Ronald D. Hedlund, and G. Robert Boynton. *Representatives and Represented: Bases of Public Support for the American Legislatures.* New York: John Wiley, 1975.

Pew Research Center. *Deconstructing Distrust: How Americans View Government.* Washington, DC: Pew Research Center, 1998.

Pitkin, Hanna F. *The Concept of Representation.* Berkeley: University of California Press, 1967.

Prewitt, Kenneth, and Heinz Eulau. "Political Matrix and Political Representation." In *The Politics of Representation.* Edited by Heinz Eulau and John C. Wahlke, 127–150. London: Sage Publications, 1978.

Ripley, Randall B., Samuel Patterson, Lynn Maurer, and Stephen Quinlan. "Constituents' Evaluations of US House Members." *American Politics Quarterly* 20 (October 1992): 442–456.

Rosenberg, Robert M., Benjamin I. Page, et. al. "Constituency, Party, and Representation in Congress." *Public Opinion Quarterly* 48 (Winter 1984): 741–756.

Stimson, James, Michael MacKuen, and Robert Erickson. "Dynamic Representation." *American Political Science Review* 89 (September 1995): 543–564.

Stone, Walter J. "The Dynamics of Constituency: Electoral Control in the House." *American Politics Quarterly* 8 (October 1980): 399–424.

Uslaner, Eric M., and Ronald E. Weber. "U.S. State Legislators' Opinions and Perceptions of Constituency Attitudes." *Legislative Studies Quarterly* 4 (November 1979): 563–585.

Wahlke, John C. "Policy Demands and System Support: The Role of the Represented." In *The Politics of Representation.* Edited by Heinz Eulau and John C. Wahlke, 73–90. London: Sage Publications, 1978.

Wahlke, John C., Heinz Eulau, William Buchanan, and LeRoy Ferguson. *The Legislative System.* New York: John Wiley, 1962.

Weissberg, Robert. "Collective vs. Dyadic Representation in Congress." *American Political Science Review* 72 (June 1978): 535–547.

Wright, Gerald C. "Policy Positions in the Senate: Who is Represented?" *Legislative Studies Quarterly* 14 (May 1989): 465–486.

Yin, Robert K. *Case Study Research: Design and Methods.* Beverly Hills, CA: Sage Publications, 1984.

Index

Access: defined in literature, 9, 27, 35, 173n11; importance of, 27–28, 66, 141, 173n13, 178n20; political sophistication and, 31–32, 178n21

Accessibility (*see also* Openness), 3, 27, 28, 42, 64, 75, 123, 138, 183n24, 187n13

Accountability, 29, 38, 55, 65, 116, 125, 130, 141

Advertising, 34, 46, 63, 65, 194n17

Albright, Madeleine, 86

Anti-Federalist view of representation, 89, 116

Asher, Herb, 17, 166n6

Attentiveness, 17, 26–28, 32, 33, 40, 42, 64, 123, 166n6, 172n6, 179n22

"Authoritative representation," 135

Barr, Mike, 17, 166n6

Behavioral tradition, 167n8

Boehlert, Sherwood, 31, 84–85

Born, Richard, 166n6

Boynton, G. Robert, 167n7

Burkean perspective, 24, 49, 188n20

Bush administration, 165n1, 185n4

C-SPAN, 182n18

Cain, Bruce, 17

Campaign contributions, 110–111

Campaign contributors, 70, 110, 114, 125

Campaign finance reform: benefits to, 114–115, 188n19; facets of, 114; popularity with respondents, 113–114, 188n18

Careerism, 115, 118, 119–120, 189n24, 189n27

Carey, John M., 188n20

Cavanaugh, Thomas E., 175n9

Checks and balances, 99, 103, 185n4

Communication: absence/superficiality of, 45–47, 66; benefits to constituents, 40–41, 124, 132, 135, 178n19; constituency focus of, 25, 75, 173n11; constituent to representative, 36–37, 75; defined in literature, 9, 34–35, 173n11; "deliberative," 66, 141, 195n23; education-persuasion and, 54, 60, 141, 176n15, 194n19, 195n23; essence of representation, 22, 34, 64–65, 129, 168n1, 173n11; explanation and, 54–55, 194n19, 195n23; impediments to effective, 44, 173n1, 173–174n2; importance to respondents, 25, 34–35, 39, 42, 44, 64–66, 75, 123–124, 129, 135; institutional dimension, 101–103, 184n3, 185n5, 189n29; one-way, 34, 35, 38, 81; pillars of, 36–37; rank scales and, 79–80, 81, 185n5, 189n29; state of contemporary, 44–47; technology and, 44; town meetings and, 37–39;

203